美国短篇小说与电影

（第二版）

马乃强 ◎ 编

图书在版编目(CIP)数据

美国短篇小说与电影 / 马乃强编. -- 2版. -- 北京：北京大学出版社，2025.6.
(21世纪英语专业系列教材). -- ISBN 978-7-301-36321-8
Ⅰ. H319.37
中国国家版本馆CIP数据核字第2025PE1904号

书　　名	美国短篇小说与电影（第二版）
	MEIGUO DUANPIAN XIAOSHUO YU DIANYING (DI-ER BAN)
著作责任者	马乃强　编
责任编辑	刘　爽
标准书号	ISBN 978-7-301-36321-8
出版发行	北京大学出版社
地　　址	北京市海淀区成府路205号　100871
网　　址	http://www.pup.cn　　新浪微博：@北京大学出版社
电子邮箱	编辑部 pupwaiwen@pup.cn　　总编室 zpup@pup.cn
电　　话	邮购部 010-62752015　发行部 010-62750672
	编辑部 010-62759634
印 刷 者	北京圣夫亚美印刷有限公司
经 销 者	新华书店
	720毫米×1020毫米　16开本　22印张　450千字
	2016年9月第1版
	2025年6月第2版　2025年6月第1次印刷
定　　价	89.00元

未经许可，不得以任何方式复制或抄袭本书之部分或全部内容。
版权所有，侵权必究
举报电话：010-62752024　电子邮箱：fd@pup.cn
图书如有印装质量问题，请与出版部联系，电话：010-62756370

Contents

Introduction ***1***
    Preface 3
    Sample   The Story of an Hour 17

Unit One: Character ***25***
    Chapter 1   Rappaccini's Daughter 27
    Chapter 2   The Blue Hotel 67

Unit Two: Symbol ***107***
    Chapter 3   Paul's Case 109
    Chapter 4   Bernice Bobs Her Hair 142

Unit Three: Narration ***181***
    Chapter 5   I'm a Fool 183
    Chapter 6   Soldier's Home 204

Unit Four: Setting ***221***
    Chapter 7   The Greatest Man in the World 223
    Chapter 8   Barn Burning 239

Unit Five: Theme **271**
    Chapter 9   Almos'a Man 273
    Chapter 10   The Sky Is Gray 296

Appendix **338**
References **345**

Introduction

Preface

Sample: The Story of an Hour

Preface

The advances in digital technology have greatly changed the practice of language teaching. We used to teach language with texts in print, and now multimedia, the integration of sound, text, graphics, and video, is enriching our instruction. Yet, the introduction of multimedia is not to help students learn how to liberate themselves from the printed texts. Rather, the broader goal is to cultivate systematic methods of inquiry, models of critique, and analytical ways of reading visual images and messages in both print and media texts. Media are the important teaching tool, but the current language teaching further requires teaching with as well as teaching about multimedia.

1. A Rationale for Teaching Literature in ELT

The teaching of language and literature is inseparable. There has been controversy on the place of literature in language teaching. The controversy, however, centers not on if literature should be used, but always on how it should be used. The opponents often argue about when and where to use literary works, but literature takes varied forms in ELT classroom, and its significance has never been ignored.

Literature has great cultural value. Besides language instruction, the students of English also require an orientation to the target culture. The world of literature provides abundant cultural insights and experiences for language students. When reading literature from the foreign culture, we would encounter different cultural barriers and problems. With their exposition and solution, we could develop the communication across cultures, and this will improve our cultural awareness.

Literature has important linguistic value. Literature in English could be called English at its best. There are rich resources of language in literary works, which are most fully and skillfully used. The literary language could help to elaborate vocabulary and syntax, grammar and context. It is also a teaching aid for all language skills, including listening and writing. And moreover, we, as students, could learn many communicative skills through various characters that English literature displays.

Literature also has much educational value. We integrate the study of literary work into teaching English, and this demands that English literature should contribute to language instruction. Literature actually does more than that. With the appreciation and enjoyment from literature, it refines our language skills, and further stimulates us toward more advanced discussion and knowledge. Learning from classic literary characters, we could even make our own personal growth.

Considering the linguistic level of college students, the exclusive use of literature in English language teaching is hard to achieve, and not necessary, either. Yet, English literature is an available and also valuable resource for our language instruction. J. F. Povey comments on the place of literature in classroom, "Literature gives evidence of the widest variety of syntax, the richest variations of vocabulary discrimination. It provides examples of the language employed at its most effective, subtle, and suggestive. As literature sets out the potential of the English language it serves as an encouragement, guide, target to the presently limited linguistic achievement of the foreign student."[1] Fully understanding the significance of literature in language arts, we could say that the integration of literature with English teaching is both feasible and inevitable.

---

[1] Povey, J. F. "The Teaching of Literature in Advanced ESL Classes." In L. McIntosh & M. Celce-Murcia, eds. *Teaching English as a Second or Foreign Language*. Rowley: Newbury House, 1979, pp. 162-186.

2. A Rationale for Using Multimedia in ELT

Multimedia means the combined use of several mass media, especially for the purpose of education or entertainment. It integrates sound, text, graphics, and video, and interacting with digital technology, multimedia invades into almost every corner of our society. Apart from the entertaining function, multimedia still "provides continuous education throughout our life, offering a popular day and night school for the nation."[①] For many educators, multimedia is only for entertainment, not worth for serious study. However, we have to realize that the students nowadays are barraged with multimedia and technique advances. Facing this challenge, we are to provide students with media skills for today and tomorrow, and that forms a rationale for using multimedia in classroom, especially of language arts. English language teaching intends to improve students' potential, so it has no reason to refuse using multimedia.

With the development of digital technology, the introduction of multimedia into curriculum expands the notion of school literacy, which used to be principally the ability to read printed texts. Following traditional communication skills, the students are likely to fall into rote memorization. We know that many students of English try to learn the language through only memorizing vocabulary list, but often in vain. Media education stimulates critical thinking and analytical reading of students, and therefore, the school literacy today should also include the critical reading of media texts. The media literacy could help students comprehend and communicate through both traditional and emerging skills of information exchange.

Actually, multimedia is not strange to English language teaching from the very beginning. The audiovisual materials have long accompanied the teaching of English listening, such as tapes, videos, and in recent years, computer courseware. Yet, most teachers use media only as a teaching tool, namely as audiovisuals to illustrate

---

[①] Semali, Ladislaus M. *Literacy in Multimedia America: Integrating Media Education across the Curriculum*. New York: Falmer Press, 2000, p. 13.

instruction or even as entertainment to compensate students' hard work. This is far from satisfactory, and we should further teach about media as a source of information, messages and texts. Semali believes that the real expansion of school literacy will "require teaching with as well as teaching about television, computers, video, and film,"[①] and only in this way could the students really become media literate.

The introduction of multimedia into language classroom does not mean exclusion of texts in print. Like the place of literature in English language teaching, the exclusive use of multimedia materials is not practical, either. Since they both function well in enriching language instruction, we are to integrate literature and multimedia into teaching English. The students would acquire systematic knowledge about analytical reading and critical thinking from the printed texts and media texts, to be specific, from the short story and video film.

3. Teaching Short Story in ELT Classroom

English literature is an available and valuable resource for teaching the language, and now the problem is how to select and prepare literary works for classroom instruction. When teaching foreign literature, we mainly worry about the linguistic and cultural barriers between literary texts and students. Still, most teachers don't favor the abridged or simplified versions, because they simply have no place in literature anthology. The students do not have to understand everything they read, as the failure in some difficult structures usually does not prevent general comprehension. Thus, English language teaching demands literature in completeness. Literature is classified in genres, such as poetry, novel, play, essay, and short story, among which short story is the most approachable and satisfying literary form for College English teaching.

Short story is relatively brief. By the classic definition of Edgar Allan Poe, a short

---

① Semali, Ladislaus M. *Literacy in Multimedia America: Integrating Media Education across the Curriculum*. New York: Falmer Press, 2000, p. 22.

story must be short enough to be read at one sitting.[①] The contemporary short story most often refers to a work of fiction no longer than 20,000 words and no shorter than 1,000. So, short stories are short enough to maintain students' interest within class, although they also vary in length. The length fits well our teaching unit, and it makes the students' reading task and teachers' coverage both easier.

Short story is complete. Poe defines that short story must have a unified plot about a single protagonist, and it must aim at producing a single effect within the complete work.[②] Short story has a beginning to initiate the main action, a middle to presume what has gone before and require something to follow, and an ending to finish the plot. The simple beginning-middle-ending structure could illustrate completeness of literature. Actually, the structure of short story is more complicated, like this classic five-part scheme: "the first stage presents the conflict or problem to be solved; the second stage complicates that conflict; the third stage brings it to climax; the fourth explores the implications of choice at the climax; and the fifth presents the resolution."[③] Reading a short story, we could experience a complete literary piece rather than some key passages, chapters, or episodes of long works.

Short story is universal. It represents different English-speaking world, and it could further cross the limitation of age, sex, class and even nation. The universal themes of short story are to involve the readers rapidly, making an immediate impact and a single impression. Although outside the target culture, the students possibly have some similar experiences in life, and they could relate to the tales in front. Focused and memorable, short story serves as an essential part of the language and cultural

---

① Poe, Edgar Allan. "Nathaniel Hawthorne." In G. R. Thompson, ed. *The Selected Writings of Edgar Allan Poe*. New York: Norton, 2004, pp. 643-647.
② Ibid.
③ Dunning, Stephen. *Teaching Literature to Adolescents*. Glenview: Scott, Foreman and Company, 1968, p. 133.

experience available to the students of English.

These are the benefits of teaching short story, which grant this literary form a safe place in English language curriculum. The inclusion of short fiction does not expel the potential of poetry, novel or play, but comparing advantages (varied literary genres and writing characteristics) and disadvantages (poetry is often very abstract, while novel or play is too long), short story is still the most approachable and satisfying. The remaining question is how to integrate selected tales into English classroom. The teaching of short story requires the active participation of students, but the teachers' elaborate instruction is the same important.

When teaching short story, the focus must be on the text of tales. Considering the linguistic and cultural barriers facing the students, it is necessary to provide some background knowledge before approaching difficult vocabulary and allusion. Text notes could always help, but the information should be related enough not to distract attention or cause confusion. Additional cultural questions are to be cleared up whenever they arise. The preview in class could also work, if not costing much time. Before coming to class for discussion, students are supposed to have read the short story. If possible, it is better to read twice, first a normal reading for general comprehension, and then a fast reading for the story line and basic relationships among characters. One possible assignment is to make plot summaries as preparation for class discussion. This summary exercise, as simple as who's-doing-what-where, does not guarantee, but does encourage the basic understanding of tales.

Only when students are ready to talk could those discussion questions function well, which are prepared elaborately and cast carefully. For fruitful discussion, literary terms are probably an annoying holdback. They should be defined in familiar language, and it is very likely to find some appropriate examples from stories we are reading. Of course, we don't have to be so ambitious as to teach all literary terms through one or two tales. Naturally, we are not satisfied with the plot summaries or literary terms, because "our ultimate aim is extension of students' skills as readers rather than consolidation of their skills as readers of simple narrative."[①] To extend beyond the narrative level, students should learn how to read between the lines, from concrete examples to abstract ideas.

Very often, classroom discussion will not yield a true consensus. Within the range of rationality, every reader could have his own interpretation of the story. When students achieve enough literary taste, they start to read out the voice, scene, image, and angle from the printed text. Now they come close to the role of screenwriter or film director. The comparative study of short story and film could expand students' vision and further inspire their desire for advanced discussion.

4. Using Film in ELT Classroom

Literature comes into being with the appearance of human beings, but film has a much shorter history, a little more than a century. "On December 28, 1895, the Lumière brothers held one of the first public showing of motion picture projected on a screen, at the Grand Café in Paris,"[②] and film critics usually agree that this date signifies the birth of movie industry. Yet, film is a medium of ever-increasing popularity, and nowadays it is attracting billions of audience every year. By and large people go to the movies for the same reason they read literature: to lose themselves in a good story. Only the nature of film is an artistic form of collaboration, and it tells a story by integrating language, costumes, makeup, music, sound effects, color, light, locations, and visual images. For many teachers, it seems that reading is considered a highbrow activity, while movies are for the mass. This preference for literature over film is not necessarily correct, for

---

① Dunning, Stephen. *Teaching Literature to Adolescents*. Glenview: Scott, Foreman and Company, 1968, p. 20.
② Bordwell, David & Kristin Thompson. *Film Art: An Introduction* (7th edition). New York: McGraw-Hill, 2004, p. 466.

in the past century, film writers, directors, and actors have produced many profound and lasting works of no less artistic value. Besides, the movies illustrate the language spoken in diverse context by native speakers and provide richly detailed cultural information. Thus, we could contend that literature and film both have a deserved place in language teaching. As we ask our students to be active readers of literature, we also challenge them to become active viewers of film, so that they could achieve both verbal and visual literacy.

Most students have positive experience of watching film, and they will not refuse the appearance of movies in English class. We are not to show films, but to teach films, teaching with as well as teaching about film. After reading a literary work, we could give a movie version as an extension or comparison, since most film adaptation is an act of effective interpretation. Film viewing imparts pleasure and always generates fruitful discussion, but teaching film language would bring more benefits. Previously, when watching movies, we focus our attention on story lines, plot conventions, and popular actors. If we favor some particular movie, we mainly like its plot or characters. This is a superficial viewing. Like fiction, film has plot, character, setting, theme, and point of view. Like play, film has actors, costumes, makeup, locations, and director. We could say that film shares a lot with literature on literary and dramatic aspects. But after all, film is another medium, and it has basic difference from printed texts. It relies on the visual image combined with spoken word, so movie has its own special language.

We are not familiar with the cinematic aspects of a film, which are hard to skip when teaching about movies. The introduction of film language becomes necessary, and this includes technical terms that describe cinematography, sound, editing, and special visual effects. Similar to teaching literary terms, we are to define and give examples of various shots, editing techniques, and sound sources. This will facilitate our discussion and enrich our viewing. Teasley & Wilder state that studying film language could "make explicit the techniques for telling a story visually, heighten our appreciation for the art of film, and increase our awareness of how subtle cues can shade meaning."[1] We cannot agree more, and only with the mastery of film language could we begin to see and hear things that have been invisible and inaudible before.

The film adaptation of literary works has a long history, and novels, plays, and even poems have been adapted into movies. No matter how hard it tries, a film cannot exactly represent its literary source, mainly because of the difference between printed text and media text. The most we can expect of a film adaptation is that it is relatively faithful to the original work and still a good film. When adapting a novel or a play, we have to compress events and simplify characters to suit the running time and match the taste of common audience, so it is easy to invite criticism. Harrison cites Béla Balázs, one of the first film theorists in adaptations, who goes to the extreme and says, "One may perhaps make a good film out of a bad novel, but never out of a good one."[2] His word proves the criticism for novel adaptation, but it seems that short story is exempted from this problem. According to Alfred Hitchcock, a film bears a closer similarity to a short story, because "they both sustain one idea that culminates when the action has reached the highest point of dramatic curve."[3] With this reassurance, we could integrate short story and film into our English teaching curriculum.

5. Selecting Short Story and Film for ELT

Short story is printed text, and film is media text, but English language teaching benefits from the combined reading of both texts. Short stories exist to be read, to be experienced, and to be interpreted, while adaptations extend, enhance, and elaborate on

---

[1] Teasley, Alan B. & Ann Wilder. *Reel Conversations: Reading Films with Young Adults*. Portsmouth: Boynton / Cook Publishers, 1997, p. 26.
[2] Harrison, Stephanie, ed. *Adaptations: From Short Story to Big Screen*. New York: Three Rivers Press, 2005, p. xv.
[3] Aquino, John. *Film in the Language Arts Class*. Washington, D.C.: National Education Association, 1977, p. 16.

their sources. Film scripts start the process of adaptation and interpret the original texts, translating the stories from one medium into another. Yet, film scripts are still words on pages, and they need another step of interpretation. When shooting films, the scripts are transmuted into visual images by directors, actors, cinematographers, designers, and other film craftspeople. The writing of a script and the making of a film, therefore, both require unfolding the original story, and "in the end the film is here and the story is there and one hopes there is a fruitful interaction."[①] As active readers and positive viewers, we experience different interpretative approaches when reading the story in print and watching the story in film. This mutual collaboration could improve our verbal and visual literacy, and hence students become more media literate.

Talking about literature in English, the amount of short stories is immense. We have the task to keep in front of students a few stories to represent those many fine ones. The Americans are said to have invented the short story, which has thrived in this country from the moment of its literary independence. American writers are "the first to define the short story as a specific literary form, different from the novel or the long narrative poem not only in length but also in kind."[②] Most great American novelists, from Nathaniel Hawthorne and Henry James in the 19th century to Ernest Hemingway and William Faulkner in the 20th century, have written great short stories. Many other American writers, such as Edgar Allan Poe, Sherwood Anderson, and Katherine Anne Porter, have especially excelled in writing short story with its own rules and values. The flourishing American magazines have been featuring in publishing short stories. With the invasive development of radio, television, and film, they only fade out gradually in the second half of last century, but still far from disappearance. Recently, the successful film adaptation of the short story "Brokeback Mountain" proves its continuous

---

① Harrison, Stephanie, ed. *Adaptations: From Short Story to Big Screen*. New York: Three Rivers Press, 2005, p. xix.

② Skaggs, Calvin, ed. *The American Short Story*. New York: Dell Publishing, 1977, p. 11.

popularity. This literary form demands the highest literary craft and still attracts many most talented writers. Thus, the heritage of American short story, reflecting the diversity of American experience, fully deserves our attention in the teaching of English language.

The amount of films adapted from short stories is equally huge. Carol Emmens' book *Short Stories on Film and Video* claims to include all the films produced between 1920 and 1984 that are based on the short stories by American authors or outstanding international authors well known in America. This book has approximately 1,375 entries. Surely many more movies have been adapted from short stories during the past forty years. Some films have achieved more success than the original stories, such as Alfred Hitchcock's *Rear Window* (Cornell Woolrich's "It Had to Be Murder"), and Stanley Kubrick's *2001: A Space Odyssey* (Arthur Clarke's "The Sentinel"). Some others are successful on their own terms, even if receiving less acclaim than their sources, and here we have Robert Siodmak's *The Killers* (Ernest Hemingway's same title story) and Richard Brooks' *The Last Time I Saw Paris* (F. Scott Fitzgerald's "Babylon Revisited"). Still others have failed, not because they are unfaithful, but because they are not good films. (One obvious example is the recent version of *Scarlet Letter* starring Demi Moore, though it is not based on a short story.) With American short story in our mind, we are to choose the corresponding and most appropriate movies for English language class.

The films adapted from short stories are not necessarily short, and the above-mentioned movies all last about two hours. We have said that the potential use of novel or play in English teaching class is limited by its length, and the same problem confronts film using. With both story and film to discuss, it is not practical to spend two hours of class time only watching a movie. One solution is to use film clips to illustrate the whole movie, and many teachers have been doing this way, but this will definitely affect its completeness. Another approach is to choose short films. Many great short stories have been adapted into short films, such as Henry James' "The Real Thing," Charlotte Perkins Gilman's "The Yellow Wallpaper," and William Faulkner's "A Rose for Emily." The American Short Story series are among the best ever shot, and they have received much acclaim from critics and audience. Funded by National Endowment for the Humanities, Learning in Focus has been shooting this series from the late 1970s, which are shown on the influential American Public Broadcasting Service. It is a collection of some finest short stories covering a diverse range of topics by some of America's greatest authors such as Mark Twain, F. Scott Fitzgerald, Ernest Hemingway, and many others.

To illustrate the integration of literature and multimedia in ELT classroom, we are to give a sample of teaching short story through film. "Rappaccini's Daughter" (story, 1844; film, 1980), the most problematic but also the most characteristic of all of Hawthorne's tales, could provide us a model worksheet. The story explores two essential Hawthorne themes: the sin of interfering with another's soul and the futility of trying to tamper with nature, both relevant till today. Starring Kathleen Beller (the Academy Award nominee) and Kristopher Tabori, the film is written by Herbert Hartig and directed by Dezsö Magyar. Vividly reproducing its mysterious, ambiguous and symbolic world, the film adaptation is faithful to but not confined by Hawthorne's text. We read the story and watch the movie, enjoying both but not to decide which is better.

6. Model Worksheet for "Rappaccini's Daughter"

6.1 Preview

1. Introduce Nathaniel Hawthorne and his tales.
2. Point out linguistic barriers: Middle English usage and Italian words.

6.2 Plot Summary

1. Read the tale and sum up story plot: who's-doing-what-where pattern.
2. Think over discussion questions, and prepare for class discussion.

6.3 Story Discussion

1. Structure: Do you like and agree with the story's conclusion? If you were the author, how would you finish the tale?
2. Style: Do you think "Rappaccini's Daughter" is a gothic story, a feminist story, or an allegorical story? Please explain why.
3. Theme: How does Hawthorne explore the nature of good and evil in this story? What do you think about the portraying of science?
4. Character: Is Beatrice an angelic figure, a seductive temptress, neither, or something else? Analyze the relationships between Beatrice and three male characters, Giovanni, Doctor Rappaccini, and Professor Baglioni.
5. Symbol: Discuss and explain the symbolic meaning of the garden and the color purple. Can you find some other symbols in the story?
6. Setting: What effect does the post-medieval Italian setting have on the action and interpretation of the story?

6.4 Visual View

1. Sketch the garden image and the final scene of the story. What would compose the foreground and background? Please explain.
2. Watch the movie together and take notes for any interesting point.

6.5 Film Analysis

1. Introduce high angle shot and low angle shot with the sequence of Giovanni throwing the bouquet to Beatrice, from his window to her in the garden. Could you find some other shooting point of view, such as the reverse angle?
2. What do you think of the color, sound, and costume of the movie? Is it necessary to use a voiceover for Giovanni?

6.6 Integration of Story and Film

1. Does the movie conform to or oppose against your impression from reading the story? Are you satisfied with the film?

2. Compare the different conclusions to the story and the film. Further talk about the addition (a servant to the landlady; the little restaurant; some friends of Giovanni) and omission (Professor Baglioni's final cry) when adapting the tale to film.

7. Beyond the Integration of Literature and Multimedia

The advances of digital society demand more literate students—literate in both printed texts and media texts. The expansion of school literacy, therefore, extends the realm of our education and also challenges the traditional instruction. Teaching the English language with literature and multimedia is a possible tendency for future media education, and it could contribute a bit to cultivating the graduates of new ages. English, as a universal language, is not only a tool; neither is multimedia in our teaching practice. We are to master language skills, but we should not exclude the culture and literature of target language. We teach the English language with help of multimedia, and the teaching about media texts is the same necessary.

Up to today, the American Short Story series have released twenty-one films. Teachers of the story-film courses could choose from, but of course not limited by this series. There are more and more choices with the flourishing of film and media industry. The collection *The American Short Story through Film* here includes ten filmed short stories, for one semester of College English teaching. With this book, we intend to teach the English language through the integration of both media. The teaching combines traditional fiction criticism and modern film study, and hence improves the students' cultural awareness, literary education, and school literacy. English language teaching benefits a lot from the development of digital technology, and looking beyond, we would like to wait for its positive influence in every corner of our coming society.

Sample
The Story of an Hour

Kate Chopin

Author Introduction:

Kate Chopin (1851—1904) was born in St. Louis to a prominent Creole-Irish family that prized books and education. On a visit to New Orleans, she met her husband-to-be and returned there to live with him when she married at twenty.

After her husband's early death, she went back to St. Louis and began to write, largely drawing on the experiences of her years in the Deep South.

She contributed to many of the popular periodicals of her time, but her writing career came to an end with the publication of her novel *The Awakening* (1899), which was sharply condemned for its frank representation of adultery and mixed marriage.

This book has subsequently been praised for its sensitive portrayal of a woman in quest of her individuality. Many of Chopin's stories were collected in *Bayou Folks* (1894) and *A Night in Acadie* (1899).

Story Summary:

The story suggests that marriage, regardless of the good intentions of the people it joins, necessarily results in repression and a loss of freedom.

Mrs. Mallard allows herself time to reflect upon learning of her husband's death. Instead of dreading the lonely years ahead of her, she stumbles upon another realization all together. The story plays with both irony and tragedy as the shock that her friends fear will kill Louise restores her freedom, and the joy they anticipate for her is the heartbreak that kills her.

We should learn from the marriage of the Mallards, which could suffocate a wife with the loss of freedom in the name of love, convention and tradition.

Key Terms:

Convention: Mrs. Mallard lives in the Deep South of America, surrounded with strong bonds of convention and tradition.

Self-Awareness: Hearing the sudden death of her husband, Mrs. Mallard comes to a new self-awareness: her freedom in marriage and future life.

Psychology: Mrs. Mallard comes to realize her self-awareness suddenly through her psychological activities, upstairs alone by herself.

Irony: The biggest irony in the story is that Mr. Mallard is alive while Mrs. Mallard dies at the end of the story. It is said that joy kills her.

Feminism: Marriage, regardless of the good intentions of the people it joins, necessarily results in repression and a loss of freedom, especially for women. The female needs to search for their identity in a male-dominated world.

The Story of an Hour[1]

Knowing that Mrs. Mallard was afflicted with[2] a heart trouble, great care was taken to break to her as gently as possible the news of her husband's death.

It was her sister Josephine who told her, in broken sentences; veiled hints that revealed in half concealing. Her husband's friend Richards was there, too, near her. It was he who had been in the newspaper office when intelligence of the railroad disaster was received, with Brently Mallard's name leading the list of "killed." He had only taken the time to assure himself of its truth by a second telegram, and had hastened to forestall[3] any less careful, less tender friend in bearing the sad message.

She did not hear the story as many women have heard the same, with a paralyzed inability to accept its significance. She wept at once, with sudden, wild abandonment, in her sister's arms. When the storm of grief had spent itself she went away to her room alone. She would have no one follow her.

There stood, facing the open window, a comfortable, roomy armchair. Into this she sank, pressed down by a physical exhaustion that haunted her body and seemed to reach into her soul.

She could see in the open square before her house the tops of trees that were all aquiver with the new spring life. The delicious breath of rain was in the air. In the street below a peddler[4] was crying his wares. The notes of a distant song which some one was singing reached her faintly, and countless sparrows were twittering in the eaves.

There were patches of blue sky showing here and there through the clouds that had met and piled one above the other in the west facing her window.

---

[1] First published in *Vogue* on December 6, 1894, under the title "The Dream of an Hour," and then reprinted in *St. Louis Life* on January 5, 1895.
[2] Suffering from.
[3] To keep from happening or arising; act in advance of; deal with ahead of time.
[4] Someone who travels about selling his wares (as on the streets or at carnivals).

She sat with her head thrown back upon the cushion of the chair, quite motionless, except when a sob came up into her throat and shook her, as a child who has cried itself to sleep continues to sob in its dreams.

She was young, with a fair, calm face, whose lines bespoke repression and even a certain strength. But now there was a dull stare in her eyes, whose gaze was fixed away off yonder on one of those patches of blue sky. It was not a glance of reflection, but rather indicated a suspension of intelligent thought.

There was something coming to her and she was waiting for it, fearfully. What was it? She did not know; it was too subtle and elusive to name. But she felt it, creeping out of the sky, reaching toward her through the sounds, the scents, the color that filled the air.

Now her bosom rose and fell tumultuously. She was beginning to recognize this thing that was approaching to possess her, and she was striving to beat it back with her will—as powerless as her two white slender hands would have been.

When she abandoned herself a little whispered word escaped her slightly parted lips. She said it over and over under her breath: "free, free, free!" The vacant stare and the look of terror that had followed it went from her eyes. They stayed keen and bright. Her pulses beat fast, and the coursing blood warmed and relaxed every inch of her body.

She did not stop to ask if it were or were not a monstrous joy that held her. A clear and exalted perception enabled her to dismiss the suggestion as trivial.

She knew that she would weep again when she saw the kind, tender hands folded in death; the face that had never looked save with love upon her, fixed and gray and dead. But she saw beyond that bitter moment a long procession of years to come that would belong to her absolutely. And she opened and spread her arms out to them in welcome.

There would be no one to live for her during those coming years; she would live for herself. There would be no powerful will bending hers in that blind persistence with which men and women believe they have a right to impose a private will upon a fellow-creature. A kind intention or a cruel intention made that act seem no less a crime as she looked upon it in that brief moment of illumination[1].

And yet she had loved him—sometimes. Often she had not. What did it matter! What could love, the unsolved mystery, count for in face of this possession of self-assertion which she suddenly recognized as the strongest impulse of her being!

"Free! Body and soul free!" she kept whispering.

Josephine was kneeling before the closed door with her lips to the keyhole, imploring for admission. "Louise, open the door! I beg; open the door—you will make yourself ill. What are you doing, Louise? For heaven's sake open the door."

"Go away. I am not making myself ill." No; she was drinking in a very elixir of life through that open window.

Her fancy was running riot along those days ahead of her. Spring days, and summer days, and all sorts of days that would be her own. She breathed a quick prayer that life might be long. It was only yesterday she had thought with a shudder that life might be long.

She arose at length and opened the door to her sister's importunities. There was a feverish triumph in her eyes, and she carried herself unwittingly like a goddess of Victory. She clasped her sister's waist, and together they descended the stairs. Richards stood waiting for them at the bottom.

Some one was opening the front door with a latchkey[2]. It was Brently Mallard who entered, a little travel-stained[3], composedly carrying his grip-sack and umbrella.

---

[1] A condition of spiritual awareness or divine illumination; an interpretation that removes obstacles to understanding.
[2] Key for raising or drawing back a latch or opening an outside door.
[3] Soiled from travel.

He had been far from the scene of accident, and did not even know there had been one. He stood amazed at Josephine's piercing cry; at Richards' quick motion to screen him from the view of his wife.

But Richards was too late.

When the doctors came they said she had died of heart disease—of joy that kills.

Film Comment:

Kate Chopin: *Five Stories of an Hour* (26:00): This program consists of five versions of the same short story, "The Story of an Hour" by Kate Chopin, who scandalized American readers in the late 19th century by questioning the social and marital mores of her time. The story examines the behavior and feelings of a woman on the day she is informed of her husband's death. The program includes a reading of the story by Zoë Wanamaker, plus dramatizations by playwrights Kathleen Potter, David Stafford, and Michelene Wandor.

(1) Narration of "The Story of an Hour" (07:09)

Zoë Wanamaker narrates Kate Chopin's story. After hearing of her husband's death, Mrs. Mallard encounters a new feeling of freedom. She receives a shock at the end and dies of joy that kills.

(2) "The Story of an Hour": Part 1 (04:46)

In this dramatization Louise reveals to her sister the freedom she feels after being told her husband has died. Thus, Josephine understands why Louise dies at the end when her husband returns home.

(3) "The Husband's Story" (04:00)

This rendition by David Stafford portrays the story through the viewpoint and narration of Louise's husband, Brently Mallard, including the reason why he missed the train that ended up crashing.

(4) "The Story of an Hour": Part 2 (07:06)

In this dramatization, Louise reflects on her wedding day. She tells her sister that she tried to love her husband. When Brently returns, Louise is ecstatic and vows to change her life for him.

(5) Kate Chopin's Life (00:38)

Born Katherine O'Flaherty in 1850, Kate grew up in St. Louis, Missouri, in an all-female household after her father's death. In 1870 she married Oscar Chopin and enjoyed a happy marriage in Louisiana.

Discussion Questions:

(1) What does Mrs. Mallard really die of?

(2) How do you think Mr. Mallard would feel if he knew how his wife really felt?

(3) Do you believe that Chopin is trying to make some grand assertion about fate or free will with the ending of the story? If so, what is it?

(4) In what ways is the last line of the story an ironic statement? What is gained by having the doctors make such a statement rather than putting it in the mouths of Josephine or Richards?

(5) If you were going to write some fan fiction inspired by "The Story of an Hour," how would you do it? Which characters would you explore? How would you imagine the personalities of Richards, Josephine, and Mr. Mallard? What would be the back-story behind Mr. and Mrs. Mallard's marriage?

Unit One: Character

Chapter 1: Rappaccini's Daughter

Chapter 2: The Blue Hotel

Chapter 1
Rappaccini's Daughter

Nathaniel Hawthorne

Author Introduction:

Nathaniel Hawthorne (1804—1864) was born in Salem, Massachusetts, into a prominent family who traced their lineage back to the Puritans. After graduating from Bowdoin College in 1825, Hawthorne returned to Salem to live a life of almost total seclusion for twelve years as he mastered his skills as a writer. Only when his first collections *Twice-Told Tales* (1837) made money, did he feel secure enough to marry Sophia Peabody and settle in the Old Manse in Concord, Massachusetts.

The Scarlet Letter (1850), his greatest novel of a woman taken into adultery, brought him recognition as a major literary figure, which was followed by three more novels, *The House of Seven Gables* (1851), a story tinged with nightmarish humor, *The Blithedale Romance* (1852), drawn from his short, disgruntled stay at a Utopian commune, Brook Farm, and *The Marble Faun* (1860), inspired by a short stay in Italy.

In 1853 he was appointed consul to Liverpool by his college friend Franklin Pierce, who had become President of the United States. After four years of service in his post, Hawthorne traveled in England and Italy until his return to America in 1860. Much of his work is centering on New England and colored by romanticism, while the weight of his Puritan heritage, with its ethical biases and emphasis on sin, radically shaped his themes.

His books of short stories are two volumes of *Twice-Told Tales* (1837 and 1842) and *Mosses from an Old Manse* (1846). Hawthorne wrote for children, too, retelling classic legends in *The Wonder Book* (1852) and *Tanglewood Tales* (1853).

Story Summary:

The story explores the definition of beauty, emotion/love versus intellect/science, and Creator/creation.

Young Giovanni comes to Padua to study. His apartment window overlooks a voluptuously beautiful garden which comforts him in his otherwise dismal surroundings and homesick state. The garden is cultivated by Dr. Rappaccini, a strange man of science who grows deadly plants for use in medicines. One day Giovanni sees Rappaccini's daughter tending the garden. Her bloom is as deep and vivid as the poisonous flowers in her care. But she has been nourished by the garden and her very breath and touch are deadly. Giovanni's love for her and fateful quest to free her begins. But he is unable to save his innocent mistress from her fate. His fears and mistrust ultimately destroy her.

We should learn from the death of Rappaccini's daughter, the innocent Beatrice, who dies for the sins of her father interfering with the laws of Nature with his experiments.

Key Terms:

Allegory: The story has parallels with that of Adam and Eve in the Book of

Genesis of the *Bible*, possibly with Giovanni and Beatrice respectively representing Adam and Eve, Dr. Rappaccini representing God, and Professor Baglioni representing Satan.

Symbolism: There are quite a few cases of symbolism in the story, such as the garden, the plants, the flowers, the colors, the insects, the fountain, the antidote, etc.

Femme Fatale: Although she is innocent and pure, Giovanni is convinced that Beatrice is corrupted or cursed by her poisonousness, and that she needs to be saved.

Ethics: Beatrice dies for the sins of her father, Dr. Rappaccini, whose experiments aim at interfering with the laws of Nature.

Feminism: Although in distress, Beatrice accepts to drink the antidote for the sake of Giovanni and dies like the heroine of a tragic romance.

Masculinity: The death of Beatrice is the result of intentional or non-intentional collaboration of three men: Dr. Rappaccini, Professor Baglioni and her lover Giovanni, illustrating the power of masculinity.

Rappaccini's Daughter[1]

A young man, named Giovanni Guasconti, came, very long ago, from the more southern region of Italy, to pursue his studies at the University of Padua[2]. Giovanni, who had but a scanty supply of gold ducats[3] in his pocket, took lodgings in a high and gloomy chamber of an old edifice, which looked not unworthy to have been the palace of a Paduan noble, and which, in fact, exhibited over its entrance the armorial bearings of a family long since extinct. The young stranger, who was not unstudied in the great

---

[1] First published in *The United States Magazine and Democratic Review*, December 1844, and then collected in *Mosses from an Old Manse* (1846).
[2] City in northern Italy, near Venice.
[3] Italian coins.

poem of his country, recollected that one of the ancestors of this family, and perhaps an occupant of this very mansion, had been pictured by Dante① as a partaker of the immortal agonies of his Inferno②. These reminiscences and associations, together with the tendency to heart-break natural to a young man for the first time out of his native sphere, caused Giovanni to sigh heavily, as he looked around the desolate and ill-furnished apartment.

"Holy Virgin, signor," cried old dame Lisabetta, who, won by the youth's remarkable beauty of person, was kindly endeavoring to give the chamber a habitable air, "what a sigh was that to come out of a young man's heart! Do you find this old mansion gloomy? For the love of heaven, then, put your head out of the window, and you will see as bright sunshine as you have left in Naples."

Guasconti mechanically did as the old woman advised, but could not quite agree with her that the Lombard③ sunshine was as cheerful as that of southern Italy. Such as it was, however, it fell upon a garden beneath the window, and expended its fostering influences on a variety of plants, which seemed to have been cultivated with exceeding care.

"Does this garden belong to the house?" asked Giovanni.

"Heaven forbid, signor!—unless it were fruitful of better pot-herbs than any that grow there now," answered old Lisabetta. "No; that garden is cultivated by the own hands of Signor Giacomo Rappaccini, the famous Doctor, who, I warrant him, has been heard of as far as Naples. It is said he distils these plants into medicines that are as potent as a charm. Oftentimes you may see the Signor Doctor at work, and perchance

---

① Italian poet, whose major work was the *Divine Comedy*, an epic tale of the poet's journey through Hell, Purgatory, and Heaven.

② Hell in Dante's *Divine Comedy*. In *Inferno* 18:71, Dante observes an unnamed Paduan nobleman among those who have committed crimes against Nature.

③ A member of a Germanic people that invaded northern Italy in the sixth century and established a kingdom in the Po River valley.

the Signora his daughter, too, gathering the strange flowers that grow in the garden."

The old woman had now done what she could for the aspect of the chamber, and, commending the young man to the protection of the saints, took her departure.

Giovanni still found no better occupation than to look down into the garden beneath his window. From its appearance, he judged it to be one of those botanic gardens, which were of earlier date in Padua than elsewhere in Italy, or in the world. Or, not improbably, it might once have been the pleasure-place of an opulent family; for there was the ruin of a marble fountain in the center, sculptured with rare art, but so woefully shattered that it was impossible to trace the original design from the chaos of remaining fragments. The water, however, continued to gush and sparkle into the sunbeams as cheerfully as ever. A little gurgling sound ascended to the young man's window, and made him feel as if a fountain were an immortal spirit, that sung its song unceasingly, and without heeding the vicissitudes[①] around it; while one century embodied it in marble, and another scattered the perishable garniture on the soil. All about the pool into which the water subsided, grew various plants, that seemed to require a plentiful supply of moisture for the nourishment of gigantic leaves, and, in some instances, flowers gorgeously magnificent. There was one shrub in particular, set in a marble vase in the midst of the pool, that bore a profusion of purple blossoms, each of which had the luster and richness of a gem; and the whole together made a show so resplendent that it seemed enough to illuminate the garden, even had there been no sunshine. Every portion of the soil was peopled with plants and herbs, which, if less beautiful, still bore tokens of assiduous care; as if all had their individual virtues, known to the scientific mind that fostered them. Some were placed in urns, rich with old carving, and others in common garden-pots; some crept serpent-like along the ground, or climbed on high, using whatever means of ascent was offered them. One

---

① Changes.

plant had wreathed itself round a statue of Vertumnus[①], which was thus quite veiled and shrouded in a drapery of hanging foliage, so happily arranged that it might have served a sculptor for a study.

While Giovanni stood at the window, he heard a rustling behind a screen of leaves, and became aware that a person was at work in the garden. His figure soon emerged into view, and showed itself to be that of no common laborer, but a tall, emaciated[②], sallow, and sickly looking man, dressed in a scholar's garb[③] of black. He was beyond the middle term of life, with gray hair, a thin gray beard, and a face singularly marked with intellect and cultivation, but which could never, even in his more youthful days, have expressed much warmth of heart.

Nothing could exceed the intentness with which this scientific gardener examined every shrub which grew in his path; it seemed as if he was looking into their inmost nature, making observations in regard to their creative essence, and discovering why one leaf grew in this shape, and another in that, and wherefore such and such flowers differed among themselves in hue and perfume. Nevertheless, in spite of the deep intelligence on his part, there was no approach to intimacy between himself and these vegetable existences. On the contrary, he avoided their actual touch, or the direct inhaling of their odors, with a caution that impressed Giovanni most disagreeably; for the man's demeanor was that of one walking among malignant influences, such as savage beasts, or deadly snakes, or evil spirits, which, should he allow them one moment of license, would wreak upon him some terrible fatality. It was strangely frightful to the young man's imagination, to see this air of insecurity in a person cultivating a garden, that most simple and innocent of human toils, and which had been

---

① The Roman god of seasons. In Ovid's *Metamorphoses* 14, Vertumnus woos and wins the modest Pomona in her secluded garden.
② Very thin especially from disease or hunger or cold.
③ Clothing of a distinctive style or for a particular occasion.

alike the joy and labor of the unfallen parents of the race[①]. Was this garden, then, the Eden of the present world?—and this man, with such a perception of harm in what his own hands caused to grow, was he the Adam?

The distrustful gardener, while plucking away the dead leaves or pruning the too luxuriant growth of the shrubs, defended his hands with a pair of thick gloves. Nor were these his only armor. When, in his walk through the garden, he came to the magnificent plant that hung its purple gems beside the marble fountain, he placed a kind of mask over his mouth and nostrils, as if all this beauty did but conceal a deadlier malice. But finding his task still too dangerous, he drew back, removed the mask, and called loudly, but in the infirm voice of a person affected with inward disease:

"Beatrice!—Beatrice!"

"Here am I, my father! What would you?" cried a rich and youthful voice from the window of the opposite house; a voice as rich as a tropical sunset, and which made Giovanni, though he knew not why, think of deep hues of purple or crimson, and of perfumes heavily delectable.—"Are you in the garden?"

"Yes, Beatrice," answered the gardener, "and I need your help."

Soon there emerged from under a sculptured portal the figure of a young girl, arrayed with as much richness of taste as the most splendid of the flowers, beautiful as the day, and with a bloom so deep and vivid that one shade more would have been too much. She looked redundant with life, health, and energy; all of which attributes were bound down and compressed, as it were, and girdled tensely, in their luxuriance, by her virgin zone[②]. Yet Giovanni's fancy must have grown morbid, while he looked down into the garden; for the impression which the fair stranger made upon him was as if here were another flower, the human sister of those vegetable ones, as beautiful as they—more beautiful than the richest of them—but still to be touched only with a

---

① Referring to Adam and Eve in Garden Eden.
② Her belt, "virgin" because Beatrice appears to be an unmarried girl.

glove, nor to be approached without a mask. As Beatrice came down the garden-path, it was observable that she handled and inhaled the odor of several of the plants, which her father had most sedulously① avoided.

"Here, Beatrice," said the latter, —"see how many needful offices require to be done to our chief treasure. Yet, shattered as I am, my life might pay the penalty of approaching it so closely as circumstances demand. Henceforth, I fear, this plant must be consigned to your sole charge."

"And gladly will I undertake it," cried again the rich tones of the young lady, as she bent towards the magnificent plant, and opened her arms as if to embrace it. "Yes, my sister, my splendor, it shall be Beatrice's task to nurse and serve thee; and thou shalt reward her with thy kisses and perfume breath, which to her is as the breath of life!"

Then, with all the tenderness in her manner that was so strikingly expressed in her words, she busied herself with such attentions as the plant seemed to require; and Giovanni, at his lofty window, rubbed his eyes, and almost doubted whether it were a girl tending her favorite flower, or one sister performing the duties of affection to another. The scene soon terminated. Whether Doctor Rappaccini had finished his labors in the garden, or that his watchful eye had caught the stranger's face, he now took his daughter's arm and retired. Night was already closing in; oppressive exhalations seemed to proceed from the plants, and steal upward past the open window; and Giovanni, closing the lattice, went to his couch, and dreamed of a rich flower and beautiful girl. Flower and maiden were different and yet the same, and fraught with some strange peril in either shape.

But there is an influence in the light of morning that tends to rectify whatever errors of fancy, or even of judgment, we may have incurred during the sun's decline, or among the shadows of the night, or in the less wholesome glow of moonshine.

---

① With diligence and intent.

Chapter 1 Rappaccini's Daughter

Giovanni's first movement on starting from sleep, was to throw open the window, and gaze down into the garden which his dreams had made so fertile of mysteries. He was surprised, and a little ashamed, to find how real and matter-of-fact an affair it proved to be, in the first rays of the sun, which gilded the dew-drops that hung upon leaf and blossom, and, while giving a brighter beauty to each rare flower, brought everything within the limits of ordinary experience. The young man rejoiced, that, in the heart of the barren city, he had the privilege of overlooking this spot of lovely and luxuriant vegetation. It would serve, he said to himself, as a symbolic language, to keep him in communion with Nature. Neither the sickly and thought-worn Doctor Giacomo Rappaccini, it is true, nor his brilliant daughter, were now visible; so that Giovanni could not determine how much of the singularity which he attributed to both, was due to their own qualities, and how much to his wonder-working fancy. But he was inclined to take a most rational view of the whole matter.

In the course of the day, he paid his respects to Signor Pietro Baglioni, Professor of Medicine in the University, a physician of eminent repute, to whom Giovanni had brought a letter of introduction. The Professor was an elderly personage, apparently of genial nature, and habits that might almost be called jovial; he kept the young man to dinner, and made himself very agreeable by the freedom and liveliness of his conversation, especially when warmed by a flask or two of Tuscan wine[①]. Giovanni, conceiving that men of science, inhabitants of the same city, must needs be on familiar terms with one another, took an opportunity to mention the name of Doctor Rappaccini. But the Professor did not respond with so much cordiality as he had anticipated.

"Ill would it become a teacher of the divine art of medicine," said Professor Pietro Baglioni, in answer to a question of Giovanni, "to withhold due and well-considered praise of a physician so eminently skilled as Rappaccini. But, on the other hand, I

---

① Tuscany is a province of Italy known for its wine.

should answer it but scantily to my conscience, were I to permit a worthy youth like yourself, Signor Giovanni, the son of an ancient friend, to imbibe erroneous ideas respecting a man who might hereafter chance to hold your life and death in his hands. The truth is, our worshipful Doctor Rappaccini has as much science as any member of the faculty—with perhaps one single exception—in Padua, or all Italy. But there are certain grave objections to his professional character."

"And what are they?" asked the young man.

"Has my friend Giovanni any disease of body or heart, that he is so inquisitive about physicians?" said the Professor, with a smile. "But as for Rappaccini, it is said of him—and I, who know the man well, can answer for its truth—that he cares infinitely more for science than for mankind. His patients are interesting to him only as subjects for some new experiment. He would sacrifice human life, his own among the rest, or whatever else was dearest to him, for the sake of adding so much as a grain of mustard-seed① to the great heap of his accumulated knowledge."

"Methinks he is an awful man, indeed," remarked Guasconti, mentally recalling the cold and purely intellectual aspect of Rappaccini. "And yet, worshipful Professor, is it not a noble spirit? Are there many men capable of so spiritual a love of science?"

"God forbid," answered the Professor, somewhat testily—"at least, unless they take sounder views of the healing art than those adopted by Rappaccini. It is his theory, that all medicinal virtues are comprised within those substances which we term vegetable poisons. These he cultivates with his own hands, and is said even to have produced new varieties of poison, more horribly deleterious② than Nature, without the assistance of this learned person, would ever have plagued the world withal. That the Signor Doctor does less mischief than might be expected, with such dangerous substances, is undeniable. Now and then, it must be owned, he has effected—or seemed

---

① Black or white seeds ground to make mustard pastes or powders.
② Harmful.

Chapter 1 Rappaccini's Daughter

to effect—a marvelous cure. But, to tell you my private mind, Signor Giovanni, he should receive little credit for such instances of success—they being probably the work of chance—but should be held strictly accountable for his failures, which may justly be considered his own work."

The youth might have taken Baglioni's opinions with many grains of allowance, had he known that there was a professional warfare of long continuance between him and Doctor Rappaccini, in which the latter was generally thought to have gained the advantage. If the reader be inclined to judge for himself, we refer him to certain black-letter tracts[①] on both sides, preserved in the medical department of the University of Padua.

"I know not, most learned Professor," returned Giovanni, after musing on what had been said of Rappaccini's exclusive zeal for science—"I know not how dearly this physician may love his art; but surely there is one object more dear to him. He has a daughter."

"Aha!" cried the Professor with a laugh. "So now our friend Giovanni's secret is out. You have heard of this daughter, whom all the young men in Padua are wild about, though not half a dozen have ever had the good hap to see her face. I know little of the Signora Beatrice, save that Rappaccini is said to have instructed her deeply in his science, and that, young and beautiful as fame reports her, she is already qualified to fill a professor's chair. Perchance her father destines her for mine! Other absurd rumors there be, not worth talking about, or listening to. So now, Signor Giovanni, drink off your glass of Lacryma[②]."

Guasconti returned to his lodgings somewhat heated with the wine he had quaffed, and which caused his brain to swim with strange fantasies in reference to Doctor Rappaccini and the beautiful Beatrice. On his way, happening to pass by a florist's, he

---

① Ancient writings done by medieval scribes.
② An Italian wine, grown near Mount Vesuvius.

bought a fresh bouquet of flowers.

Ascending to his chamber, he seated himself near the window, but within the shadow thrown by the depth of the wall, so that he could look down into the garden with little risk of being discovered. All beneath his eye was a solitude. The strange plants were basking in the sunshine, and now and then nodding gently to one another, as if in acknowledgment of sympathy and kindred. In the midst, by the shattered fountain, grew the magnificent shrub, with its purple gems clustering all over it; they glowed in the air, and gleamed back again out of the depths of the pool, which thus seemed to overflow with colored radiance from the rich reflection that was steeped in it. At first, as we have said, the garden was a solitude. Soon, however,—as Giovanni had half hoped, half feared, would be the case,—a figure appeared beneath the antique sculptured portal, and came down between the rows of plants, inhaling their various perfumes, as if she were one of those beings of old classic fable, that lived upon sweet odors. On again beholding Beatrice, the young man was even startled to perceive how much her beauty exceeded his recollection of it; so brilliant, so vivid in its character, that she glowed amid the sunlight, and, as Giovanni whispered to himself, positively illuminated the more shadowy intervals of the garden path. Her face being now more revealed than on the former occasion, he was struck by its expression of simplicity and sweetness; qualities that had not entered into his idea of her character, and which made him ask anew, what manner of mortal she might be. Nor did he fail again to observe, or imagine, an analogy between the beautiful girl and the gorgeous shrub that hung its gem-like flowers over the fountain; a resemblance which Beatrice seemed to have indulged a fantastic humor in heightening, both by the arrangement of her dress and the selection of its hues.

Approaching the shrub, she threw open her arms, as with a passionate ardor, and drew its branches into an intimate embrace; so intimate, that her features were hidden in its leafy bosom, and her glistening ringlets all intermingled with the flowers.

Chapter 1 Rappaccini's Daughter

"Give me thy breath, my sister," exclaimed Beatrice; "for I am faint with common air! And give me this flower of thine, which I separate with gentlest fingers from the stem, and place it close beside my heart."

With these words, the beautiful daughter of Rappaccini plucked one of the richest blossoms of the shrub, and was about to fasten it in her bosom. But now, unless Giovanni's draughts[①] of wine had bewildered his senses, a singular incident occurred. A small orange colored reptile, of the lizard or chameleon species, chanced to be creeping along the path, just at the feet of Beatrice. It appeared to Giovanni—but, at the distance from which he gazed, he could scarcely have seen anything so minute—it appeared to him, however, that a drop or two of moisture from the broken stem of the flower descended upon the lizard's head. For an instant, the reptile contorted itself violently, and then lay motionless in the sunshine. Beatrice observed this remarkable phenomenon, and crossed herself, sadly, but without surprise; nor did she therefore hesitate to arrange the fatal flower in her bosom. There it blushed, and almost glimmered with the dazzling effect of a precious stone, adding to her dress and aspect the one appropriate charm, which nothing else in the world could have supplied. But Giovanni, out of the shadow of his window, bent forward and shrank back, and murmured and trembled.

"Am I awake? Have I my senses?" said he to himself. "What is this being?—beautiful, shall I call her?—or inexpressibly terrible?"

Beatrice now strayed carelessly through the garden, approaching closer beneath Giovanni's window, so that he was compelled to thrust his head quite out of its concealment, in order to gratify the intense and painful curiosity which she excited. At this moment, there came a beautiful insect over the garden wall; it had perhaps wandered through the city and found no flowers nor verdure[②] among those antique

---

① A serving of drink (usually alcoholic) drawn from a keg.
② The lush greenness of flourishing vegetation.

haunts of men, until the heavy perfumes of Doctor Rappaccini's shrubs had lured it from afar. Without alighting on the flowers, this winged brightness seemed to be attracted by Beatrice, and lingered in the air and fluttered about her head. Now here it could not be but that Giovanni Guasconti's eyes deceived him. Be that as it might, he fancied that while Beatrice was gazing at the insect with childish delight, it grew faint and fell at her feet;—its bright wings shivered; it was dead—from no cause that he could discern, unless it were the atmosphere of her breath. Again Beatrice crossed herself and sighed heavily, as she bent over the dead insect.

An impulsive movement of Giovanni drew her eyes to the window. There she beheld the beautiful head of the young man—rather a Grecian than an Italian head, with fair, regular features, and a glistening of gold among his ringlets—gazing down upon her like a being that hovered in mid-air. Scarcely knowing what he did, Giovanni threw down the bouquet which he had hitherto held in his hand.

"Signora," said he, "there are pure and healthful flowers. Wear them for the sake of Giovanni Guasconti!"

"Thanks, Signor," replied Beatrice, with her rich voice that came forth as it were like a gush of music; and with a mirthful expression half childish and half woman-like. "I accept your gift, and would fain recompense it with this precious purple flower; but if I toss it into the air, it will not reach you. So Signor Guasconti must even content himself with my thanks."

She lifted the bouquet from the ground, and then as if inwardly ashamed at having stepped aside from her maidenly reserve to respond to a stranger's greeting, passed swiftly homeward through the garden. But, few as the moments were, it seemed to Giovanni when she was on the point of vanishing beneath the sculptured portal, that his beautiful bouquet was already beginning to wither in her grasp. It was an idle thought; there could be no possibility of distinguishing a faded flower from a fresh one, at so great a distance.

Chapter 1 Rappaccini's Daughter

For many days after this incident, the young man avoided the window that looked into Doctor Rappaccini's garden, as if something ugly and monstrous would have blasted his eye-sight, had he been betrayed into a glance. He felt conscious of having put himself, to a certain extent, within the influence of an unintelligible power, by the communication which he had opened with Beatrice. The wisest course would have been, if his heart were in any real danger, to quit his lodgings and Padua itself, at once; the next wiser, to have accustomed himself, as far as possible, to the familiar and day-light view of Beatrice; thus bringing her rigidly and systematically within the limits of ordinary experience. Least of all, while avoiding her sight, should Giovanni have remained so near this extraordinary being, that the proximity and possibility even of intercourse, should give a kind of substance and reality to the wild vagaries① which his imagination ran riot continually in producing. Guasconti had not a deep heart—or at all events, its depths were not sounded now—but he had a quick fancy, and an ardent southern temperament, which rose every instant to a higher fever-pitch. Whether or no Beatrice possessed those terrible attributes—that fatal breath—the affinity with those so beautiful and deadly flowers—which were indicated by what Giovanni had witnessed, she had at least instilled a fierce and subtle poison into his system. It was not love, although her rich beauty was a madness to him; nor horror, even while he fancied her spirit to be imbued with the same baneful essence that seemed to pervade her physical frame; but a wild offspring of both love and horror that had each parent in it, and burned like one and shivered like the other. Giovanni knew not what to dread; still less did he know what to hope; yet hope and dread kept a continual warfare in his breast, alternately vanquishing one another and starting up afresh to renew the contest. Blessed are all simple emotions, be they dark or bright! It is the lurid intermixture of the two that produces the illuminating blaze of the infernal regions.

---

① Extravagant or erratic notion or action.

Sometimes he endeavored to assuage the fever of his spirit by a rapid walk through the streets of Padua, or beyond its gates; his footsteps kept time with the throbbings of his brain, so that the walk was apt to accelerate itself to a race. One day, he found himself arrested; his arm was seized by a portly personage who had turned back on recognizing the young man, and expended much breath in overtaking him.

"Signor Giovanni!—stay, my young friend!"—cried he. "Have you forgotten me? That might well be the case, if I were as much altered as yourself."

It was Baglioni, whom Giovanni had avoided, ever since their first meeting, from a doubt that the Professor's sagacity would look too deeply into his secrets. Endeavoring to recover himself, he stared forth wildly from his inner world into the outer one, and spoke like a man in a dream.

"Yes; I am Giovanni Guasconti. You are Professor Pietro Baglioni. Now let me pass!"

"Not yet—not yet, Signor Giovanni Guasconti," said the Professor, smiling, but at the same time scrutinizing the youth with an earnest glance. "What, did I grow up side by side with your father, and shall his son pass me like a stranger, in these old streets of Padua? Stand still, Signor Giovanni; for we must have a word or two before we part."

"Speedily, then, most worshipful Professor, speedily!" said Giovanni, with feverish impatience. "Does not your worship see that I am in haste?"

Now, while he was speaking, there came a man in black along the street, stooping and moving feebly, like a person in inferior health. His face was all overspread with a most sickly and sallow hue, but yet so pervaded with an expression of piercing and active intellect, that an observer might easily have overlooked the merely physical attributes, and have seen only this wonderful energy. As he passed, this person exchanged a cold and distant salutation with Baglioni, but fixed his eyes upon Giovanni with an intentness that seemed to bring out whatever was within him worthy of notice. Nevertheless, there was a peculiar quietness in the look, as if taking merely a

Chapter 1 Rappaccini's Daughter

speculative, not a human interest, in the young man.

"It is Doctor Rappaccini!" whispered the Professor, when the stranger had passed.—"Has he ever seen your face before?"

"Not that I know," answered Giovanni, starting at the name.

"He *has* seen you!—he must have seen you!" said Baglioni, hastily. "For some purpose or other, this man of science is making a study of you. I know that look of his! It is the same that coldly illuminates his face, as he bends over a bird, a mouse, or a butterfly, which, in pursuit of some experiment, he has killed by the perfume of a flower;—a look as deep as Nature itself, but without Nature's warmth of love. Signor Giovanni, I will stake① my life upon it, you are the subject of one of Rappaccini's experiments!"

"Will you make a fool of me?" cried Giovanni, passionately. "*That*, Signor Professor, were an untoward experiment."

"Patience, patience!" replied the imperturbable② Professor. "I tell thee, my poor Giovanni, that Rappaccini has a scientific interest in thee. Thou hast fallen into fearful hands! And the Signora Beatrice? What part does she act in this mystery?"

But Guasconti, finding Baglioni's pertinacity intolerable, here broke away, and was gone before the Professor could again seize his arm. He looked after the young man intently, and shook his head.

"This must not be," said Baglioni to himself. "The youth is the son of my old friend, and shall not come to any harm from which the arcana③ of medical science can preserve him. Besides, it is too insufferable an impertinence in Rappaccini thus to snatch the lad out of my own hands, as I may say, and make use of him for his infernal experiments. This daughter of his! It shall be looked to. Perchance, most learned

---

① To place a bet on.
② Calm and even-tempered.
③ Elixirs.

Rappaccini, I may foil you where you little dream of it!"

Meanwhile, Giovanni had pursued a circuitous route, and at length found himself at the door of his lodgings. As he crossed the threshold, he was met by old Lisabetta, who smirked and smiled, and was evidently desirous to attract his attention; vainly, however, as the ebullition① of his feelings had momentarily subsided into a cold and dull vacuity②. He turned his eyes full upon the withered face that was puckering itself into a smile, but seemed to behold it not. The old dame, therefore, laid her grasp upon his cloak.

"Signor!—Signor!" whispered she, still with a smile over the whole breadth of her visage, so that it looked not unlike a grotesque carving in wood, darkened by centuries—"Listen, Signor! There is a private entrance into the garden!"

"What do you say?" exclaimed Giovanni, turning quickly about, as if an inanimate thing should start into feverish life.—"A private entrance into Doctor Rappaccini's garden!"

"Hush! hush!—not so loud!" whispered Lisabetta, putting her hand over his mouth. "Yes; into the worshipful Doctor's garden, where you may see all his fine shrubbery. Many a young man in Padua would give gold to be admitted among those flowers."

Giovanni put a piece of gold into her hand.

"Show me the way," said he.

A surmise, probably excited by his conversation with Baglioni, crossed his mind, that this interposition of old Lisabetta might perchance be connected with the intrigue, whatever were its nature, in which the Professor seemed to suppose that Doctor Rappaccini was involving him. But such a suspicion, though it disturbed Giovanni, was inadequate to restrain him. The instant he was aware of the possibility of approaching

---

① Enthusiasm; liveliness.
② Emptiness.

Chapter 1 Rappaccini's Daughter

Beatrice, it seemed an absolute necessity of his existence to do so. It mattered not whether she were angel or demon; he was irrevocably within her sphere, and must obey the law that whirled him onward, in ever lessening circles, towards a result which he did not attempt to foreshadow. And yet, strange to say, there came across him a sudden doubt, whether this intense interest on his part were not delusory①—whether it were really of so deep and positive a nature as to justify him in now thrusting himself into an incalculable position—whether it were not merely the fantasy of a young man's brain, only slightly, or not at all, connected with his heart!

He paused—hesitated—turned half about—but again went on. His withered guide led him along several obscure passages, and finally undid a door, through which, as it was opened, there came the sight and sound of rustling leaves, with the broken sunshine glimmering among them. Giovanni stepped forth, and forcing himself through the entanglement of a shrub that wreathed its tendrils over the hidden entrance, he stood beneath his own window, in the open area of Doctor Rappaccini's garden.

How often is it the case, that, when impossibilities have come to pass, and dreams have condensed their misty substance into tangible realities, we find ourselves calm, and even coldly self-possessed, amid circumstances which it would have been a delirium of joy or agony to anticipate! Fate delights to thwart us thus. Passion will choose his own time to rush upon the scene, and lingers sluggishly behind, when an appropriate adjustment of events would seem to summon his appearance. So was it now with Giovanni. Day after day, his pulses had throbbed with feverish blood, at the improbable idea of an interview with Beatrice, and of standing with her, face to face, in this very garden, basking in the oriental sunshine of her beauty, and snatching from her full gaze the mystery which he deemed the riddle of his own existence. But now there was a singular and untimely equanimity② within his breast. He threw a glance around

---

① Deceptive; artificial.
② Calmness; serenity.

the garden to discover if Beatrice or her father were present, and perceiving that he was alone, began a critical observation of the plants.

The aspect of one and all of them dissatisfied him; their gorgeousness seemed fierce, passionate, and even unnatural. There was hardly an individual shrub which a wanderer, straying by himself through a forest, would not have been startled to find growing wild, as if an unearthly face had glared at him out of the thicket. Several, also, would have shocked a delicate instinct by an appearance of artificialness, indicating that there had been such commixture, and, as it were, adultery of various vegetable species, that the production was no longer of God's making, but the monstrous offspring of man's depraved fancy, glowing with only an evil mockery of beauty. They were probably the result of experiment, which, in one or two cases, had succeeded in mingling plants individually lovely into a compound possessing the questionable and ominous character that distinguished the whole growth of the garden. In fine, Giovanni recognized but two or three plants in the collection, and those of a kind that he well knew to be poisonous. While busy with these contemplations, he heard the rustling of a silken garment, and turning, beheld Beatrice emerging from beneath the sculptured portal.

Giovanni had not considered with himself what should be his deportment; whether he should apologize for his intrusion into the garden, or assume that he was there with the privity, at least, if not by the desire, of Doctor Rappaccini or his daughter. But Beatrice's manner placed him at his ease, though leaving him still in doubt by what agency he had gained admittance. She came lightly along the path, and met him near the broken fountain. There was surprise in her face, but brightened by a simple and kind expression of pleasure.

"You are a connoisseur in flowers, Signor," said Beatrice with a smile, alluding to the bouquet which he had flung her from the window. "It is no marvel, therefore, if the sight of my father's rare collection has tempted you to take a nearer view. If he were

Chapter 1 Rappaccini's Daughter

here, he could tell you many strange and interesting facts as to the nature and habits of these shrubs, for he has spent a life-time in such studies, and this garden is his world."

"And yourself, lady"—observed Giovanni—"if fame says true—you, likewise, are deeply skilled in the virtues indicated by these rich blossoms, and these spicy perfumes. Would you deign① to be my instructress, I should prove an apter scholar than under Signor Rappaccini himself."

"Are there such idle rumors?" asked Beatrice, with the music of a pleasant laugh. "Do people say that I am skilled in my father's science of plants? What a jest is there! No; though I have grown up among these flowers, I know no more of them than their hues and perfume; and sometimes, methinks I would fain rid myself of even that small knowledge. There are many flowers here, and those not the least brilliant, that shock and offend me, when they meet my eye. But, pray, Signor, do not believe these stories about my science. Believe nothing of me save what you see with your own eyes."

"And must I believe all that I have seen with my own eyes?" asked Giovanni pointedly, while the recollection of former scenes made him shrink. "No, Signora, you demand too little of me. Bid me believe nothing, save what comes from your own lips."

It would appear that Beatrice understood him. There came a deep flush to her cheek; but she looked full into Giovanni's eyes, and responded to his gaze of uneasy suspicion with a queen-like haughtiness.

"I do so bid you, Signor!" she replied. "Forget whatever you may have fancied in regard to me. If true to the outward senses, still it may be false in its essence. But the words of Beatrice Rappaccini's lips are true from the heart outward. Those you may believe!"

A fervor glowed in her whole aspect, and beamed upon Giovanni's consciousness like the light of truth itself. But while she spoke, there was a fragrance in the

---

① To condescend to give or grant; stoop.

atmosphere around her rich and delightful, though evanescent[①], yet which the young man, from an indefinable reluctance, scarcely dared to draw into his lungs. It might be the odor of the flowers. Could it be Beatrice's breath, which thus embalmed her words with a strange richness, as if by steeping them in her heart? A faintness passed like a shadow over Giovanni, and flitted away; he seemed to gaze through the beautiful girl's eyes into her transparent soul, and felt no more doubt or fear.

    The tinge of passion that had colored Beatrice's manner vanished; she became gay, and appeared to derive a pure delight from her communion with the youth, not unlike what the maiden of a lonely island might have felt, conversing with a voyager from the civilized world. Evidently her experience of life had been confined within the limits of that garden. She talked now about matters as simple as the day-light or summer-clouds, and now asked questions in reference to the city, or Giovanni's distant home, his friends, his mother, and his sisters; questions indicating such seclusion, and such lack of familiarity with modes and forms, that Giovanni responded as if to an infant. Her spirit gushed out before him like a fresh rill, that was just catching its first glimpse of the sunlight, and wondering, at the reflections of earth and sky which were flung into its bosom. There came thoughts, too, from a deep source, and fantasies of a gem-like brilliancy, as if diamonds and rubies sparkled upward among the bubbles of the fountain. Ever and anon, there gleamed across the young man's mind a sense of wonder, that he should be walking side by side with the being who had so wrought upon his imagination—whom he had idealized in such hues of terror—in whom he had positively witnessed such manifestations of dreadful attributes—that he should be conversing with Beatrice like a brother, and should find her so human and so maiden-like. But such reflections were only momentary; the effect of her character was too real, not to make itself familiar at once.

---

①   Vanishing.

Chapter 1 Rappaccini's Daughter

In this free intercourse, they had strayed through the garden, and now, after many turns among its avenues, were come to the shattered fountain, beside which grew the magnificent shrub with its treasury of glowing blossoms. A fragrance was diffused from it, which Giovanni recognized as identical with that which he had attributed to Beatrice's breath, but incomparably more powerful. As her eyes fell upon it, Giovanni beheld her press her hand to her bosom, as if her heart were throbbing suddenly and painfully.

"For the first time in my life," murmured she, addressing the shrub, "I had forgotten thee!"

"I remember, Signora," said Giovanni, "that you once promised to reward me with one of these living gems for the bouquet, which I had the happy boldness to fling to your feet. Permit me now to pluck it as a memorial of this interview."

He made a step towards the shrub, with extended hand. But Beatrice darted forward, uttering a shriek that went through his heart like a dagger. She caught his hand, and drew it back with the whole force of her slender figure. Giovanni felt her touch thrilling through his fibers.

"Touch it not!" exclaimed she, in a voice of agony. "Not for thy life! It is fatal!"

Then, hiding her face, she fled from him, and vanished beneath the sculptured portal. As Giovanni followed her with his eyes, he beheld the emaciated figure and pale intelligence of Doctor Rappaccini, who had been watching the scene, he knew not how long, within the shadow of the entrance.

No sooner was Guasconti alone in his chamber, than the image of Beatrice came back to his passionate musings, invested with all the witchery that had been gathering around it ever since his first glimpse of her, and now likewise imbued with a tender warmth of girlish womanhood. She was human: her nature was endowed with all gentle and feminine qualities; she was worthiest to be worshipped; she was capable, surely, on her part, of the height and heroism of love. Those tokens, which he had hitherto considered as proofs of a frightful peculiarity in her physical and moral system, were now either forgotten, or, by the subtle sophistry① of passion, transmuted into a golden crown of enchantment, rendering Beatrice the more admirable, by so much as she was the more unique. Whatever had looked ugly, was now beautiful; or, if incapable of such a change, it stole away and hid itself among those shapeless half-ideas, which throng the dim region beyond the daylight of our perfect consciousness. Thus did Giovanni spend the night, nor fell asleep, until the dawn had begun to awake the slumbering flowers in Doctor Rappaccini's garden, whither his dreams doubtless led him. Up rose the sun in his due season, and flinging his beams upon the young man's eyelids, awoke him to a sense of pain. When thoroughly aroused, he became sensible of a burning and tingling agony in his hand—in his right hand—the very hand which Beatrice had grasped in her own, when he was on the point of plucking one of the gem-like flowers. On the back of that hand there was now a purple print, like that of four small fingers, and the likeness of a slender thumb upon his wrist.

Oh, how stubbornly does love—or even that cunning semblance of love which flourishes in the imagination, but strikes no depth of root into the heart—how stubbornly does it hold its faith, until the moment come, when it is doomed to vanish into thin mist! Giovanni wrapt a handkerchief about his hand, and wondered what evil thing had stung him, and soon forgot his pain in a reverie of Beatrice.

After the first interview, a second was in the inevitable course of what we call fate. A third; a fourth; and a meeting with Beatrice in the garden was no longer an incident in Giovanni's daily life, but the whole space in which he might be said to live; for the anticipation and memory of that ecstatic hour made up the remainder. Nor was it otherwise with the daughter of Rappaccini. She watched for the youth's appearance, and flew to his side with confidence② as unreserved as if they had been playmates

---

① Plausible but fallacious argumentation.
② A feeling of trust (in someone or something).

Chapter 1 Rappaccini's Daughter

from early infancy—as if they were such playmates still. If, by any unwonted chance, he failed to come at the appointed moment, she stood beneath the window, and sent up the rich sweetness of her tones to float around him in his chamber, and echo and reverberate throughout his heart—"Giovanni! Giovanni! Why tarriest thou? Come down!" And down he hastened into that Eden of poisonous flowers.

But, with all this intimate familiarity, there was still a reserve in Beatrice's demeanor, so rigidly and invariably sustained, that the idea of infringing[①] it scarcely occurred to his imagination. By all appreciable signs, they loved; they had looked love, with eyes that conveyed the holy secret from the depths of one soul into the depths of the other, as if it were too sacred to be whispered by the way; they had even spoken love, in those gushes of passion when their spirits darted forth in articulated breath, like tongues of long-hidden flame; and yet there had been no seal of lips, no clasp of hands, nor any slightest caress, such as love claims and hallows. He had never touched one of the gleaming ringlets of her hair; her garment—so marked was the physical barrier between them—had never been waved against him by a breeze. On the few occasions when Giovanni had seemed tempted to overstep the limit, Beatrice grew so sad, so stern, and withal wore such a look of desolate separation, shuddering at itself, that not a spoken word was requisite to repel him. At such times, he was startled at the horrible suspicions that rose, monster-like, out of the caverns of his heart, and stared him in the face; his love grew thin and faint as the morning-mist; his doubts alone had substance. But when Beatrice's face brightened again, after the momentary shadow, she was transformed at once from the mysterious, questionable being, whom he had watched with so much awe and horror; she was now the beautiful and unsophisticated girl, whom he felt that his spirit knew with a certainty beyond all other knowledge.

A considerable time had now passed since Giovanni's last meeting with Baglioni.

---

① Violating.

One morning, however, he was disagreeably surprised by a visit from the Professor, whom he had scarcely thought of for whole weeks, and would willingly have forgotten still longer. Given up, as he had long been, to a pervading excitement, he could tolerate no companions, except upon condition of their perfect sympathy with his present state of feeling. Such sympathy was not to be expected from Professor Baglioni.

The visitor chatted carelessly, for a few moments, about the gossip of the city and the University, and then took up another topic.

"I have been reading an old classic author lately," said he, "and met with a story[①] that strangely interested me. Possibly you may remember it. It is of an Indian prince, who sent a beautiful woman as a present to Alexander the Great. She was as lovely as the dawn, and gorgeous as the sunset; but what especially distinguished her was a certain rich perfume in her breath—richer than a garden of Persian roses. Alexander, as was natural to a youthful conqueror, fell in love at first sight with this magnificent stranger. But a certain sage physician, happening to be present, discovered a terrible secret in regard to her."

"And what was that?" asked Giovanni, turning his eyes downward to avoid those of the Professor.

"That this lovely woman," continued Baglioni, with emphasis, "had been nourished with poisons from her birth upward, until her whole nature was so imbued with them, that she herself had become the deadliest poison in existence. Poison was her element of life. With that rich perfume of her breath, she blasted the very air. Her love would have been poison!—her embrace death! Is not this a marvelous tale?"

"A childish fable," answered Giovanni, nervously starting from his chair. "I marvel how your worship finds time to read such nonsense, among your graver studies."

---

① Hawthorne met with the story in Sir Thomas Browne's *Vulgar Errors* (1646), an "old classic" for New England readers.

Chapter 1 Rappaccini's Daughter

"By the bye," said the Professor, looking uneasily about him, "what singular fragrance is this in your apartment? Is it the perfume of your gloves? It is faint, but delicious, and yet, after all, by no means agreeable. Were I to breathe it long, methinks it would make me ill. It is like the breath of a flower—but I see no flowers in the chamber."

"Nor are there any," replied Giovanni, who had turned pale as the Professor spoke; "nor, I think, is there any fragrance, except in your worship's imagination. Odors, being a sort of element combined of the sensual and the spiritual, are apt to deceive us in this manner. The recollection of a perfume—the bare idea of it—may easily be mistaken for a present reality."

"Aye; but my sober imagination does not often play such tricks," said Baglioni; "and were I to fancy any kind of odor, it would be that of some vile apothecary drug, wherewith my fingers are likely enough to be imbued. Our worshipful friend Rappaccini, as I have heard, tinctures his medicaments with odors richer than those of Araby[①]. Doubtless, likewise, the fair and learned Signora Beatrice would minister to her patients with draughts as sweet as a maiden's breath. But woe to him that sips them!"

Giovanni's face evinced many contending emotions. The tone in which the Professor alluded to the pure and lovely daughter of Rappaccini was a torture to his soul; and yet, the intimation of a view of her character, opposite to his own, gave instantaneous distinctness to a thousand dim suspicions, which now grinned at him like so many demons. But he strove hard to quell them, and to respond to Baglioni with a true lover's perfect faith.

"Signor Professor," said he, "you were my father's friend—perchance, too, it is your purpose to act a friendly part towards his son. I would fain feel nothing towards

---

① Arabia.

you save respect and deference. But I pray you to observe, Signor, that there is one subject on which we must not speak. You know not the Signora Beatrice. You cannot, therefore, estimate the wrong—the blasphemy, I may even say—that is offered to her character by a light or injurious word."

"Giovanni!—my poor Giovanni!" answered the Professor, with a calm expression of pity, "I know this wretched girl far better than yourself. You shall hear the truth in respect to the poisoner Rappaccini, and his poisonous daughter. Yes; poisonous as she is beautiful! Listen; for even should you do violence to my gray hairs, it shall not silence me. That old fable of the Indian woman has become a truth, by the deep and deadly science of Rappaccini, and in the person of the lovely Beatrice!"

Giovanni groaned and hid his face.

"Her father," continued Baglioni, "was not restrained by natural affection from offering up his child, in this horrible manner, as the victim of his insane zeal for science. For—let us do him justice—he is as true a man of science as ever distilled his own heart in an alembic[①]. What, then, will be your fate? Beyond a doubt, you are selected as the material of some new experiment. Perhaps the result is to be death—perhaps a fate more awful still! Rappaccini, with what he calls the interest of science before his eyes, will hesitate at nothing."

"It is a dream!" muttered Giovanni to himself, "surely it is a dream!"

"But," resumed the Professor, "be of good cheer, son of my friend! It is not yet too late for the rescue. Possibly, we may even succeed in bringing back this miserable child within the limits of ordinary nature, from which her father's madness has estranged her. Behold this little silver vase! It was wrought by the hands of the renowned Benvenuto Cellini[②], and is well worthy to be a love-gift to the fairest dame in Italy. But its contents

---

① Device for distilling. In other words, Rappaccini's heart was in his work.
② Benvenuto Cellini (1500—1571), Italian sculptor and metalworker.

Chapter 1 Rappaccini's Daughter

are invaluable. One little sip of this antidote① would have rendered the most virulent poisons of the Borgias② innocuous. Doubt not that it will be as efficacious against those of Rappaccini. Bestow the vase, and the precious liquid within it, on your Beatrice, and hopefully await the result."

Baglioni laid a small, exquisitely wrought silver phial on the table, and withdrew, leaving what he had said to produce its effect upon the young man's mind.

"We will thwart Rappaccini yet!" thought he, chuckling to himself, as he descended the stairs. "But, let us confess the truth of him, he is a wonderful man!—a wonderful man indeed! A vile empiric, however, in his practice, and therefore not to be tolerated by those who respect the good old rules of the medical profession!"

Throughout Giovanni's whole acquaintance with Beatrice, he had occasionally, as we have said, been haunted by dark surmises as to her character. Yet, so thoroughly had she made herself felt by him as a simple, natural, most affectionate and guileless creature, that the image now held up by Professor Baglioni, looked as strange and incredible, as if it were not in accordance with his own original conception. True, there were ugly recollections connected with his first glimpses of the beautiful girl; he could not quite forget the bouquet that withered in her grasp, and the insect that perished amid the sunny air, by no ostensible agency save the fragrance of her breath. These incidents, however, dissolving in the pure light of her character, had no longer the efficacy of facts, but were acknowledged as mistaken fantasies, by whatever testimony of the senses they might appear to be substantiated. There is something truer and more real, than what we can see with the eyes, and touch with the finger. On such better evidence, had Giovanni founded his confidence in Beatrice, though rather by the necessary force of her high attributes, than by any deep and generous faith on his part. But, now, his spirit was incapable of sustaining itself at the height to which the early enthusiasm

---

① A remedy that stops or controls the effects of a poison.
② Infamous Italian family supposed to have poisoned their enemies.

of passion had exalted it; he fell down, groveling among earthly doubts, and defiled therewith the pure whiteness of Beatrice's image. Not that he gave her up; he did but distrust. He resolved to institute some decisive test that should satisfy him, once for all, whether there were those dreadful peculiarities in her physical nature, which could not be supposed to exist without some corresponding monstrosity① of soul. His eyes, gazing down afar, might have deceived him as to the lizard, the insect, and the flowers. But if he could witness, at the distance of a few paces, the sudden blight of one fresh and healthful flower in Beatrice's hand, there would be room for no further question. With this idea, he hastened to the florist's, and purchased a bouquet that was still gemmed with the morning dew-drops.

It was now the customary hour of his daily interview with Beatrice. Before descending into the garden, Giovanni failed not to look at his figure in the mirror; a vanity to be expected in a beautiful young man, yet, as displaying itself at that troubled and feverish moment, the token of a certain shallowness of feeling and insincerity of character. He did gaze, however, and said to himself, that his features had never before possessed so rich a grace, nor his eyes such vivacity, nor his cheeks so warm a hue of superabundant life.

"At least," thought he, "her poison has not yet insinuated itself into my system. I am no flower to perish in her grasp!"

With that thought, he turned his eyes on the bouquet, which he had never once laid aside from his hand. A thrill of indefinable horror shot through his frame, on perceiving that those dewy flowers were already beginning to droop; they wore the aspect of things that had been fresh and lovely, yesterday. Giovanni grew white as marble, and stood motionless before the mirror, staring at his own reflection there, as at the likeness of something frightful. He remembered Baglioni's remark about the fragrance that

---

① Being abnormal.

Chapter 1　Rappaccini's Daughter

seemed to pervade the chamber. It must have been the poison in his breath! Then he shuddered—shuddered at himself! Recovering from his stupor①, he began to watch, with curious eye, a spider that was busily at work, hanging its web from the antique cornice of the apartment, crossing and re-crossing the artful system of interwoven lines, as vigorous and active a spider as ever dangled from an old ceiling. Giovanni bent towards the insect, and emitted a deep, long breath. The spider suddenly ceased its toil; the web vibrated with a tremor originating in the body of the small artizan. Again Giovanni sent forth a breath, deeper, longer, and imbued with a venomous feeling out of his heart; he knew not whether he were wicked or only desperate. The spider made a convulsive gripe with his limbs, and hung dead across the window.

"Accursed! Accursed!" muttered Giovanni, addressing himself. "Hast thou grown so poisonous, that this deadly insect perishes by thy breath?"

At that moment, a rich, sweet voice came floating up from the garden: "Giovanni! Giovanni! It is past the hour! Why tarriest thou! Come down!"

"Yes," muttered Giovanni again. "She is the only being whom my breath may not slay! Would that it might!"

He rushed down, and in an instant, was standing before the bright and loving eyes of Beatrice. A moment ago, his wrath and despair had been so fierce that he could have desired nothing so much as to wither her by a glance. But, with her actual presence, there came influences which had too real an existence to be at once shaken off; recollections of the delicate and benign power of her feminine nature, which had so often enveloped him in a religious calm; recollections of many a holy and passionate outgush of her heart, when the pure fountain had been unsealed from its depths, and made visible in its transparency to his mental eye; recollections which, had Giovanni known how to estimate them, would have assured him that all this ugly mystery was

---

① Mental numbness, resulting from shock.

but an earthly illusion, and that, whatever mist of evil might seem to have gathered over her, the real Beatrice was a heavenly angel. Incapable as he was of such high faith, still her presence had not utterly lost its magic. Giovanni's rage was quelled into an aspect of sullen insensibility. Beatrice, with a quick spiritual sense, immediately felt that there was a gulf of blackness between them, which neither he nor she could pass. They walked on together, sad and silent, and came thus to the marble fountain, and to its pool of water on the ground, in the midst of which grew the shrub that bore gem-like blossoms. Giovanni was affrighted at the eager enjoyment—the appetite, as it were—with which he found himself inhaling the fragrance of the flowers.

"Beatrice," asked he abruptly, "whence came this shrub?"

"My father created it," answered she, with simplicity.

"Created it! created it!" repeated Giovanni. "What mean you, Beatrice?"

"He is a man fearfully acquainted with the secrets of nature," replied Beatrice; "and, at the hour when I first drew breath, this plant sprang from the soil, the offspring of his science, of his intellect, while I was but his earthly child. Approach it not!" continued she, observing with terror that Giovanni was drawing nearer to the shrub. "It has qualities that you little dream of. But I, dearest Giovanni—I grew up and blossomed with the plant, and was nourished with its breath. It was my sister, and I loved it with a human affection: for—alas! hast thou not suspected it? there was an awful doom."

Here Giovanni frowned so darkly upon her that Beatrice paused and trembled. But her faith in his tenderness reassured her, and made her blush that she had doubted for an instant.

"There was an awful doom," she continued,—"the effect of my father's fatal love of science—which estranged me from all society of my kind. Until Heaven sent thee, dearest Giovanni, Oh! how lonely was thy poor Beatrice!"

"Was it a hard doom?" asked Giovanni, fixing his eyes upon her.

"Only of late have I known how hard it was," answered she tenderly. "Oh, yes; but my heart was torpid①, and therefore quiet."

Giovanni's rage broke forth from his sullen gloom like a lightning-flash out of a dark cloud.

"Accursed one!" cried he, with venomous scorn and anger. "And finding thy solitude wearisome, thou hast severed me, likewise, from all the warmth of life, and enticed me into thy region of unspeakable horror!"

"Giovanni!" exclaimed Beatrice, turning her large bright eyes upon his face. The force of his words had not found its way into her mind; she was merely thunder-struck.

"Yes, poisonous thing!" repeated Giovanni, beside himself with passion. "Thou hast done it! Thou hast blasted me! Thou hast filled my veins with poison! Thou hast made me as hateful, as ugly, as loathsome and deadly a creature as thyself—a world's wonder of hideous monstrosity! Now—if our breath be happily as fatal to ourselves as to all others—let us join our lips in one kiss of unutterable hatred, and so die!"

"What has befallen me?" murmured Beatrice, with a low moan out of her heart. "Holy Virgin pity me, a poor heartbroken child!"

"Thou! Dost thou pray?" cried Giovanni, still with the same fiendish scorn. "Thy very prayers, as they come from thy lips, taint the atmosphere with death. Yes, yes; let us pray! Let us to church, and dip our fingers in the holy water at the portal! They that come after us will perish as by a pestilence②. Let us sign crosses in the air! It will be scattering curses abroad in the likeness of holy symbols!"

"Giovanni," said Beatrice calmly, for her grief was beyond passion, "Why dost thou join thyself with me thus in those terrible words? I, it is true, am the horrible thing thou namest me. But thou!—what hast thou to do, save with one other shudder at my hideous misery, to go forth out of the garden and mingle with thy race, and forget that there ever crawled on earth such a monster as poor Beatrice?"

---

① Slow-moving; sluggish.
② Epidemic; plague.

"Dost thou pretend ignorance?" asked Giovanni, scowling upon her. "Behold! This power have I gained from the pure daughter of Rappaccini!"

There was a swarm of summer-insects flitting through the air, in search of the food promised by the flower-odors of the fatal garden. They circled round Giovanni's head, and were evidently attracted towards him by the same influence which had drawn them, for an instant, within the sphere of several of the shrubs. He sent forth a breath among them, and smiled bitterly at Beatrice, as at least a score of the insects fell dead upon the ground.

"I see it! I see it!" shrieked Beatrice. "It is my father's fatal science? No, no, Giovanni; it was not I! Never, never! I dreamed only to love thee, and be with thee a little time, and so to let thee pass away, leaving but thine image in mine heart. For, Giovanni—believe it—though my body be nourished with poison, my spirit is God's creature, and craves love as its daily food. But my father!—he has united us in this fearful sympathy. Yes; spurn me!—tread upon me!—kill me! Oh, what is death, after such words as thine? But it was not I! Not for a world of bliss would I have done it!"

Giovanni's passion had exhausted itself in its outburst from his lips. There now came across him a sense, mournful, and not without tenderness, of the intimate and peculiar relationship between Beatrice and himself. They stood, as it were, in an utter solitude, which would be made none the less solitary by the densest throng of human life. Ought not, then, the desert of humanity around them to press this insulated pair closer together? If they should be cruel to one another, who was there to be kind to them? Besides, thought Giovanni, might there not still be a hope of his returning within the limits of ordinary nature, and leading Beatrice—the redeemed Beatrice—by the hand? Oh, weak, and selfish, and unworthy spirit, that could dream of an earthly union and earthly happiness as possible, after such deep love had been so bitterly wronged as was Beatrice's love by Giovanni's blighting words! No, no; there could be no such hope. She must pass heavily, with that broken heart, across the borders of Time—

she must bathe her hurts in some fount of Paradise, and forget her grief in the light of immortality—and *there* be well!

But Giovanni did not know it.

"Dear Beatrice," said he, approaching her, while she shrank away, as always at his approach, but now with a different impulse—"dearest Beatrice, our fate is not yet so desperate. Behold! There is a medicine, potent, as a wise physician has assured me, and almost divine in its efficacy[①]. It is composed of ingredients the most opposite to those by which thy awful father has brought this calamity upon thee and me. It is distilled of blessed herbs. Shall we not quaff it together, and thus be purified from evil?"

"Give it me!" said Beatrice, extending her hand to receive the little silver phial which Giovanni took from his bosom. She added, with a peculiar emphasis: "I will drink—but do thou await the result."

She put Baglioni's antidote to her lips; and, at the same moment, the figure of Rappaccini emerged from the portal, and came slowly towards the marble fountain. As he drew near, the pale man of science seemed to gaze with a triumphant expression at the beautiful youth and maiden, as might an artist who should spend his life in achieving a picture or a group of statuary, and finally be satisfied with his success. He paused—his bent form grew erect with conscious power, he spread out his hand over them, in the attitude of a father imploring a blessing upon his children. But those were the same hands that had thrown poison into the stream of their lives! Giovanni trembled. Beatrice shuddered very nervously, and pressed her hand upon her heart.

"My daughter," said Rappaccini, "thou art no longer lonely in the world! Pluck one of those precious gems from thy sister shrub, and bid thy bridegroom wear it in his bosom. It will not harm him now! My science, and the sympathy between thee and him, have so wrought within his system, that he now stands apart from common men,

---

① Effectiveness.

as thou dost, daughter of my pride and triumph, from ordinary women. Pass on, then, through the world, most dear to one another, and dreadful to all besides!"

"My father," said Beatrice, feebly—and still, as she spoke, she kept her hand upon her heart—"wherefore didst thou inflict this miserable doom upon thy child?"

"Miserable!" exclaimed Rappaccini. "What mean you, foolish girl? Dost thou deem it misery to be endowed with marvelous gifts, against which no power nor strength could avail an enemy? Misery, to be able to quell the mightiest with a breath? Misery, to be as terrible as thou art beautiful? Wouldst thou, then, have preferred the condition of a weak woman, exposed to all evil, and capable of none?"

"I would fain have been loved, not feared," murmured Beatrice, sinking down upon the ground.—"But now it matters not; I am going, father, where the evil, which thou hast striven to mingle with my being, will pass away like a dream—like the fragrance of these poisonous flowers, which will no longer taint my breath among the flowers of Eden. Farewell, Giovanni! Thy words of hatred are like lead within my heart—but they, too, will fall away as I ascend. Oh, was there not, from the first, more poison in thy nature than in mine?"

To Beatrice—so radically had her earthly part been wrought upon by Rappaccini's skill—as poison had been life, so the powerful antidote was death. And thus the poor victim of man's ingenuity and of thwarted nature, and of the fatality that attends all such efforts of perverted wisdom, perished there, at the feet of her father and Giovanni. Just at that moment, Professor Pietro Baglioni looked forth from the window, and called loudly, in a tone of triumph mixed with horror, to the thunder-stricken man of science:

"Rappaccini! Rappaccini! And is *this* the upshot[①] of your experiment?"

[①] The final result.

Film Comment:

Nathaniel Hawthorne's *Rappaccini's Daughter*: 57 minutes, color
Starring: Kathleen Beller & Kristopher Tabori
Screenplay by: Herbert Hartig
Directed by: Dezsö Magyar

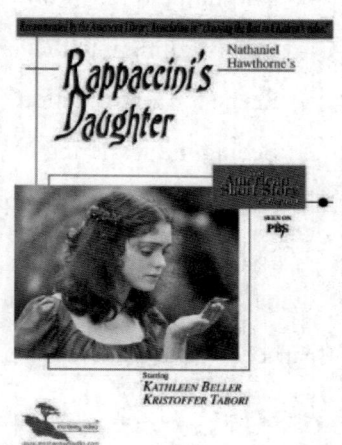

Set in 18th Century Italy, "Rappaccini's Daughter" is the tale of a young scholar named Giovanni (Kristopher Tabori) who falls in love with a beautiful, yet forbidden, girl who tends her father's poison garden.

However, the strange and unearthly beauty of Beatrice (Kathleen Beller) masks a terrifying curse which Giovanni must tragically discover. Her father, the mysterious Dr. Rappaccini, has made her the subject of a diabolical experiment. In Giovanni's attempt to free Beatrice from the control of her father and to escape the poisonous effect she begins to have on him, he unwittingly destroys her.

From the short story of master American novelist Nathaniel Hawthorne, two quintessential Hawthorne themes are explored: the sins of interfering with another's soul and the futility of trying to tamper with nature.

Film Scenes:

Scene 1: The poison garden
Taking lodging in an old mansion, Giovanni discovers outside his window a beautiful garden, cultivated with poisonous plants and shrubs.

Scene 2: The forbidden daughter
Looking down into the garden, Giovanni sees the beautiful daughter of Dr.

Rappaccini, Beatrice, whose breath kills a beautiful butterfly.

Scene 3: The meeting

With the help of the landlady, Giovanni secretly comes into the garden, meeting with the innocent Beatrice.

Scene 4: Fever or poison?

The daily interview with Beatrice has become the whole space to live, and Giovanni is falling into the hands of Dr. Rappaccini together with her.

Scene 5: Confrontation

Seeing the withering of bouquet and the death of spider, Giovanni realizes that he himself has become poisonous, and thus confronts Beatrice with his accusations.

Scene 6: The kiss

The kiss with Beatrice will not harm Giovanni, but the antidote, which he gives Beatrice to save her, takes her life instead, for poison has been life to Beatrice.

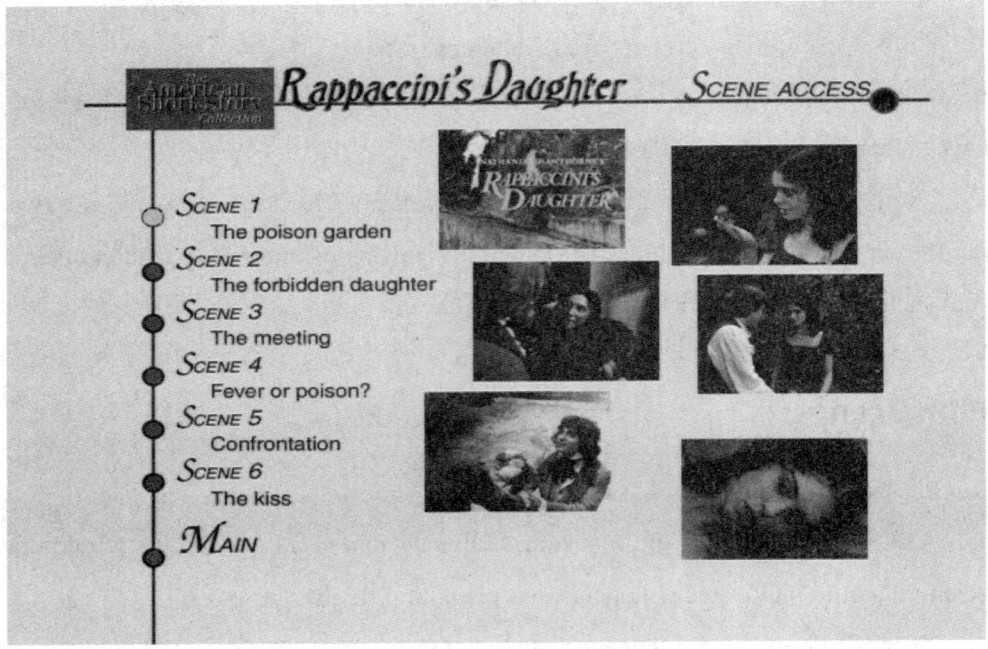

Film Clip:

The Antidote

Giovanni suggests they should drink the antidote together and thus be purified from evil. Yet, Beatrice would rather drink first and make Giovanni await the result. She kisses Giovanni and takes the antidote without any hesitation. Dr. Rappaccini emerges from the portal and comes slowly towards the young couple. Gazing with a triumphant expression at the beautiful youth and maiden, Dr. Rappaccini tells them that Giovanni stands apart from common men, the same as Beatrice different from ordinary women. Beatrice is no longer lonely in the world. Therefore, Beatrice could pluck one gem from her sister shrub, and bid Giovanni wear it in his bosom. It will not harm him now, but they can only live in the garden, like Adam and Eve.

Beatrice says that she would fain have been loved, not feared or hated, but it doesn't matter anymore, for she is dying. She falls to the ground. As poison has been life to Beatrice, the powerful antidote means death to her. Beatrice is clear about that, but she still drinks, and she accuses Giovanni that there is more poison in his nature than in hers from the first. Beatrice is the poor victim of man's ingenuity, thwarted nature, and the fatality of perverted wisdom. She dies at the feet of her father and Giovanni, who would be shocked and hurt for the rest of their lives.

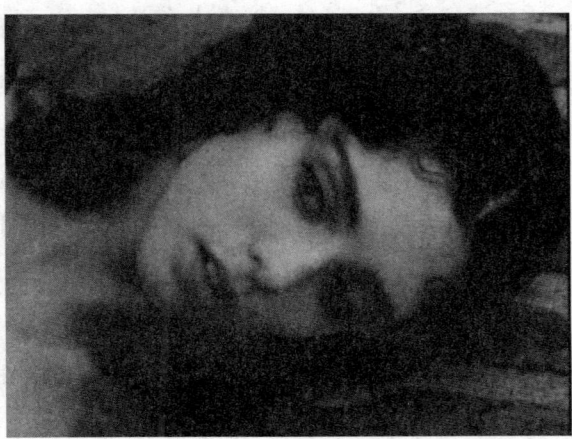

Discussion Questions:

Story Discussion

(1) How does Giovanni meet Beatrice and fall in love with her? Is she a suitable lover?

(2) As a scientist, Dr. Rappaccini has made his daughter the subject of a diabolical experiment. What kind of sacrifice is this?

(3) Dr. Rappaccini's garden is the whole world for young Beatrice. What does this garden image imply?

(4) Giovanni attempts to free Beatrice from her father's control and experiment. What does his good intention bring to her?

(5) What are the relations between science and nature in the story? How dangerous is it to tamper with nature?

Film Appreciation

(1) How does Giovanni watch the garden below from his window?

(2) How does Giovanni observe Dr. Rappaccini from his window? What about the first sight of Beatrice?

(3) How does the film illustrate the death of the butterfly before Beatrice? What about the withering of the bouquet?

(4) How does Giovanni realize that he himself has become poisonous?

(5) What's the function of the antidote? How does Beatrice come to her death?

(6) Why is the final call of Professor Baglioni missing from the film?

(7) What's the symbolic meaning of the Garden in the film?

(8) What are the adapted scenes in the film?

Further Reading and Watching:

Young Goodman Brown

Chapter 2
The Blue Hotel

Stephen Crane

Author Introduction:

Stephen Crane (1871—1900) was born in Newark, New Jersey, the last and fourteenth child of a Methodist minister. After schooling at Lafayette College and Syracuse University, he worked in New York as a freelance journalist.

In 1893 he published at his own expense the novel *Maggie: A Girl of the Streets*, a pioneering work of American literary Naturalism. Without having any battle experience, Crane brought out his famous short novel about the Civil War, *The Red Badge of Courage* (1895), which in theme and technique foreshadows the war novels of the twentieth century.

In his brief and energetic life, he published fourteen books while acting out, in his personal adventures, the legend of the writer as soldier of fortune. On his way to Cuba for the first time he picked up a mistress at the Hotel de Dream in Jacksonville, Florida—a woman who accompanied him when he went on to Greece as a war correspondent. Malicious gossip about his private life subsequently drove him from America to England, where he settled in 1897 and made friends with leading English writers such as Joseph Conrad and H. G. Wells. Hounded by creditors and afflicted by tuberculosis, he died in Germany at the age of 28.

In Crane, the contradictions and tensions present in many writers seem to be intensified, and his common themes involve fear, spiritual crises and social isolation. His short stories were collected in *The Open Boat and Other Tales of Adventure* (1898), *The Monster and Other Stories* (1899), and *Wounds in the Rain* (1900). His complete works in prose and verse were published in 1925—1926.

Story Summary:

Defining many of the overarching themes, the story breaks free from the norms of the period, often entering the realms of Expressionism.

A century ago, a foreigner (a Swede) travels to a Nebraska hotel, his mind filled with the romantic violence of Western dime novels. He soon finds his expectations fulfilled, confronting a disturbing fate whose mysterious cause ultimately seems to elude us. Being accused of cheating at cards, the young man must defend his personal identity, his father must give up some protection of his son, and the Swede must prove his worth. The tensions created by this scenario come to a head, when the two have to fight to prove they are worthy of the reputations of the West. After the battle is decided, the final duel with fear proves to be the most significant of them all.

We should learn from the death of the Swede, an outsider who is affected by the Dime Novel and whose death further proves the violence of the wild West.

Key Terms:

Naturalism: Stephen Crane is the master of naturalism, and there are many naturalistic elements in the story, such as the description of snowflakes and snow storm.

Dime Novel: It is a cheap melodramatic novel, usually in paperback and mostly set in the wild West. The Swede is very possibly affected by such kind of novel.

Impressionist: Breaking from the norms of the period, Stephen Crane often enters the realms of impressionism, showing the effects of light and color rather than on clear and exact detail.

Realism: Transiting from realism to naturalism, Stephen Crane also takes realistic writing in the story, like the hotel scene and the fight scene in the wild Nebraska.

Community: The Western people treasure a lot about their community and community culture, protecting every guest under their roof, but the Swede considers the Western community dangerous.

Outsider: All the guests coming to the hotel are outsiders to the community, especially the Swede, who are supposed to follow the local rules.

The Blue Hotel[1]

I

The Palace Hotel at Fort Romper was painted a light blue, a shade that is on the legs of a kind of heron, causing the bird to declare its position against any background. The Palace Hotel, then, was always screaming and howling in a way that made the dazzling winter landscape of Nebraska seem only a gray swampish hush. It stood alone on the prairie, and when the snow was falling the town two hundred yards away was not visible. But when the traveler alighted at the railway station he was obliged to pass the Palace Hotel before he could come upon the company of low clapboard houses

---

[1] First published in two installments in *Collier's Weekly* for November 26 and December 3, 1898, and then collected in *The Monster and Other Stories* (1899).

which composed Fort Romper, and it was not to be thought that any traveler could pass the Palace Hotel without looking at it. Pat Scully, the proprietor, had proved himself a master of strategy when he chose his paints. It is true that on clear days, when the great trans-continental expresses, long lines of swaying Pullmans[①], swept through Fort Romper, passengers were overcome at the sight, and the cult that knows the brown-reds and the subdivisions of the dark greens of the East expressed shame, pity, horror, in a laugh. But to the citizens of this prairie town and to the people who would naturally stop there, Pat Scully had performed a feat. With this opulence and splendor, these creeds, classes, egotisms, that streamed through Romper on the rails day after day, they had no color in common.

As if the displayed delights of such a blue hotel were not sufficiently enticing, it was Scully's habit to go every morning and evening to meet the leisurely trains that stopped at Romper and work his seductions upon any man that he might see wavering, gripsack[②] in hand.

One morning, when a snow-crusted engine dragged its long string of freight cars and its one passenger coach to the station, Scully performed the marvel of catching three men. One was a shaky and quick-eyed Swede, with a great shining cheap valise; one was a tall bronzed cowboy, who was on his way to a ranch near the Dakota line; one was a little silent man from the East, who didn't look it, and didn't announce it. Scully practically made them prisoners. He was so nimble and merry and kindly that each probably felt it would be the height of brutality to try to escape. They trudged off over the creaking board sidewalks in the wake of the eager little Irishman. He wore a heavy fur cap squeezed tightly down on his head. It caused his two red ears to stick out stiffly, as if they were made of tin.

At last, Scully, elaborately, with boisterous hospitality, conducted them through

---

① Railroad cars with sleeping accommodations.
② Suitcase.

Chapter 2　The Blue Hotel

the portals of the blue hotel. The room which they entered was small. It seemed to be merely a proper temple for an enormous stove, which, in the center, was humming with godlike violence. At various points on its surface the iron had become luminous and glowed yellow from the heat. Beside the stove Scully's son Johnnie was playing High-Five[①] with an old farmer who had whiskers both gray and sandy. They were quarrelling. Frequently the old farmer turned his face towards a box of sawdust—colored brown from tobacco juice—that was behind the stove, and spat with an air of great impatience and irritation. With a loud flourish of words Scully destroyed the game of cards, and bustled his son up-stairs with part of the baggage of the new guests. He himself conducted them to three basins of the coldest water in the world. The cowboy and the Easterner burnished themselves fiery-red with this water, until it seemed to be some kind of a metal polish. The Swede, however, merely dipped his fingers gingerly and with trepidation. It was notable that throughout this series of small ceremonies the three travelers were made to feel that Scully was very benevolent. He was conferring great favors upon them. He handed the towel from one to the other with an air of philanthropic impulse.

　　Afterwards they went to the first room, and, sitting about the stove, listened to Scully's officious clamor at his daughters, who were preparing the mid-day meal. They reflected in the silence of experienced men who tread carefully amid new people. Nevertheless, the old farmer, stationary, invincible in his chair near the warmest part of the stove, turned his face from the sawdust box frequently and addressed a glowing commonplace to the strangers. Usually he was answered in short but adequate sentences by either the cowboy or the Easterner. The Swede said nothing. He seemed to be occupied in making furtive estimates of each man in the room. One might have thought that he had the sense of silly suspicion which comes to guilt. He resembled a

---

① Cinch, a card game.

badly frightened man.

Later, at dinner, he spoke a little, addressing his conversation entirely to Scully. He volunteered that he had come from New York, where for ten years he had worked as a tailor. These facts seemed to strike Scully as fascinating, and afterwards he volunteered that he had lived at Romper for fourteen years. The Swede asked about the crops and the price of labor. He seemed barely to listen to Scully's extended replies. His eyes continued to rove from man to man.

Finally, with a laugh and a wink, he said that some of these Western communities were very dangerous; and after his statement he straightened his legs under the table, tilted his head, and laughed again, loudly. It was plain that the demonstration had no meaning to the others. They looked at him wondering and in silence.

II

As the men trooped heavily back into the front-room, the two little windows presented views of a turmoiling sea of snow. The huge arms of the wind were making attempts—mighty, circular, futile—to embrace the flakes as they sped. A gate-post like a still man with a blanched face stood aghast amid this profligate fury. In a hearty voice Scully announced the presence of a blizzard. The guests of the blue hotel, lighting their pipes, assented with grunts of lazy masculine contentment. No island of the sea could be exempt in the degree of this little room with its humming stove. Johnnie, son of Scully, in a tone which defined his opinion of his ability as a card-player, challenged the old farmer of both gray and sandy whiskers to a game of High-Five. The farmer agreed with a contemptuous and bitter scoff. They sat close to the stove, and squared their knees under a wide board. The cowboy and the Easterner watched the game with interest. The Swede remained near the window, aloof, but with a countenance that showed signs of an inexplicable excitement.

The play of Johnnie and the gray-beard was suddenly ended by another quarrel.

Chapter 2   The Blue Hotel

The old man arose while casting a look of heated scorn at his adversary. He slowly buttoned his coat, and then stalked with fabulous dignity from the room. In the discreet silence of all other men the Swede laughed. His laughter rang somehow childish. Men by this time had begun to look at him askance, as if they wished to inquire what ailed him.

A new game was formed jocosely. The cowboy volunteered to become the partner of Johnnie, and they all then turned to ask the Swede to throw in his lot with the little Easterner. He asked some questions about the game, and, learning that it wore many names, and that he had played it when it was under an alias, he accepted the invitation. He strode towards the men nervously, as if he expected to be assaulted. Finally, seated, he gazed from face to face and laughed shrilly. This laugh was so strange that the Easterner looked up quickly, the cowboy sat intent and with his mouth open, and Johnnie paused, holding the cards with still fingers.

Afterwards there was a short silence. Then Johnnie said, "Well, let's get at it. Come on now!" They pulled their chairs forward until their knees were bunched under the board. They began to play, and their interest in the game caused the others to forget the manner of the Swede.

The cowboy was a board-whacker. Each time that he held superior cards he whanged them, one by one, with exceeding force, down upon the improvised table, and took the tricks with a glowing air of prowess and pride that sent thrills of indignation into the hearts of his opponents. A game with a board-whacker in it is sure to become intense. The countenances of the Easterner and the Swede were miserable whenever the cowboy thundered down his aces and kings, while Johnnie, his eyes gleaming with joy, chuckled and chuckled.

Because of the absorbing play none considered the strange ways of the Swede. They paid strict heed to the game. Finally, during a lull caused by a new deal, the Swede suddenly addressed Johnnie: "I suppose there have been a good many men killed in this room." The jaws of the others dropped and they looked at him.

"What in hell are you talking about?" said Johnnie.

The Swede laughed again his blatant laugh, full of a kind of false courage and defiance. "Oh, you know what I mean all right," he answered.

"I'm a liar if I do!" Johnnie protested. The card was halted, and the men stared at the Swede. Johnnie evidently felt that as the son of the proprietor he should make a direct inquiry. "Now, what might you be drivin' at, mister?" he asked. The Swede winked at him. It was a wink full of cunning. His fingers shook on the edge of the board. "Oh, maybe you think I have been to nowheres. Maybe you think I'm a tenderfoot?"

"I don't know nothin' about you," answered Johnnie, "and I don't give a damn where you've been. All I got to say is that I don't know what you're driving at. There hain't never been nobody killed in this room."

The cowboy, who had been steadily gazing at the Swede, then spoke: "What's wrong with you, mister?"

Apparently it seemed to the Swede that he was formidably menaced. He shivered and turned white near the corners of his mouth. He sent an appealing glance in the direction of the little Easterner. During these moments he did not forget to wear his air of advanced pot-valor[①]. "They say they don't know what I mean," he remarked mockingly to the Easterner.

The latter answered after prolonged and cautious reflection. "I don't understand you," he said, impassively.

The Swede made a movement then which announced that he thought he had encountered treachery from the only quarter where he had expected sympathy, if not help. "Oh, I see you are all against me. I see—"

---

① Drunken bravado.

Chapter 2   The Blue Hotel

The cowboy was in a state of deep stupefaction. "Say." he cried, as he tumbled the deck violently down upon the board "—say, what are you gittin' at, hey?"

The Swede sprang up with the celerity of a man escaping from a snake on the floor. "I don't want to fight!" he shouted. "I don't want to fight!"

The cowboy stretched his long legs indolently and deliberately. His hands were in his pockets. He spat into the sawdust box. "Well, who the hell thought you did?" he inquired.

The Swede backed rapidly towards a corner of the room. His hands were out protectingly in front of his chest, but he was making an obvious struggle to control his fright. "Gentlemen," he quavered, "I suppose I am going to be killed before I can leave this house! I suppose I am going to be killed before I can leave this house!" In his eyes was the dying-swan look. Through the windows could be seen the snow turning blue in the shadow of dusk. The wind tore at the house and some loose thing beat regularly against the clap-boards like a spirit tapping.

A door opened, and Scully himself entered. He paused in surprise as he noted the tragic attitude of the Swede. Then he said, "What's the matter here?"

The Swede answered him swiftly and eagerly: "These men are going to kill me."

"Kill you!" ejaculated Scully. "Kill you! What are you talkin'?"

The Swede made the gesture of a martyr.

Scully wheeled sternly upon his son. "What is this, Johnnie?"

The lad had grown sullen. "Damned if I know," he answered. "I can't make no sense to it." He began to shuffle the cards, fluttering them together with an angry snap. "He says a good many men have been killed in this room, or something like that. And he says he's goin' to be killed here too. I don't know what ails him. He's crazy, I shouldn't wonder."

Scully then looked for explanation to the cowboy, but the cowboy simply shrugged his shoulders.

"Kill you?" said Scully again to the Swede. "Kill you? Man, you're off your nut."

"Oh, I know." burst out the Swede. "I know what will happen. Yes, I'm crazy—yes. Yes, of course, I'm crazy—yes. But I know one thing—" There was a sort of sweat of misery and terror upon his face. "I know I won't get out of here alive."

The cowboy drew a deep breath, as if his mind was passing into the last stages of dissolution. "Well, I'm dog-goned," he whispered to himself.

Scully wheeled suddenly and faced his son. "You've been troublin' this man!"

Johnnie's voice was loud with its burden of grievance. "Why, good Gawd, I ain't done nothin' to 'im."

The Swede broke in. "Gentlemen, do not disturb yourselves. I will leave this house. I will go away because"—he accused them dramatically with his glance—"because I do not want to be killed."

Scully was furious with his son. "Will you tell me what is the matter, you young divil? What's the matter, anyhow? Speak out!"

"Blame it!" cried Johnnie in despair, "don't I tell you I don't know. He—he says we want to kill him, and that's all I know. I can't tell what ails him."

The Swede continued to repeat: "Never mind, Mr. Scully; never mind. I will leave this house. I will go away, because I do not wish to be killed. Yes, of course, I am crazy—yes. But I know one thing! I will go away. I will leave this house. Never mind, Mr. Scully; never mind. I will go away."

"You will not go 'way," said Scully. "You will not go 'way until I hear the reason of this business. If anybody has troubled you I will take care of him. This is my house. You are under my roof, and I will not allow any peaceable man to be troubled here." He cast a terrible eye upon Johnnie, the cowboy, and the Easterner.

"Never mind, Mr. Scully; never mind. I will go away. I do not wish to be killed." The Swede moved towards the door, which opened upon the stairs. It was evidently his intention to go at once for his baggage.

"No, no," shouted Scully peremptorily; but the white-faced man slid by him and disappeared. "Now," said Scully severely, "what does this mane?"

Johnnie and the cowboy cried together: "Why, we didn't do nothin' to 'im!"

Scully's eyes were cold. "No," he said, "you didn't?"

Johnnie swore a deep oath. "Why this is the wildest loon I ever see. We didn't do nothin' at all. We were jest sittin' here playin' cards, and he—"

The father suddenly spoke to the Easterner. "Mr. Blanc," he asked, "what has these boys been doin'?"

The Easterner reflected again. "I didn't see anything wrong at all," he said at last, slowly.

Scully began to howl. "But what does it mane?" He stared ferociously at his son. "I have a mind to lather you for this, me boy."

Johnnie was frantic. "Well, what have I done?" he bawled at his father.

III

"I think you are tongue-tied," said Scully finally to his son, the cowboy, and the Easterner; and at the end of this scornful sentence he left the room.

Up-stairs the Swede was swiftly fastening the straps of his great valise. Once his back happened to be half turned towards the door, and, hearing a noise there, he wheeled and sprang up, uttering a loud cry. Scully's wrinkled visage showed grimly in the light of the small lamp he carried. This yellow effulgence, streaming upward, colored only his prominent features, and left his eyes, for instance, in mysterious shadow. He resembled a murderer.

"Man! man!" he exclaimed, "have you gone daffy?"

"Oh, no! Oh, no!" rejoined the other. "There are people in this world who know pretty nearly as much as you do—understand?"

For a moment they stood gazing at each other. Upon the Swede's deathly pale checks were two spots brightly crimson and sharply edged, as if they had been carefully painted. Scully placed the light on the table and sat himself on the edge of the bed. He spoke ruminatively. "By cracky, I never heard of such a thing in my life. It's a complete muddle. I can't, for the soul of me, think how you ever got this idea into your head." Presently he lifted his eyes and asked: "And did you sure think they were going to kill you?"

The Swede scanned the old man as if he wished to see into his mind. "I did," he said at last. He obviously suspected that this answer might precipitate an outbreak. As he pulled on a strap his whole arm shook, the elbow wavering like a bit of paper.

Scully banged his hand impressively on the foot-board of the bed. "Why, man, we're goin' to have a line of ilictric street-cars in this town next spring."

"'A line of electric street-cars,'" repeated the Swede, stupidly.

"And," said Scully, "there's a new railroad goin' to be built down from Broken Arm to here. Not to mintion the four churches and the smashin' big brick school-house. Then there's the big factory, too. Why, in two years Romper'll be a *metropolis*."

Having finished the preparation of his baggage, the Swede straightened himself. "Mr. Scully," he said, with sudden hardihood, "how much do I owe you?"

"You don't owe me anythin'," said the old man, angrily.

"Yes, I do," retorted the Swede. He took seventy-five cents from his pocket and tendered it to Scully; but the latter snapped his fingers in disdainful refusal. However, it happened that they both stood gazing in a strange fashion at three silver pieces on the Swede's open palm.

"I'll not take your money," said Scully at last. "Not after what's been goin' on here." Then a plan seemed to strike him. "Here," he cried, picking up his lamp and moving towards the door. "Here! Come with me a minute."

"No," said the Swede, in overwhelming alarm.

"Yes," urged the old man. "Come on! I want you to come and see a picter—just

Chapter 2 The Blue Hotel

across the hall—in my room."

The Swede must have concluded that his hour was come. His jaw dropped and his teeth showed like a dead man's. He ultimately followed Scully across the corridor, but he had the step of one hung in chains.

Scully flashed the light high on the wall of his own chamber. There was revealed a ridiculous photograph of a little girl. She was leaning against a balustrade of gorgeous decoration, and the formidable bang to her hair was prominent. The figure was as graceful as an upright sled-stake, and, withal, it was of the hue of lead. "There," said Scully, tenderly, "that's the picter of my little girl that died. Her name was Carrie. She had the purtiest hair you ever saw! I was that fond of her, she—"

Turning then, he saw that the Swede was not contemplating the picture at all, but, instead, was keeping keen watch on the gloom in the rear.

"Look, man!" cried Scully, heartily. "That's the picter of my little gal that died. Her name was Carrie. And then here's the picter of my oldest boy, Michael. He's a lawyer in Lincoln, an' doin' well. I gave that boy a grand eddycation, and I'm glad for it now. He's a fine boy. Look at 'im now. Ain't he bold as blazes, him there in Lincoln, an honored an' respicted gintleman. An honored an' respicted gintleman," concluded Scully with a flourish. And, so saying, he smote the Swede jovially on the back.

The Swede faintly smiled.

"Now," said the old man, "there's only one more thing." He dropped suddenly to the floor and thrust his head beneath the bed. The Swede could hear his muffled voice. "I'd keep it under me piller if it wasn't for that boy Johnnie. Then there's the old woman—Where is it now? I never put it twice in the same place. Ah, now come out with you!"

Presently he backed clumsily from under the bed, dragging with him an old coat rolled into a bundle. "I've fetched him," he muttered. Kneeling on the floor, he unrolled the coat and extracted from its heart a large yellow-brown whiskey bottle.

His first maneuver was to hold the bottle up to the light. Reassured, apparently, that nobody had been tampering with it, he thrust it with a generous movement towards the Swede.

The weak-kneed Swede was about to eagerly clutch this element of strength, but he suddenly jerked his hand away and cast a look of horror upon Scully.

"Drink," said the old man affectionately. He had risen to his feet, and now stood facing the Swede.

There was a silence. Then again Scully said: "Drink!"

The Swede laughed wildly. He grabbed the bottle, put it to his mouth, and as his lips curled absurdly around the opening and his throat worked, he kept his glance, burning with hatred, upon the old man's face.

IV

After the departure of Scully the three men, with the card-board still upon their knees, preserved for a long time an astounded silence. Then Johnnie said: "That's the dod-dangest Swede I ever see."

"He ain't no Swede," said the cowboy, scornfully.

"Well, what is he then?" cried Johnnie. "What is he then?"

"It's my opinion," replied the cowboy deliberately, "he's some kind of a Dutchman." It was a venerable custom of the country to entitle as Swedes all light-haired men who spoke with a heavy tongue. In consequence the idea of the cowboy was not without its daring. "Yes, sir," he repeated. "It's my opinion this feller is some kind of a Dutchman."

"Well, he says he's a Swede, anyhow," muttered Johnnie, sulkily. He turned to the Easterner: "What do you think, Mr. Blanc?"

"Oh, I don't know," replied the Easterner.

"Well, what do you think makes him act that way?" asked the cowboy.

Chapter 2   The Blue Hotel

"Why, he's frightened." The Easterner knocked his pipe against a rim of the stove. "He's clear frightened out of his boots."

"What at?" cried Johnnie and cowboy together.

The Easterner reflected over his answer.

"What at?" cried the others again.

"Oh, I don't know, but it seems to me this man has been reading dime-novels, and he thinks he's right out in the middle of it—the shootin' and stabbin' and all."

"But," said the cowboy, deeply scandalized, "this ain't Wyoming, ner none of them places. This is Nebrasker."

"Yes," added Johnnie, "an' why don't he wait till he gits *out West?*"

The travelled Easterner laughed. "It isn't different there even—not in these days. But he thinks he's right in the middle of hell."

Johnnie and the cowboy mused long.

"It's awful funny," remarked Johnnie at last.

"Yes," said the cowboy. "This is a queer game. I hope we don't git snowed in, because then we'd have to stand this here man bein' around with us all the time. That wouldn't be no good."

"I wish pop would throw him out," said Johnnie.

Presently they heard a loud stamping on the stairs, accompanied by ringing jokes in the voice of old Scully, and laughter, evidently from the Swede. The men around the stove stared vacantly at each other. "Gosh!" said the cowboy. The door flew open, and old Scully, flushed and anecdotal, came into the room. He was jabbering at the Swede, who followed him, laughing bravely. It was the entry of two roisterers from a banquet-hall.

"Come now," said Scully sharply to the three seated men, "move up and give us a chance at the stove." The cowboy and the Easterner obediently sidled their chairs to make room for the new-comers. Johnnie, however, simply arranged himself in a more indolent attitude, and then remained motionless.

"Come! Git over, there," said Scully.

"Plenty of room on the other side of the stove," said Johnnie.

"Do you think we want to sit in the draught?" roared the father.

But the Swede here interposed with a grandeur of confidence. "No, no. Let the boy sit where he likes," he cried in a bullying voice to the father.

"All right! All right!" said Scully, deferentially. The cowboy and the Easterner exchanged glances of wonder.

The five chairs were formed in a crescent about one side of the stove. The Swede began to talk; he talked arrogantly, profanely, angrily. Johnnie, the cowboy, and the Easterner maintained a morose silence, while old Scully appeared to be receptive and eager, breaking in constantly with sympathetic ejaculations.

Finally the Swede announced that he was thirsty. He moved in his chair, and said that he would go for a drink of water.

"I'll git it for you," cried Scully at once.

"No," said the Swede, contemptuously. "I'll get it for myself." He arose and stalked with the air of an owner off into the executive parts of the hotel.

As soon as the Swede was out of hearing Scully sprang to his feet and whispered intensely to the others: "Up-stairs he thought I was tryin' to poison 'im."

"Say," said Johnnie, "this makes me sick. Why don't you throw 'im out in the snow?"

"Why, he's all right now," declared Scully. "It was only that he was from the East, and he thought this was a tough place. That's all. He's all right now."

The cowboy looked with admiration upon the Easterner. "You were straight," he said. "You were on to that there Dutchman."

"Well," said Johnnie to his father, "he may be all right now, but I don't see it. Other time he was scared, but now he's too fresh."

Chapter 2   The Blue Hotel

Scully's speech was always a combination of Irish brogue and idiom, Western twang and idiom, and scraps of curiously formal diction taken from the story-books and newspapers. He now hurled a strange mass of language at the head of his son. "What do I keep? What do I keep? What do I keep?" he demanded, in a voice of thunder. He slapped his knee impressively, to indicate that he himself was going to make reply, and that all should heed. "I keep a hotel," he shouted. "A hotel, do you mind? A guest under my roof has sacred privileges. He is to be intimidated by none. Not one word shall he hear that would prejudice him in favor of goin' away. I'll not have it. There's no place in this here town where they can say they iver took in a guest of mine because he was afraid to stay here." He wheeled suddenly upon the cowboy and the Easterner. "Am I right?"

"Yes, Mr. Scully," said the cowboy, "I think you're right."

"Yes, Mr. Scully," said the Easterner, "I think you're right."

V

At six-o'clock supper, the Swede fizzed like a fire-wheel. He sometimes seemed on the point of bursting into riotous song, and in all his madness he was encouraged by old Scully. The Easterner was incased in reserve; the cowboy sat in wide-mouthed amazement, forgetting to eat, while Johnnie wrathily demolished great plates of food. The daughters of the house, when they were obliged to replenish the biscuits, approached as warily as Indians, and, having succeeded in their purpose, fled with ill-concealed trepidation. The Swede domineered the whole feast, and he gave it the appearance of a cruel bacchanal[①]. He seemed to have grown suddenly taller; he gazed, brutally disdainful, into every face. His voice rang through the room. Once when he jabbed out harpoon-fashion with his fork to pinion a biscuit, the weapon nearly impaled

---

①   Someone who engages in drinking bouts.

the hand of the Easterner which had been stretched quietly out for the same biscuit.

After supper, as the men filed towards the other room, the Swede smote Scully ruthlessly on the shoulder. "Well, old boy, that was a good, square meal." Johnnie looked hopefully at his father; he knew that shoulder was tender from an old fall; and, indeed, it appeared for a moment as if Scully was going to flame out over the matter, but in the end he smiled a sickly smile and remained silent. The others understood from his manner that he was admitting his responsibility for the Swede's new view-point.

Johnnie, however, addressed his parent in an aside. "Why don't you license somebody to kick you down-stairs?" Scully scowled darkly by way of reply.

When they were gathered about the stove, the Swede insisted on another game of High Five. Scully gently deprecated the plan at first, but the Swede turned a wolfish glare upon him. The old man subsided, and the Swede canvassed the others. In his tone there was always a great threat. The cowboy and the Easterner both remarked indifferently that they would play. Scully said that he would presently have to go to meet the 6:58 train, and so the Swede turned menacingly upon Johnnie. For a moment their glances crossed like blades, and then Johnnie smiled and said, "Yes, I'll play."

They formed a square, with the little board on their knees. The Easterner and the Swede were again partners. As the play went on, it was noticeable that the cowboy was not board-whacking as usual. Meanwhile, Scully, near the lamp, had put on his spectacles and, with an appearance curiously like an old priest, was reading a newspaper. In time he went out to meet the 6:58 train, and, despite his precautions, a gust of polar wind whirled into the room as he opened the door. Besides scattering the cards, it dulled the players to the marrow. The Swede cursed frightfully. When Scully returned, his entrance disturbed a cosey and friendly scene. The Swede again cursed. But presently they were once more intent, their heads bent forward and their hands moving swiftly. The Swede had adopted the fashion of board-whacking.

Scully took up his paper and for a long time remained immersed in matters which

Chapter 2   The Blue Hotel

were extraordinarily remote from him. The lamp burned badly, and once he stopped to adjust the wick. The newspaper, as he turned from page to page, rustled with a slow and comfortable sound. Then suddenly he heard three terrible words: "You are cheatin'!"

Such scenes often prove that there can be little of dramatic import in environment. Any room can present a tragic front; any room can be comic. This little den was now hideous as a torture-chamber. The new faces of the men themselves had changed it upon the instant. The Swede held a huge fist in front of Johnnie's face, while the latter looked steadily over it into the blazing orbs of his accuser. The Easterner had grown pallid; the cowboy's jaw had dropped in that expression of bovine amazement which was one of his important mannerisms. After the three words, the first sound in the room was made by Scully's paper as it floated forgotten to his feet. His spectacles had also fallen from his nose, but by a clutch he had saved them in air. His hand, grasping the spectacles, now remained poised awkwardly and near his shoulder. He stared at the card-players.

Probably the silence was while a second elapsed. Then, if the floor had been suddenly twitched out from under the men they could not have moved quicker. The five had projected themselves headlong towards a common point. It happened that Johnnie, in rising to hurl himself upon the Swede, had stumbled slightly because of his curiously instinctive care for the cards and the board. The loss of the moment allowed time for the arrival of Scully, and also allowed the cowboy time to give the Swede a great push which sent him staggering back. The men found tongue together, and hoarse shouts of rage, appeal, or fear burst from every throat. The cowboy pushed and jostled feverishly at the Swede, and the Easterner and Scully clung wildly to Johnnie; but, through the smoky air, above the swaying bodies of the peace-compellers, the eyes of the two warriors ever sought each other in glances of challenge that were at once hot and steely.

Of course the board had been overturned, and now the whole company of cards was scattered over the floor, where the boots of the men trampled the fat and painted kings and queens as they gazed with their silly eyes at the war that was waging above them.

Scully's voice was dominating the yells. "Stop now? Stop, I say! Stop, now—"

Johnnie, as he struggled to burst through the rank formed by Scully and the Easterner, was crying, "Well, he says I cheated! He says I cheated! I won't allow no man to say I cheated! If he says I cheated, he's a—!"

The cowboy was telling the Swede, "Quit, now! Quit, d'ye hear—"

The screams of the Swede never ceased: "He did cheat! I saw him! I saw him—"

As for the Easterner, he was importuning in a voice that was not heeded: "Wait a moment, can't you? Oh, wait a moment. What's the good of a fight over a game of cards? Wait a moment—"

In this tumult no complete sentences were clear. "Cheat"—"Quit"—"He says"—these fragments pierced the uproar and rang out sharply. It was remarkable that, whereas Scully undoubtedly made the most noise, he was the least heard of any of the riotous band.

Then suddenly there was a great cessation. It was as if each man had paused for breath; and although the room was still lighted with the anger of men, it could be seen that there was no danger of immediate conflict, and at once Johnnie, shouldering his way forward, almost succeeded in confronting the Swede. "What did you say I cheated for? What did you say I cheated for? I don't cheat, and I won't let no man say I do!"

The Swede said, "I saw you! I saw you!"

"Well," cried Johnnie, "I'll fight any man what says I cheat!"

"No, you won't," said the cowboy. "Not here."

"Ah, be still, can't you?" said Scully, coming between them.

The quiet was sufficient to allow the Easterner's voice to be heard. He was repealing, "Oh, wait a moment, can't you? What's the good of a fight over a game of cards? Wait a moment!"

Chapter 2　The Blue Hotel

Johnnie, his red face appearing above his father's shoulder, hailed the Swede again. "Did you say I cheated?"

The Swede showed his teeth. "Yes."

"Then," said Johnnie, "we must fight."

"Yes, fight," roared the Swede. He was like a demoniac. "Yes, fight! I'll show you what kind of a man I am! I'll show you who you want to fight! Maybe you think I can't fight! Maybe you think I can't! I'll show you, you skin①, you card-sharp! Yes, you cheated! You cheated! You cheated!"

"Well, let's go at it, then, mister," said Johnnie, coolly.

The cowboy's brow was beaded with sweat from his efforts in intercepting all sorts of raids. He turned in despair to Scully. "What are you goin' to do now?"

A change had come over the Celtic visage of the old man. He now seemed all eagerness; his eyes glowed.

"We'll let them fight," he answered, stalwartly. "I can't put up with it any longer. I've stood this damned Swede till I'm sick. We'll let them fight."

VI

The men prepared to go out-of-doors. The Easterner was so nervous that he had great difficulty in getting his arms into the sleeves of his new leather coat. As the cowboy drew his fur cap down over his ears his hands trembled. In fact, Johnnie and old Scully were the only ones who displayed no agitation. These preliminaries were conducted without words.

Scully threw open the door. "Well, come on," he said. Instantly a terrific wind caused the flame of the lamp to struggle at its wick, while a puff of black smoke sprang from the chimney-top. The stove was in mid-current of the blast, and its voice swelled

---

① Cheat (colloquial).

to equal the roar of the storm. Some of the scarred and bedabbled cards were caught up from the floor and dashed helplessly against the farther wall. The men lowered their heads and plunged into the tempest as into a sea.

No snow was falling, but great whirls and clouds of flakes, swept up from the ground by the frantic winds, were streaming southward with the speed of bullets. The covered land was blue with the sheen of an unearthly satin, and there was no other hue save where, at the low, black railway station—which seemed incredibly distant—one light gleamed like a tiny jewel. As the men floundered into a thigh deep drift, it was known that the Swede was bawling out something. Scully went to him, put a hand on his shoulder and projected an ear. "What's that you say?" he shouted.

"I say," bawled the Swede again, "I won't stand much show against this gang. I know you'll all pitch on me."

Scully smote him reproachfully on the arm. "Tut, man!" he yelled. The wind tore the words from Scully's lips and scattered them far alee.

"You are all a gang of—" boomed the Swede, but the storm also seized the remainder of this sentence.

Immediately turning their backs upon the wind, the men had swung around a corner to the sheltered side of the hotel. It was the function of the little house to preserve here, amid this great devastation of snow, an irregular V-shape of heavily incrusted grass, which crackled beneath the feet. One could imagine the great drifts piled against the windward side. When the party reached the comparative peace of this spot it was found that the Swede was still bellowing.

"Oh, I know what kind of a thing this is! I know you'll all pitch on me. I can't lick you all!"

Scully turned upon him panther fashion. "You'll not have to whip all of us. You'll have to whip my son Johnnie. An' the man what troubles you durin' that time will have me to dale with."

Chapter 2 The Blue Hotel

The arrangements were swiftly made. The two men faced each other, obedient to the harsh commands of Scully, whose face, in the subtly luminous gloom, could be seen set in the austere impersonal lines that are pictured on the countenances of the Roman veterans. The Easterner's teeth were chattering, and he was hopping up and down like a mechanical toy. The cowboy stood rock-like.

The contestants had not stripped off any clothing. Each was in his ordinary attire. Their fists were up, and they eyed each other in a calm that had the elements of leonine cruelty in it.

During this pause, the Easterner's mind, like a film, took lasting impressions of three men—the iron-nerved master of the ceremony; the Swede, pale, motionless, terrible; and Johnnie, serene yet ferocious, brutish yet heroic. The entire prelude had in it a tragedy greater than the tragedy of action, and this aspect was accentuated by the long, mellow cry of the blizzard, as it sped the tumbling and wailing flakes into the black abyss of the south.

"Now!" said Scully.

The two combatants leaped forward and crashed together like bullocks. There was heard the cushioned sound of blows, and of a curse squeezing out from between the tight teeth of one.

As for the spectators, the Easterner's pent-up breath exploded from him with a pop of relief, absolute relief from the tension of the preliminaries. The cowboy bounded into the air with a yowl. Scully was immovable as from supreme amazement and fear at the fury of the fight which he himself had permitted and arranged.

For a time the encounter in the darkness was such a perplexity of flying arms that it presented no more detail than would a swiftly revolving wheel. Occasionally a face, as if illumined by a flash of light, would shine out, ghastly and marked with pink spots. A moment later, the men might have been known as shadows, if it were not for the involuntary utterance of oaths that came from them in whispers.

Suddenly a holocaust of warlike desire caught the cowboy, and he bolted forward with the speed of a broncho. "Go it, Johnnie! Go it! Kill him! Kill him!"

Scully confronted him. "Kape back," he said; and by his glance the cowboy could tell that this man was Johnnie's father.

To the Easterner there was a monotony of unchangeable fighting that was an abomination. This confused mingling was eternal to his sense, which was concentrated in a longing for the end, the priceless end. Once the fighters lurched near him, and as he scrambled hastily backward he heard them breathe like men on the rack.

"Kill him, Johnnie! Kill him! Kill him! Kill him!" The cowboy's face was contorted like one of those agony masks in museums.

"Keep still," said Scully, icily.

Then there was a sudden loud grunt, incomplete, cut short, and Johnnie's body swung away from the Swede and fell with sickening heaviness to the grass. The cowboy was barely in time to prevent the mad Swede from flinging himself upon his prone adversary. "No, you don't," said the cowboy, interposing an arm. "Wait a second."

Scully was at his son's side. "Johnnie! Johnnie, me boy!" His voice had a quality of melancholy tenderness. "Johnnie! Can you go on with it?" He looked anxiously down into the bloody, pulpy face of his son.

There was a moment of silence, and then Johnnie answered in his ordinary voice, "Yes, I—it—yes."

Assisted by his father he struggled to his feet. "Wait a bit now till you git your wind," said the old man.

A few paces away the cowboy was lecturing the Swede. "No, you don't! Wait a second!"

The Easterner was plucking at Scully's sleeve. "Oh, this is enough," he pleaded. "This is enough! Let it go as it stands. This is enough!"

Chapter 2   The Blue Hotel

"Bill," said Scully, "git out of the road." The cowboy stepped aside. "Now." The combatants were actuated by a new caution as they advanced towards collision. They glared at each other, and then the Swede aimed a lightning blow that carried with it his entire weight. Johnnie was evidently half stupid from weakness, but he miraculously dodged, and his fist sent the over-balanced Swede sprawling.

The cowboy, Scully, and the Easterner burst into a cheer that was like a chorus of triumphant soldiery, but before its conclusion the Swede had scuffled agilely to his feet and come in berserk abandon at his foe. There was another perplexity of flying arms, and Johnnie's body again swung away and fell, even as a bundle might fall from a roof. The Swede instantly staggered to a little wind-waved tree and leaned upon it, breathing like an engine, while his savage and flame-lit eyes roamed from face to face as the men bent over Johnnie. There was a splendor of isolation in his situation at this time which the Easterner felt once when, lifting his eyes from the man on the ground, he beheld that mysterious and lonely figure, waiting.

"Are you any good yet, Johnnie?" asked Scully in a broken voice.

The son gasped and opened his eyes languidly. After a moment he answered, "No—I ain't—any good—any—more." Then, from shame and bodily ill he began to weep, the tears furrowing down through the blood-stains on his face. "He was too—too—too heavy for me."

Scully straightened and addressed the waiting figure. "Stranger," he said, evenly, "it's all up with our side." Then his voice changed into that vibrant huskiness which is commonly the tone of the most simple and deadly announcements. "Johnnie is whipped."

Without replying, the victor moved off on the route to the front door of the hotel.

The cowboy was formulating new and un-spellable blasphemies. The Easterner was startled to find that they were out in a wind that seemed to come direct from the shadowed arctic floes. He heard again the wail of the snow as it was flung to its grave in the south. He knew now that all this time the cold had been sinking into him deeper and deeper, and he wondered that he had not perished. He felt indifferent to the condition of the vanquished man.

"Johnnie, can you walk?" asked Scully.

"Did I hurt—hurt him any?" asked the son.

"Can you walk, boy? Can you walk?"

Johnnie's voice was suddenly strong. There was a robust impatience in it. "I asked you whether I hurt him any!"

"Yes, yes, Johnnie," answered the cowboy, consolingly; "he's hurt a good deal."

They raised him from the ground, and as soon as he was on his feet he went tottering off, rebuffing all attempts at assistance. When the party rounded the corner they were fairly blinded by the pelting of the snow. It burned their faces like fire. The cowboy carried Johnnie through the drift to the door. As they entered some cards again rose from the floor and beat against the wall.

The Easterner rushed to the stove. He was so profoundly chilled that he almost dared to embrace the glowing iron. The Swede was not in the room. Johnnie sank into a chair, and, folding his arms on his knees, buried his face in them. Scully, warming one foot and then the other at a rim of the stove, muttered to himself with Celtic mournfulness. The cowboy had removed his fur cap, and with a dazed and rueful air he was running one hand through his tousled locks. From overhead they could hear the creaking of boards, as the Swede tramped here and there in his room.

The sad quiet was broken by the sudden flinging open of a door that led towards the kitchen. It was instantly followed by an inrush of women. They precipitated themselves upon Johnnie amid a chorus of lamentation. Before they carried their prey off to the kitchen, there to be bathed and harangued with that mixture of sympathy and abuse which is a feat of their sex, the mother straightened herself and fixed old Scully with an eye of stern reproach. "Shame be upon you, Patrick Scully!" she cried. "Your own son, too. Shame be upon you!"

"There, now! Be quiet, now!" said the old man, weakly.

"Shame be upon you, Patrick Scully!" The girls, rallying to this slogan, sniffed disdainfully in the direction of those trembling accomplices, the cowboy and the Easterner. Presently they bore Johnnie away, and left the three men to dismal reflection.

VII

"I'd like to fight this here Dutchman myself," said the cowboy, breaking a long silence.

Scully wagged his head sadly. "No, that wouldn't do. It wouldn't be right. It wouldn't be right."

"Well, why wouldn't it?" argued the cowboy. "I don't see no harm in it."

"No," answered Scully, with mournful heroism. "It wouldn't be right. It was Johnnie's fight, and now we mustn't whip the man just because he whipped Johnnie."

"Yes, that's true enough," said the cowboy; "but—he better not get fresh with me, because I couldn't stand no more of it."

"You'll not say a word to him," commanded Scully, and even then they heard the tread of the Swede on the stairs. His entrance was made theatric. He swept the door back with a bang and swaggered to the middle of the room. No one looked at him. "Well," he cried, insolently, at Scully, "I s'pose you'll tell me now how much I owe you?"

The old man remained stolid. "You don't owe me nothin'."

"Huh!" said the Swede, "huh! Don't owe 'im nothin'."

The cowboy addressed the Swede. "Stranger, I don't see how you come to be so gay around here."

Old Scully was instantly alert. "Stop!" he shouted, holding his hand forth, fingers upward. "Bill, you shut up!"

The cowboy spat carelessly into the sawdust box. "I didn't say a word, did I?" he asked.

"Mr. Scully," called the Swede, "how much do I owe you?" It was seen that he was attired for departure, and that he had his valise in his hand.

"You don't owe me nothin'," repeated Scully in his same imperturbable way.

"Huh!" said the Swede. "I guess you're right. I guess if it was any way at all, you'd owe me somethin'. That's what I guess." He turned to the cowboy. "'Kill him! Kill him! Kill him!'" he mimicked, and then guffawed victoriously. "'Kill him!'" He was convulsed with ironical humor.

But he might have been jeering the dead. The three men were immovable and silent, staring with glassy eyes at the stove.

The Swede opened the door and passed into the storm, giving one derisive glance backward at the still group.

As soon as the door was closed, Scully and the cowboy leaped to their feet and began to curse. They trampled to and fro, waving their arms and smashing into the air with their fists. "Oh, but that was a hard minute!" wailed Scully. "That was a hard minute! Him there leerin' and scoffin'! One bang at his nose was worth forty dollars to me that minute! How did you stand it, Bill?"

"How did I stand it?" cried the cowboy in a quivering voice. "How did I stand it? Oh!"

The old man burst into sudden brogue. "I'd loike to take that Swade," he wailed, "and hould 'im down on a shtone flure and bate 'im to a jelly wid a shtick!"

The cowboy groaned in sympathy. "I'd like to git him by the neck and ha-ammer him"—he brought his hand down on a chair with a noise like a pistol-shot—"hammer that there Dutchman until he couldn't tell himself from a dead coyote!"

"I'd bate 'im until he—"

"I'd show *him* some things—"

And then together they raised a yearning, fanatic cry—"Oh-o-oh! if we only could—"

"Yes!"

"Yes!"

"And then I'd—"

"O-o-oh!"

VIII

The Swede, tightly gripping his valise, tacked across the face of the storm as if he carried sails. He was following a line of little naked, gasping trees, which he knew must mark the way of the road. His face, fresh from the pounding of Johnnie's fists, felt more pleasure than pain in the wind and the driving snow. A number of square shapes loomed upon him finally, and he knew them as the houses of the main body of the town. He found a street and made travel along it, leaning heavily upon the wind whenever, at a corner, a terrific blast caught him.

He might have been in a deserted village. We picture the world as thick with conquering and elate humanity, but here, with the bugles of the tempest pealing, it was hard to imagine a peopled earth. One viewed the existence of man then as a marvel, and conceded a glamour of wonder to these lice which were caused to cling to a whirling, fire-smote, ice-locked, disease-stricken, space-lost bulb. The conceit of man was explained by this storm to be the very engine of life. One was a coxcomb not to die in it. However, the Swede found a saloon.

In front of it an indomitable red light was burning, and the snow-flakes were made blood-color as they flew through the circumscribed territory of the lamp's shining. The Swede pushed open the door of the saloon and entered. A sanded expanse was before him, and at the end of it four men sat about a table drinking. Down one side of the room extended a radiant bar, and its guardian was leaning upon his elbows listening to the talk of the men at the table. The Swede dropped his valise upon the floor, and, smiling fraternally upon the barkeeper, said, "Gimme some whiskey, will you?" The man placed a bottle, a whiskey-glass, and a glass of ice-thick water upon the bar. The Swede poured himself an abnormal portion of whiskey and drank it in three gulps. "Pretty bad night," remarked the bartender, indifferently. He was making the pretension of blindness which is usually a distinction of his class; but it could have been seen that he was furtively studying the half-erased blood-stains on the face of the Swede. "Bad night," he said again.

"Oh, it's good enough for me," replied the Swede, hardily, as he poured himself some more whiskey. The barkeeper took his coin and maneuvered it through its reception by the highly nickelled cash-machine. A bell rang; a card labelled "20 cts." had appeared.

"No," continued the Swede, "this isn't too bad weather. It's good enough for me."

"So?" murmured the barkeeper, languidly.

The copious drams made the Swede's eyes swim, and he breathed a trifle heavier. "Yes, I like this weather. I like it. It suits me." It was apparently his design to impart a deep significance to these words.

"So?" murmured the bartender again. He turned to gaze dreamily at the scroll-like birds and bird-like scrolls which had been drawn with soap upon the mirrors back of the bar.

"Well, I guess I'll take another drink," said the Swede, presently. "Have something?"

"No, thanks; I'm not drinkin'," answered the bartender. Afterwards he asked, "How did you hurt your face?"

The Swede immediately began to boast loudly. "Why, in a fight. I thumped the soul out of a man down here at Scully's hotel."

The interest of the four men at the table was at last aroused.

Chapter 2 The Blue Hotel

"Who was it?" said one.

"Johnnie Scully," blustered the Swede. "Son of the man what runs it. He will be pretty near dead for some weeks, I can tell you. I made a nice thing of him, I did. He couldn't get up. They carried him in the house. Have a drink?"

Instantly the men in some subtle way incased themselves in reserve. "No, thanks," said one. The group was of curious formation. Two were prominent local business men; one was the district-attorney; and one was a professional gambler of the kind known as "square"[①]. But a scrutiny of the group would not have enabled an observer to pick the gambler from the men of more reputable pursuits. He was, in fact, a man so delicate in manner, when among people of fair class, and so judicious in his choice of victims, that in the strictly masculine part of the town's life he had come to be explicitly trusted and admired. People called him a thoroughbred. The fear and contempt with which his craft was regarded was undoubtedly the reason that his quiet dignity shone conspicuous above the quiet dignity of men who might be merely hatters, billiard markers[②], or grocery-clerks. Beyond an occasional unwary traveler, who came by rail, this gambler was supposed to prey solely upon reckless and senile farmers, who, when flush with good crops, drove into town in all the pride and confidence of an absolutely invulnerable stupidity. Hearing at times in circuitous fashion of the despoilment of such a farmer, the important men of Romper invariably laughed in contempt of the victim, and, if they thought of the wolf at all, it was with a kind of pride at the knowledge that he would never dare think of attacking their wisdom and courage. Besides, it was popular that this gambler had a real wife and two real children in a neat cottage in a suburb, where he led an exemplary home life; and when any one even suggested a discrepancy in his character, the crowd immediately vociferated descriptions of this virtuous family circle. Then men who led exemplary home lives, and men who did not

---

①   Honest.
②   Scorekeepers at billiards matches.

lead exemplary home lives, all subsided in a bunch, remarking that there was nothing more to be said.

However, when a restriction was placed upon him—as, for instance, when a strong clique of members of the new Pollywog Club refused to permit him, even as a spectator, to appear in the rooms of the organization—the candor and gentleness with which he accepted the judgment disarmed many of his foes and made his friends more desperately partisan. He invariably distinguished between himself and a respectable Romper man so quickly and frankly that his manner actually appeared to be a continual broadcast compliment.

And one must not forget to declare the fundamental fact of his entire position in Romper. It is irrefutable that in all affairs outside of his business, in all matters that occur eternally and commonly between man and man, this thieving card-player was so generous, so just, so moral, that, in a contest, he could have put to flight the consciences of nine-tenths of the citizens of Romper.

And so it happened that he was seated in this saloon with the two prominent local merchants and the district-attorney.

The Swede continued to drink raw whiskey, meanwhile babbling at the barkeeper and trying to induce him to indulge in potations. "Come on. Have a drink. Come on. What—no? Well, have a little one, then. By gawd, I've whipped a man to-night, and I want to celebrate. I whipped him good, too. Gentlemen," the Swede cried to the men at the table, "have a drink?"

"Ssh!" said the barkeeper.

The group at the table, although furtively attentive, had been pretending to be deep in talk, but now a man lifted his eyes towards the Swede and said, shortly, "Thanks. We don't want any more."

At this reply the Swede ruffled out his chest like a rooster. "Well," he exploded, "it seems I can't get anybody to drink with me in this town. Seems so, don't it? Well!"

Chapter 2   The Blue Hotel

"Ssh!" said the barkeeper.

"Say," snarled the Swede, "don't you try to shut me up. I won't have it. I'm a gentleman, and I want people to drink with me. And I want 'em to drink with me now. *Now*—do you understand?" He rapped the bar with his knuckles.

Years of experience had calloused the bartender. He merely grew sulky. "I hear you," he answered.

"Well," cried the Swede, "listen hard then. See those men over there? Well, they're going to drink with me, and don't you forget it. Now you watch."

"Hi!" yelled the barkeeper, "this won't do!"

"Why won't it?" demanded the Swede. He stalked over to the table, and by chance laid his hand upon the shoulder of the gambler. "How about this?" he asked, wrathfully. "I asked you to drink with me."

The gambler simply twisted his head and spoke over his shoulder. "My friend, I don't know you."

"Oh, hell!" answered the Swede, "come and have a drink."

"Now, my boy," advised the gambler, kindly, "take your hand off my shoulder and go 'way and mind your own business." He was a little, slim man, and it seemed strange to hear him use this tone of heroic patronage to the burly Swede. The other men at the table said nothing.

"What! You won't drink with me, you little dude? I'll make you then! I'll make you!" The Swede had grasped the gambler frenziedly at the throat, and was dragging him from his chair. The other men sprang up. The barkeeper dashed around the corner of his bar. There was a great tumult, and then was seen a long blade in the hand of the gambler. It shot forward, and a human body, this citadel of virtue, wisdom, power, was pierced as easily as if it had been a melon. The Swede fell with a cry of supreme astonishment.

The prominent merchants and the district attorney must have at once tumbled out of the place backward. The bartender found himself hanging limply to the arm of a chair and gazing into the eyes of a murderer.

"Henry," said the latter, as he wiped his knife on one of the towels that hung beneath the bar-rail, "you tell 'em where to find me. I'll be home, waiting for 'em." Then he vanished. A moment afterwards the barkeeper was in the street dinning through the storm for help, and, moreover, companionship.

The corpse of the Swede, alone in the saloon, had its eyes fixed upon a dreadful legend that dwelt atop of the cash-machine: "This registers the amount of your purchase."

IX

Months later, the cowboy was frying pork over the stove of a little ranch near the Dakota line, when there was a quick thud of hoofs outside, and presently the Easterner entered with the letters and the papers.

"Well," said the Easterner at once, "the chap that killed the Swede has got three years. Wasn't much, was it?"

"He has? Three years?" The cowboy poised his pan of pork, while he ruminated upon the news. "Three years. That ain't much."

"No. It was a light sentence," replied the Easterner as he unbuckled his spurs. "Seems there was a good deal of sympathy for him in Romper."

"If the bartender had been any good," observed the cowboy, thoughtfully, "he would have gone in and cracked that there Dutchman on the head with a bottle in the beginnin' of it and stopped all this here murderin'."

"Yes, a thousand things might have happened," said the Easterner, tartly.

The cowboy returned his pan of pork to the fire, but his philosophy continued. "It's funny, ain't it? If he hadn't said Johnnie was cheatin' he'd be alive this minute. He was an awful fool. Game played for fun, too. Not for money. I believe he was crazy."

"I feel sorry for that gambler," said the Easterner.

"Oh, so do I," said the cowboy. "He don't deserve none of it for killin' who he did."

"The Swede might not have been killed if everything had been square."

"Might not have been killed?" exclaimed the cowboy. "Everythin' square? Why, when he said that Johnnie was cheatin' and acted like such a jackass? And then in the saloon he fairly walked up to git hurt?" With these arguments the cowboy browbeat the Easterner and reduced him to rage.

"You're a fool!" cried the Easterner, viciously. "You're a bigger jackass than the Swede by a million majority. Now let me tell you one thing. Let me tell you something. Listen! Johnnie *was* cheating!"

"Johnnie," said the cowboy, blankly. There was a minute of silence, and then he said, robustly, "Why, no. The game was only for fun."

"Fun or not," said the Easterner, "Johnnie was cheating. I saw him. I know it. I saw him. And I refused to stand up and be a man. I let the Swede fight it out alone. And you—you were simply puffing around the place and wanting to fight. And then old Scully himself! We are all in it! This poor gambler isn't even a noun. He is kind of an adverb. Every sin is the result of a collaboration. We, five of us, have collaborated in the murder of this Swede. Usually there are from a dozen to forty women really involved in every murder, but in this case it seems to be only five men—you, I, Johnnie, old Scully, and that fool of an unfortunate gambler came merely as a culmination, the apex of a human movement, and gets all the punishment."

The cowboy, injured and rebellious, cried out blindly into this fog of mysterious theory: "Well, I didn't do anything, did I?"

Film Comment:

Stephen Crane's *The Blue Hotel*: 55 minutes, color
Starring: David Warner & James Keach
Screenplay by: Harry M. Petrakis
Directed by: Jan Kadar

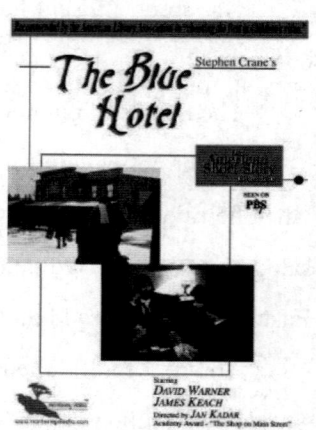

Nebraska in the 1880s...bleak, lonely, and far from what you'd expect the wild West to be. But for a naïve Swedish immigrant, the frontier parlor of "The Blue Hotel" represents the quintessential western fantasy.

No one can convince the Swede that his dime-store notions about the West are foolish. He sees murderous intentions all around him...and in his terror he turns everyone against him.

Inevitably the Swede attracts tragedy. However, who is responsible? The negative Swede? Or the cliquish hotel guests? Academy Award-winner Jan Kadar ("The Shop on Main Street") directs this timely story of how society punishes outsiders for being different.

Film Scenes:

Scene 1: The Blue Hotel

Scully paints his hotel in the conspicuous color of blue, and he is hospitable and skillful in attracting the travelers to his hotel.

Scene 2: A card game

Johnnie, the son of Scully, is playing a card game with an old farmer, which is interrupted by the arrival of the guests and ends with a sudden quarrel.

Scene 3: Crazy Swede

The Swede gets somewhat crazy: he speaks out that a good many men must have been killed in the room, and fears that he could be killed before leaving the hotel, making Johnnie angry but soothed by Scully.

Scene 4: Deadly game

After dinner the guests and Johnnie resume the card play, and the game becomes deadly because the Swede accuses Johnnie of cheating in the play, which leads to a ferocious fight, ending with the victory of the Swede.

Scene 5: The stranger

A stranger comes into the hotel, but he refuses to listen to the bragging of the Swede. When angered by his pushy behavior, the stranger pulls out a knife and kills the Swede.

Scene 6: The truth

The Easterner talks with the cowboy about who is responsible for the death of the Swede, and reveals the truth that Johnnie is indeed cheating in the card play, implying that everybody at the hotel should be responsible.

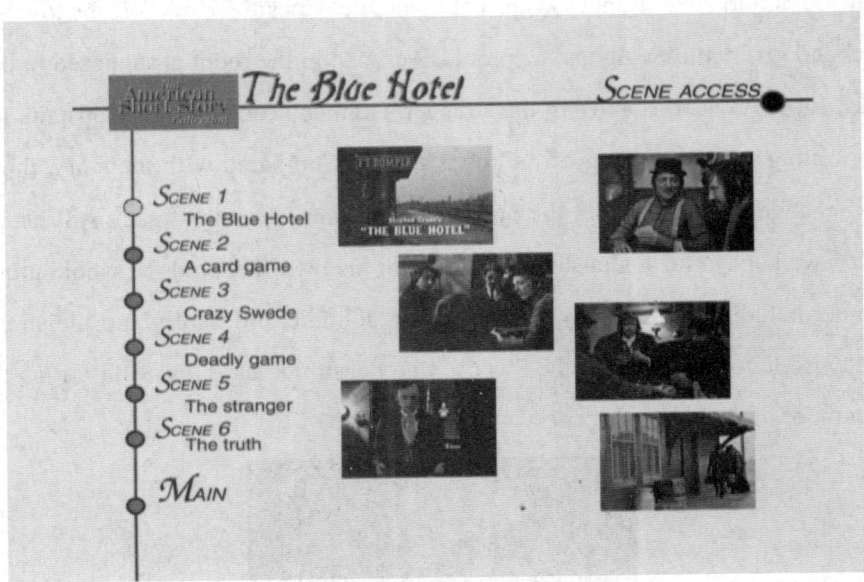

Film Clip:

The Murder

After the fierce fight with Johnnie, the son of Scully the hotel owner, the Swede has to leave and find another hotel, despite that he is the winner of the fight. When hearing owing nothing to the hotel, the Swede boasts that Scully should owe him something for teaching his son a precious lesson. When a stranger comes into the hotel for a room, Scully accepts him warmly, allocating him the room the Swede is ready to check out. The Swede is yet not willing to leave the hotel, and he insistently tells the stranger the story of his fighting with Johnnie and how he has won the fight with glory and courage, paying no attention to the impatience of the people in the room.

The stranger has no interest listening to the story of the Swede, but he forces the stranger to turn his back when talking to him, considering it impolite. When touched upon his shoulder by the Swede, the stranger pulls out a knife, stabs into the Swede, and thus kills him. The stranger keeps calm, and he wipes the blood off the knife with a towel and gives it to Scully as the proof. Everyone in the room is supposed to be the witness, for the Swede is abusing the stranger. He then peacefully goes upstairs to his room, waiting for the coming of the town sheriff. Compared with the story, the film doesn't change its setting from the hotel to the saloon. Yet, the tragedy still happens, and the Swede pays for his pushy behavior with his own life. And the whole group at the hotel, including the cowboy, the Easterner, Johnnie, old Scully and the stranger, are responsible for the death of the Swede, who doesn't deserve his death for his fancy perception of the wild West.

Discussion Questions:

Story Discussion

(1) What is the source of the Swede's fear? To what extent does it spring from a distorted view of reality and his own preconceived ideas?

(2) Is Scully acting from good motives in trying to keep peace in his hotel? Does the purity or impurity of his motives have anything to do with the outcome of the action?

(3) Is Johnnie a victim or an aggressor? What does the story as a whole say about innocence and guilt?

(4) How does the natural setting reinforce the theme and meaning of the story? What other kinds of imagery does Crane employ?

(5) What does Crane mean at the end of the story when he has the Easterner say that "Every sin is the result of a collaboration"? How are all five major characters implicated in the Swede's death?

Film Appreciation

(1) How does Scully attract the guests into his hotel?

(2) What's the image of the Blue Hotel in the winter of the prairie?

(3) How is the Swede different from the other guests when cleaning themselves? What's the source of the Swede's fear?

(4) Why does Scully show the Swede his family pictures?

(5) How do they invite the Swede to play at the card game? Why does the Swede board-whack during the game?

(6) What's the hidden meaning of those three terrible words, "You are cheating," especially for the fighting?

(7) How does the Swede come to his death? Does he deserve such a death? Who are

responsible for his death?

(8) What are the adapted scenes in the film?

Further Reading and Watching:

The Open Boat

Unit Two: Symbol

Chapter 3: Paul's Case

Chapter 4: Bernice Bobs Her Hair

Chapter 3
Paul's Case

Willa Cather

Author Introduction:

Willa Cather (1873—1947) was born of Anglo-Irish parents in Back Creek Valley, Virginia. At ten she moved with her family to Red Cloud, Nebraska, where she grew up, exploring the prairies on horseback and making friends with the immigrant farmers of the area.

After graduating from the University of Nebraska, Cather lived in Pittsburgh for ten years, where the short story "Paul's Case" opens, working first as a journalist and then as a high-school teacher of English and Latin.

At the age of 33, she moved to New York City, and held editorial positions for the popular magazine *McClure's*, but her poetry and fiction looked to the Midwest and Southwest for their subject matters and to the depths of the American past for their values. She never married.

The last part of her life was spent in New York, with occasional European travels that never swayed her from nostalgia or the conservatism of her views. Once she declared that the world had "broken apart" about 1922; unmistakably she preferred the manners, styles, and virtues that prevailed before that date.

Incidentally she was awarded the Pulitzer Prize that year for *One of Ours* (1922), a novel set during the First World War. With remarkable skill, Cather might tell a story from a man's point of view, but her favorite characters are likely to be women of strong will who triumph over obstacles.

Among her novels are *My Antonia* (1918), *A Lost Lady* (1923), *The Professor's House* (1925), and *Death Comes for the Archbishop* (1927). Her collections of short stories are *The Troll Garden* (1905), *Youth and the Bright Medusa* (1920), *Obscure Destinies* (1932), and *The Old Beauty and Others* (1948). *Not under Forty* (1936) contains many of her essays.

Story Summary:

The events of "Paul's Case" were modeled on an actual incident that occurred while Cather was teaching English and Latin in Pittsburgh, Pennsylvania.

Paul was born into a respectable neighborhood in turn-of-the-century Pittsburgh. He comes to hate its "ugliness and commonness." His defiant manner, red buttonhole carnation and "hysterical brilliant" blue eyes infuriate his teachers. But Paul simply lives for the hours after school when he works as an usher in a concert hall. He loses himself in the majesty of the arts. Finally, his widower father takes him out of school and puts him to work at a job that won't "heat his brain…" Paul retaliates by stealing money and flees to New York. He just wants to float on waves of beauty. Briefly he lives in luxury and illusion—until reality comes crashing down.

We should learn from the death of Paul, an artistically inclined young man, who commits suicide because of the false belief that money could change one's identity.

Chapter 3 Paul's Case

Key Terms:

Adolescence: Paul is a high-school student, at the age of 16 or 17, just within the period of adolescence.

Rebellion: Adolescent young boys are usually rebellious, against their parents, teachers, and religion. Paul is no exception.

Family Relationships: Paul's mother dies when he is still very young, only months old, and the relationship between Paul and his father is rather tense.

Symbolic Power: There are quite a few cases of symbols, such as flowers, colors, train, rain and snow, which have strong symbolic power.

Romance: The romance between Paul and girls is not mentioned much, while there are some boys hanging around Paul.

Suicide: Suicide is never easy, especially for religious people. Yet, Paul would rather commit suicide than go back home with his father.

Paul's Case[1]

A Study in Temperament

It was Paul's afternoon to appear before the faculty of the Pittsburgh High School to account for his various misdemeanors[2]. He had been suspended[3] a week ago, and his father had called at the Principal's office and confessed his perplexity about his son. Paul entered the faculty room suave[4] and smiling. His clothes were a trifle outgrown,

---

[1] First published in *McClure's Magazine* on May 25, 1905, later collected in *The Troll Garden* (1905), and then reprinted in *Youth and the Bright Medusa* (1920).
[2] A crime less serious than a felony.
[3] To bar temporarily from school.
[4] Charming, polite, and elegant, but may be insincere.

and the tan velvet on the collar of his open overcoat was frayed and worn; but for all that there was something of the dandy① about him, and he wore an opal pin in his neatly knotted black four-in-hand②, and a red carnation in his buttonhole. This latter adornment the faculty somehow felt was not properly significant of the contrite③ spirit befitting a boy under the ban of suspension.

Paul was tall for his age and very thin, with high, cramped shoulders and a narrow chest. His eyes were remarkable for a certain hysterical brilliancy, and he continually used them in a conscious, theatrical sort of way, peculiarly offensive in a boy. The pupils were abnormally large, as though he were addicted to belladonna④, but there was a glassy glitter about them which that drug does not produce.

When questioned by the Principal as to why he was there Paul stated, politely enough, that he wanted to come back to school. This was a lie, but Paul was quite accustomed to lying; found it, indeed, indispensable for overcoming friction. His teachers were asked to state their respective charges against him, which they did with such a rancor and aggrievedness as evinced that this was not a usual case. Disorder and impertinence were among the offenses named, yet each of his instructors felt that it was scarcely possible to put into words the real cause of the trouble, which lay in a sort of hysterically defiant manner of the boy's; in the contempt which they all knew he felt for them, and which he seemingly made not the least effort to conceal. Once, when he had been making a synopsis of a paragraph at the blackboard, his English teacher had stepped to his side and attempted to guide his hand. Paul had started back with a shudder and thrust his hands violently behind him. The astonished woman could

---

① A man who is much concerned with his dress and appearance.
② A long necktie tied in a slipknot with the ends hanging.
③ Feeling regret for a fault or offence.
④ A poisonous plant whose leaves yield a medicine for stomach aches; taking it, however, dilates the eyes.

scarcely have been more hurt and embarrassed had he struck at her. The insult was so involuntary and definitely personal as to be unforgettable. In one way and another he had made all his teachers, men and women alike, conscious of the same feeling of physical aversion. In one class he habitually sat with his hand shading his eyes; in another he always looked out of the window during the recitation; in another he made a running commentary on the lecture, with humorous intention.

His teachers felt this afternoon that his whole attitude was symbolized by his shrug and his flippantly red carnation flower, and they fell upon him without mercy, his English teacher leading the pack. He stood through it smiling, his pale lips parted over his white teeth. (His lips were continually twitching, and he had a habit of raising his eyebrows that was contemptuous and irritating to the last degree.) Older boys than Paul had broken down and shed tears under that baptism of fire, but his set smile did not once desert him, and his only sign of discomfort was the nervous trembling of the fingers that toyed with the buttons of his overcoat, and an occasional jerking of the other hand that held his hat. Paul was always smiling, always glancing about him, seeming to feel that people might be watching him and trying to detect something. This conscious expression, since it was as far as possible from boyish mirthfulness, was usually attributed to insolence or "smartness."

As the inquisition proceeded one of his instructors repeated an impertinent remark of the boy's, and the Principal asked him whether he thought that a courteous speech to have made a woman. Paul shrugged his shoulders slightly and his eyebrows twitched.

"I don't know," he replied. "I didn't mean to be polite or impolite, either. I guess it's a sort of way I have of saying things regardless."

The Principal, who was a sympathetic man, asked him whether he didn't think that a way it would be well to get rid of. Paul grinned and said he guessed so. When he was told that he could go he bowed gracefully and went out. His bow was but a repetition of the scandalous red carnation.

His teachers were in despair, and his drawing master[①] voiced the feeling of them all when he declared there was something about the boy which none of them understood. He added: "I don't really believe that smile of his comes altogether from insolence; there's something sort of haunted about it. The boy is not strong, for one thing. I happen to know that he was born in Colorado, only a few months before his mother died out there of a long illness. There is something wrong about the fellow."

The drawing master had come to realize that, in looking at Paul, one saw only his white teeth and the forced animation of his eyes. One warm afternoon the boy had gone to sleep at his drawing board, and his master had noted with amazement what a white, blue-veined face it was; drawn and wrinkled like an old man's about the eyes, the lips twitching even in his sleep, and stiff with a nervous tension that drew them back from his teeth.

His teachers left the building dissatisfied and unhappy; humiliated to have felt so vindictive toward a mere boy, to have uttered this feeling in cutting terms, and to have set each other on, as it were, in the gruesome game of intemperate reproach. Some of them remembered having seen a miserable street cat set at bay by a ring of tormentors.

As for Paul, he ran down the hill whistling the "Soldiers' Chorus" from *Faust*[②], looking wildly behind him now and then to see whether some of his teachers were not there to writhe under his lightheartedness. As it was now late in the afternoon and Paul was on duty that evening as usher at Carnegie Hall[③], he decided that he would not go home to supper. When he reached the concert hall the doors were not yet open and, as it was chilly outside, he decided to go up into the picture gallery—always deserted at this

---

① Art teacher.
② An opera by French composer Charles Gounod (1818—1893).
③ A Pittsburg music hall named for Andrew Carnegie (1835—1919), famous industrialist and philanthropist.

Chapter 3 Paul's Case

hour—where there were some of Raffaelli's[①] gay studies of Paris streets and an airy blue Venetian scene or two that always exhilarated him. He was delighted to find no one in the gallery but the old guard, who sat in one corner, a newspaper on his knee, a black patch over one eye and the other closed. Paul possessed himself of the peace and walked confidently up and down, whistling under his breath. After a while he sat down before a blue Rico[②] and lost himself. When he bethought him to look at his watch, it was after seven o'clock, and he rose with a start and ran downstairs, making a face at Augustus[③], peering out from the cast room, and an evil gesture at the Venus de Milo[④] as he passed her on the stairway.

When Paul reached the ushers' dressing room half a dozen boys were there already, and he began excitedly to tumble into his uniform. It was one of the few that at all approached fitting, and Paul thought it very becoming—though he knew that the tight, straight coat accentuated his narrow chest, about which he was exceedingly sensitive. He was always considerably excited while he dressed, twanging all over to the tuning of the strings and the preliminary flourishes of the horns in the music room; but tonight he seemed quite beside himself, and he teased and plagued the boys until, telling him that he was crazy, they put him down on the floor and sat on him.

Somewhat calmed by his suppression, Paul dashed out to the front of the house to seat the early comers. He was a model usher; gracious and smiling he ran up and down the aisles; nothing was too much trouble for him; he carried messages and brought programs as though it were his greatest pleasure in life, and all the people in his section thought him a charming boy, feeling that he remembered and admired them. As the house filled, he grew more and more vivacious and animated, and the color came to his

---

① Jean-Francois Raffaelli (1850—1924), French painter, sculptor, and etcher.
② Andreas Rico (1500—1550), Cretan-Italian painter.
③ First emperor of Rome (27 B.C.—A.D.14) and grand-nephew of Julius Caesar.
④ A famous Greek statue; the original is in the Louvre, Paris.

cheeks and lips. It was very much as though this were a great reception and Paul were the host. Just as the musicians came out to take their places, his English teacher arrived with checks for the seats which a prominent manufacturer had taken for the season. She betrayed some embarrassment when she handed Paul the tickets, and a *hauteur*[1] which subsequently made her feel very foolish. Paul was startled for a moment, and had the feeling of wanting to put her out; what business had she here among all these fine people and gay colors? He looked her over and decided that she was not appropriately dressed and must be a fool to sit downstairs in such togs. The tickets had probably been sent her out of kindness, he reflected as he put down a seat for her, and she had about as much right to sit there as he had.

When the symphony began Paul sank into one of the rear seats with a long sigh of relief, and lost himself as he had done before the Rico. It was not that symphonies, as such, meant anything in particular to Paul, but the first sigh of the instruments seemed to free some hilarious and potent spirit within him; something that struggled there like the genie in the bottle found by the Arab fisherman[2]. He felt a sudden zest of life; the lights danced before his eyes and the concert hall blazed into unimaginable splendor. When the soprano soloist came on Paul forgot even the nastiness of his teacher's being there and gave himself up to the peculiar stimulus such personages always had for him. The soloist chanced to be a German woman, by no means in her first youth, and the mother of many children; but she wore an elaborate gown and a tiara, and above all she had that indefinable air of achievement, that world-shine upon her, which, in Paul's eyes, made her a veritable queen of Romance.

After a concert was over Paul was always irritable and wretched until he got to

---

[1] (French) haughtiness; loftiness.

[2] In one of the tales of the *Arabian Nights* (also called *Thousand and One Nights*), the fisherman Ali Baba finds a genie imprisoned in a bottle who is able to perform miracles.

sleep, and tonight he was even more than usually restless. He had the feeling of not being able to let down, of its being impossible to give up this delicious excitement which was the only thing that could be called living at all. During the last number he withdrew and, after hastily changing his clothes in the dressing room, slipped out to the side door where the soprano's carriage stood. Here he began pacing rapidly up and down the walk, waiting to see her come out.

Over yonder, the Schenley, in its vacant stretch, loomed big and square through the fine rain, the windows of its twelve stories glowing like those of a lighted cardboard house under a Christmas tree. All the actors and singers of the better class stayed there when they were in the city, and a number of the big manufacturers of the place lived there in the winter. Paul had often hung about the hotel, watching the people go in and out, longing to enter and leave schoolmasters and dull care behind him forever.

At last the singer came out, accompanied by the conductor, who helped her into her carriage and closed the door with a cordial *auf wiedersehen*[①] which set Paul to wondering whether she were not an old sweetheart of his. Paul followed the carriage over to the hotel, walking so rapidly as not to be far from the entrance when the singer alighted, and disappeared behind the swinging glass doors that were opened by a Negro in a tall hat and a long coat. In the moment that the door was ajar it seemed to Paul that he, too, entered. He seemed to feel himself go after her up the steps, into the warm, lighted building, into an exotic, tropical world of shiny, glistening surfaces and basking ease. He reflected upon the mysterious dishes that were brought into the dining room, the green bottles in buckets of ice, as he had seen them in the supper party pictures of the *Sunday World* supplement. A quick gust of wind brought the rain down with sudden vehemence, and Paul was startled to find that he was still outside in the slush of the gravel driveway; that his boots were letting in the water and his scanty overcoat was

---

① (German) Good-bye. Literally, "to again see."

clinging wet about him; that the lights in front of the concert hall were out and that the rain was driving in sheets between him and the orange glow of the windows above him. There it was, what he wanted—tangibly before him, like the fairy world of a Christmas pantomime, but mocking spirits stood guard at the doors, and, as the rain beat in his face, Paul wondered whether he were destined always to shiver in the black night outside, looking up at it.

He turned and walked reluctantly toward the car① tracks. The end had to come sometime; his father in his nightclothes at the top of the stairs, explanations that did not explain, hastily improvised fictions that were forever tripping him up, his upstairs room and its horrible yellow wallpaper, the creaking bureau with the greasy plush collar-box, and over his painted wooden bed the pictures of George Washington and John Calvin②, and the framed motto, "Feed my Lambs," which had been worked in red worsted by his mother.

Half an hour later Paul alighted from his car and went slowly down one of the side streets off the main thoroughfare. It was a highly respectable street, where all the houses were exactly alike, and where businessmen of moderate means③ begot and reared large families of children, all of whom went to Sabbath school and learned the shorter catechism④, and were interested in arithmetic; all of whom were as exactly alike as their homes, and of a piece with the monotony⑤ in which they lived. Paul never went up Cordelia Street without a shudder of loathing⑥. His home was next to the house of

---

① Streetcar.
② John Calvin (1509—1564), French Protestant reformer, lived in Geneva.
③ Middle income.
④ The more widely used and influential of two catechisms of religious instruction drawn up in 1647.
⑤ The quality of boring constancy, routine, and lack of variety.
⑥ A feeling of great dislike and disgust.

the Cumberland[①] minister. He approached it tonight with the nerveless sense of defeat, the hopeless feeling of sinking back forever into ugliness and commonness that he had always had when he came home. The moment he turned into Cordelia Street he felt the waters close above his head. After each of these orgies of living he experienced all the physical depression which follows a debauch; the loathing of respectable beds, of common food, of a house penetrated by kitchen odors; a shuddering repulsion for the flavorless, colorless mass of everyday existence; a morbid desire for cool things and soft lights and fresh flowers.

The nearer he approached the house, the more absolutely unequal Paul felt to the sight of it all: his ugly sleeping chamber; the cold bathroom with the grimy zinc tub, the cracked mirror, the dripping spigots; his father, at the top of the stairs, his hairy legs sticking out from his nightshirt, his feet thrust into carpet slippers. He was so much later than usual that there would certainly be inquiries and reproaches. Paul stopped short before the door. He felt that he could not be accosted by his father tonight; that he could not toss again on that miserable bed. He would not go in. He would tell his father that he had no carfare and it was raining so hard he had gone home with one of the boys and stayed all night.

Meanwhile, he was wet and cold. He went around to the back of the house and tried one of the basement windows, found it open, raised it cautiously, and scrambled down the cellar wall to the floor. There he stood, holding his breath, terrified by the noise he had made, but the floor above him was silent, and there was no creak on the stairs. He found a soapbox, and carried it over to the soft ring of light that streamed from the furnace door, and sat down. He was horribly afraid of rats, so he did not try to sleep, but sat looking distrustfully at the dark, still terrified lest he might have awakened his father. In such reactions, after one of the experiences which made days

---

① A division of the Presbyterian Church in the United States.

and nights out of the dreary blanks of the calendar, when his senses were deadened, Paul's head was always singularly clear. Suppose his father had heard him getting in at the window and had come down and shot him for a burglar①? Then, again, suppose his father had come down, pistol in hand, and he had cried out in time to save himself, and his father had been horrified to think how nearly he had killed him? Then, again, suppose a day should come when his father would remember that night, and wish there had been no warning cry to stay his hand? With this last supposition Paul entertained himself until daybreak.

The following Sunday was fine; the sodden November chill was broken by the last flash of autumnal summer. In the morning Paul had to go to church and Sabbath school, as always. On seasonable Sunday afternoons the burghers② of Cordelia Street always sat out on their front stoops and talked to their neighbors on the next stoop, or called to those across the street in neighborly fashion. The men usually sat on gay cushions placed upon the steps that led down to the sidewalk, while the women, in their Sunday "waists"③, sat in rockers on the cramped porches, pretending to be greatly at their ease. The children played in the streets; there were so many of them that the place resembled the recreation grounds of a kindergarten. The men on the steps—all in their shirt sleeves, their vests unbuttoned—sat with their legs well apart, their stomachs comfortably protruding, and talked of the prices of things, or told anecdotes of the sagacity of their various chiefs and overlords. They occasionally looked over the multitude of squabbling children, listened affectionately to their high-pitched, nasal voices, smiling to see their own proclivities reproduced in their offspring, and interspersed their legends of the iron kings④ with remarks about their sons' progress at

---

① A thief who enters a house or another building by force.
② Comfortable or complacent members of the middle class.
③ Bodices or blouses.
④ Tycoons of the iron and steel industry.

school, their grades in arithmetic, and the amounts they had saved in their toy banks.

On this last Sunday of November Paul sat all the afternoon on the lowest step of his stoop, staring into the street, while his sisters, in their rockers, were talking to the minister's daughters next door about how many shirtwaists they had made in the last week, and how many waffles someone had eaten at the last church supper. When the weather was warm, and his father was in a particularly jovial frame of mind, the girls made lemonade, which was always brought out in a red-glass pitcher, ornamented with forget-me-nots in blue enamel. This the girls thought very fine, and the neighbors always joked about the suspicious color of the pitcher.

Today Paul's father sat on the top step, talking to a young man who shifted a restless baby from knee to knee. He happened to be the young man who was daily held up to Paul as a model, and after whom it was his father's dearest hope that he would pattern. This young man was of a ruddy complexion, with a compressed, red mouth, and faded, nearsighted eyes, over which he wore thick spectacles[1], with gold bows that curved about his ears. He was clerk to one of the magnates[2] of a great steel corporation, and was looked upon in Cordelia Street as a young man with a future. There was a story that, some five years ago—he was now barely twenty-six—he had been a trifle dissipated[3], but in order to curb his appetites and save the loss of time and strength that a sowing of wild oats[4] might have entailed, he had taken his chief's advice, oft reiterated[5] to his employees, and at twenty-one had married the first woman whom he could persuade to share his fortunes. She happened to be an angular schoolmistress, much older than he, who also wore thick glasses, and who had now

---

[1] Glasses.
[2] A very wealthy or powerful businessman.
[3] Preoccupied with the pursuit of pleasure and especially games of chance.
[4] Living promiscuously and self-indulgently.
[5] To say, state, or perform again.

borne him four children, all nearsighted, like herself.

The young man was relating how his chief, now cruising in the Mediterranean, kept in touch with all the details of the business, arranging his office hours on his yacht just as though he were at home, and "knocking off work enough to keep two stenographers busy." His father told, in turn, the plan his corporation was considering, of putting in an electric railway plant in Cairo. Paul snapped his teeth; he had an awful apprehension that they might spoil it all before he got there. Yet he rather liked to hear these legends of the iron kings that were told and retold on Sundays and holidays; these stories of palaces in Venice, yachts on the Mediterranean, and high play at Monte Carlo① appealed to his fancy, and he was interested in the triumphs of these cash boys who had become famous, though he had no mind for the cash-boy stage.

After supper was over and he had helped to dry the dishes, Paul nervously asked his father whether he could go to George's to get some help in his geometry, and still more nervously asked for carfare. This latter request he had to repeat, as his father, on principle, did not like to hear requests for money, whether much or little. He asked Paul whether he could not go to some boy who lived nearer, and told him that he ought not to leave his schoolwork until Sunday; but he gave him the dime②. He was not a poor man, but he had a worthy ambition to come up in the world. His only reason for allowing Paul to usher was that he thought a boy ought to be earning a little.

Paul bounded upstairs, scrubbed the greasy odor of the dishwater from his hands with the ill-smelling soap he hated, and then shook over his fingers a few drops of violet water from the bottle he kept hidden in his drawer. He left the house with his geometry conspicuously under his arm, and the moment he got out of Cordelia Street and boarded a downtown car, he shook off the lethargy of two deadening days and began to live again.

---

① High-stakes gambling in Monaco's chief city.
② A coin of the United States; worth ten cents.

Chapter 3 Paul's Case

The leading juvenile① of the permanent stock company② which played at one of the downtown theaters was an acquaintance of Paul's, and the boy had been invited to drop in at the Sunday-night rehearsals whenever he could. For more than a year Paul had spent every available moment loitering③ about Charley Edwards's dressing room. He had won a place among Edwards's following not only because the young actor, who could not afford to employ a dresser④, often found him useful, but because he recognized in Paul something akin to what churchmen term "vocation."

It was at the theater and at Carnegie Hall that Paul really lived; the rest was but a sleep and a forgetting. This was Paul's fairy tale, and it had for him all the allurement of a secret love. The moment he inhaled the gassy, painty, dusty odor behind the scenes, he breathed like a prisoner set free, and felt within him the possibility of doing or saying splendid, brilliant, poetic things. The moment the cracked orchestra beat out the overture from *Martha*⑤, or jerked at the serenade from *Rigoletto*⑥, all stupid and ugly things slid from him, and his senses were deliciously, yet delicately fired.

Perhaps it was because, in Paul's world, the natural nearly always wore the guise of ugliness, that a certain element of artificiality seemed to him necessary in beauty. Perhaps it was because his experience of life elsewhere was so full of Sabbath-school picnics, petty economies, wholesome advice as to how to succeed in life, and the inescapable odors of cooking, that he found this existence so alluring, these smartly clad men and women so attractive, that he was so moved by these starry apple orchards

---

① The juvenile is the male actor who takes youthful parts; his female equivalent is called an ingénue.
② A theatrical company that performs several plays in one theater.
③ To hang around, hang out.
④ A person employed to assist actors in putting on and taking off their costumes.
⑤ A romantic opera by Friedrich von Flotow (1812—1883).
⑥ A tragic opera by Giuseppe Verdi (1813—1901).

that bloomed perennially under the limelight①.

It would be difficult to put it strongly enough how convincingly the stage entrance of that theater was for Paul the actual portal of Romance. Certainly none of the company ever suspected it, least of all Charley Edwards. It was very like the old stories that used to float about London of fabulously rich Jews, who had subterranean halls there, with palms, and fountains, and soft lamps and richly appareled women who never saw the disenchanting light of London day. So, in the midst of that smoke-palled city, enamored of figures and grimy toil, Paul had his secret temple, his wishing carpet, his bit of blue-and-white Mediterranean shore bathed in perpetual sunshine.

Several of Paul's teachers had a theory that his imagination had been perverted by garish fiction, but the truth was that he scarcely ever read at all. The books at home were not such as would either tempt or corrupt a youthful mind, and as for reading the novels that some of his friends urged upon him—well, he got what he wanted much more quickly from music; any sort of music, from an orchestra to a barrel organ. He needed only the spark②, the indescribable thrill that made his imagination master of his senses, and he could make plots and pictures enough of his own. It was equally true that he was not stage struck—not, at any rate, in the usual acceptation of that expression. He had no desire to become an actor, any more than he had to become a musician. He felt no necessity to do any of these things; what he wanted was to see, to be in the atmosphere, float on the wave of it, to be carried out, blue league③ after blue league, away from everything.

After a night behind the scenes Paul found the schoolroom more than ever repulsive; the bare floors and naked walls; the prosy men who never wore frock coats, or violets in their buttonholes; the women with their dull gowns, shrill voices, and

---

① A focus of public attention.
② A momentary flash of light.
③ A unit of distance equal to 3.0 statute miles (4.8 kilometers).

Chapter 3 Paul's Case

pitiful seriousness about prepositions that govern the dative. He could not bear to have the other pupils think, for a moment, that he took these people seriously; he must convey to them that he considered it all trivial, and was there only by way of a jest, anyway. He had autographed pictures of all the members of the stock company which he showed his classmates, telling them the most incredible stories of his familiarity with these people, of his acquaintance with the soloists who came to Carnegie Hall, his suppers with them and the flowers he sent them. When these stories lost their effect, and his audience grew listless, he became desperate and would bid all the boys good-by, announcing that he was going to travel for a while; going to Naples, to Venice, to Egypt. Then, next Monday, he would slip back, conscious and nervously smiling; his sister was ill, and he should have to defer his voyage until spring.

Matters went steadily worse with Paul at school. In the itch to let his instructors know how heartily he despised them and their homilies, and how thoroughly he was appreciated elsewhere, he mentioned once or twice that he had no time to fool with theorems; adding—with a twitch of the eyebrows and a touch of that nervous bravado which so perplexed them—that he was helping the people down at the stock company; they were old friends of his.

The upshot① of the matter was that the Principal went to Paul's father, and Paul was taken out of school and put to work. The manager at Carnegie Hall was told to get another usher in his stead; the doorkeeper at the theater was warned not to admit him to the house; and Charley Edwards remorsefully② promised the boy's father not to see him again.

The members of the stock company were vastly amused when some of Paul's stories reached them—especially the women. They were hard-working women, most

---

① The final result.
② Regretfully.

of them supporting indigent① husbands or brothers, and they laughed rather bitterly at having stirred the boy to such fervid② and florid③ inventions. They agreed with the faculty and with his father that Paul's was a bad case.

    The east-bound train was plowing through a January snowstorm; the dull dawn was beginning to show gray when the engine whistled a mile out of Newark④. Paul started up from the seat where he had lain curled in uneasy slumber, rubbed the breath-misted window glass with his hand, and peered out. The snow was whirling in curling eddies above the white bottom lands, and the drifts lay already deep in the fields and along the fences, while here and there the long dead grass and dried weed stalks protruded black above it. Lights shone from the scattered houses, and a gang of laborers who stood beside the track waved their lanterns.

    Paul had slept very little, and he felt grimy and uncomfortable. He had made the all-night journey in a day coach, partly because he was ashamed, dressed as he was, to go into a Pullman⑤, and partly because he was afraid of being seen there by some Pittsburgh businessman, who might have noticed him in Denny & Carson's office. When the whistle awoke him, he clutched quickly at his breast pocket, glancing about him with an uncertain smile. But the little, clay-bespattered Italians were still sleeping, the slatternly women across the aisle were in open-mouthed oblivion, and even the crumby, crying babies were for the nonce stilled. Paul settled back to struggle with his impatience as best he could.

    When he arrived at the Jersey City station he hurried through his breakfast,

---

①   Very poor.
②   Characterized by intense emotion.
③   Elaborately or excessively ornamented.
④   The city in New Jersey just outside of New York City.
⑤   The luxurious sleeping car designed by American inventor George M. Pullman.

manifestly ill at ease and keeping a sharp eye about him. After he reached the Twenty-third Street station①, he consulted a cabman and had himself driven to a men's-furnishings establishment that was just opening for the day. He spent upward of two hours there, buying with endless reconsidering and great care. His new street suit he put on in the fitting room; the frock coat and dress clothes he had bundled into the cab with his linen. Then he drove to a hatter's and a shoe house. His next errand was at Tiffany's②, where he selected his silver③ and a new scarf pin. He would not wait to have his silver marked④, he said. Lastly, he stopped at a trunk shop on Broadway⑤ and had his purchases packed into various traveling bags.

It was a little after one o'clock when he drove up to the Waldorf⑥, and after settling with the cabman, went into the office. He registered from Washington; said his mother and father had been abroad, and that he had come down to await the arrival of their steamer⑦. He told his story plausibly⑧ and had no trouble, since he volunteered to pay for them in advance, in engaging his rooms; a sleeping room, sitting room, and bath.

Not once, but a hundred times, Paul had planned this entry into New York. He had gone over every detail of it with Charley Edwards, and in his scrapbook at home there were pages of description about New York hotels, cut from the Sunday papers. When he was shown to his sitting room on the eighth floor he saw at a glance that everything was as it should be; there was but one detail in his mental picture that the place did

① Railway terminal in Manhattan.
② A fashionable jewelry store in Manhattan.
③ A comb and brush set.
④ Monogrammed.
⑤ A street in Manhattan that passes through Times Square; famous for its theaters.
⑥ A fashionable hotel in Manhattan.
⑦ A ship that has an engine powered by steam.
⑧ Easy to believe on the basis of available evidence.

not realize, so he rang for the bellboy and sent him down for flowers. He moved about nervously until the boy returned, putting away his new linen and fingering it delightedly as he did so. When the flowers came he put them hastily into water, and then tumbled into a hot bath. Presently he came out of his white bathroom, resplendent in his new silk underwear, and playing with the tassels of his red robe. The snow was whirling so fiercely outside his windows that he could scarcely see across the street, but within the air was deliciously soft and fragrant. He put the violets and jonquils on the taboret[①] beside the couch, and threw himself down, with a long sigh, covering himself with a Roman blanket. He was thoroughly tired; he had been in such haste, he had stood up to such a strain, covered so much ground in the last twenty-four hours, that he wanted to think how it had all come about. Lulled by the sound of the wind, the warm air, and the cool fragrance of the flowers, he sank into deep, drowsy retrospection.

It had been wonderfully simple; when they had shut him out of the theater and concert hall, when they had taken away his bone, the whole thing was virtually determined. The rest was a mere matter of opportunity. The only thing that at all surprised him was his own courage—for he realized well enough that he had always been tormented by fear, a sort of apprehensive dread that, of late years, as the meshes of the lies he had told closed about him, had been pulling the muscles of his body tighter and tighter. Until now he could not remember the time when he had not been dreading something. Even when he was a little boy it was always there—behind him, or before, or on either side. There had always been the shadowed corner, the dark place into which he dared not look, but from which something seemed always to be watching him—and Paul had done things that were not pretty to watch, he knew.

But now he had a curious sense of relief, as though he had at last thrown down the gauntlet to the thing in the corner.

---

① A small, cylindrical stand.

Chapter 3 Paul's Case

Yet it was but a day since he had been sulking in the traces①; but yesterday afternoon that he had been sent to the bank with Denny & Carson's deposit, as usual—but this time he was instructed to leave the book to be balanced. There was above two thousand dollars in checks, and nearly a thousand in the bank notes which he had taken from the book and quietly transferred to his pocket. At the bank he had made out a new deposit slip. His nerves had been steady enough to permit of his returning to the office, where he had finished his work and asked for a full day's holiday tomorrow, Saturday, giving a perfectly reasonable pretext②. The bankbook, he knew, would not be returned before Monday or Tuesday, and his father would be out of town for the next week. From the time he slipped③ the bank notes into his pocket until he boarded the night train for New York, he had not known a moment's hesitation. It was not the first time Paul had steered through treacherous④ waters.

How astonishingly easy it had all been; here he was, the thing done; and this time there would be no awakening, no figure at the top of the stairs. He watched the snowflakes whirling by his window until he fell asleep.

When he awoke, it was three o'clock in the afternoon. He bounded up with a start; half of one of his precious days gone already! He spent more than an hour in dressing, watching every stage of his toilet carefully in the mirror. Everything was quite perfect; he was exactly the kind of boy he had always wanted to be.

When he went downstairs Paul took a carriage and drove up Fifth Avenue toward the Park⑤. The snow had somewhat abated; carriages and tradesmen's wagons were hurrying soundlessly to and fro in the winter twilight; boys in woolen mufflers were

---

① Traces were straps, ropes, or chains by which an animal pulled a wagon or a carriage. Here, the phrase is metaphoric, referring to Paul's sulky attitude toward the bonds of work.
② A fictitious reason.
③ To insert quickly or quietly.
④ Very dangerous and unpredictable.
⑤ Central Park, the principal park in Manhattan.

shoveling off the doorsteps; the avenue stages① made fine spots of color against the white street. Here and there on the corners were stands, with whole flower gardens blooming under glass cases, against the sides of which the snowflakes stuck and melted; violets, roses, carnations, lilies of the valley—somehow vastly more lovely and alluring that they blossomed thus unnaturally in the snow. The Park itself was a wonderful stage winterpiece.

When he returned, the pause of the twilight had ceased and the tune of the streets had changed. The snow was falling faster, lights streamed from the hotels that reared their dozen stories fearlessly up into the storm, defying the raging Atlantic winds. A long, black stream of carriages poured down the avenue, intersected here and there by other streams, tending horizontally. There were a score of cabs about the entrance of his hotel, and his driver had to wait. Boys in livery were running in and out of the awning stretched across the sidewalk, up and down the red velvet carpet laid from the door to the street. Above, about, within it all was the rumble and roar, the hurry and toss of thousands of human beings as hot for pleasure as himself, and on every side of him towered the glaring affirmation of the omnipotence of wealth.

The boy set his teeth and drew his shoulders together in a spasm of realization; the plot of all dramas, the text of all romances, the nerve-stuff of all sensations was whirling about him like the snowflakes. He burnt like a faggot② in a tempest.

When Paul went down to dinner the music of the orchestra came floating up the elevator shaft to greet him. His head whirled as he stepped into the thronged corridor, and he sank back into one of the chairs against the wall to get his breath. The lights, the chatter, the perfumes, the bewildering medley of color—he had, for a moment, the feeling of not being able to stand it. But only for a moment; these were his own people, he told himself. He went slowly about the corridors, through the writing rooms,

---

① Window displays.

② A bundle of sticks or twigs, tied together for burning.

smoking rooms, reception rooms, as though he were exploring the chambers of an enchanted palace, built and peopled for him alone.

When he reached the dining room he sat down at a table near a window. The flowers, the white linen, the many-colored wineglasses, the gay toilettes of the women, the low popping of corks, the undulating repetitions of the *Blue Danube*[①] from the orchestra, all flooded Paul's dream with bewildering radiance. When the roseate tinge of his champagne was added—that cold, precious, bubbling stuff that creamed and foamed in his glass—Paul wondered that there were honest men in the world at all. This was what all the world was fighting for, he reflected; this was what all the struggle was about. He doubted the reality of his past. Had he ever known a place called Cordelia Street, a place where fagged-looking businessmen got on the early car; mere rivets in a machine they seemed to Paul,—sickening men, with combings of children's hair always hanging to their coats, and the smell of cooking in their clothes. Cordelia Street—Ah, that belonged to another time and country; had he not always been thus, had he not sat here night after night, from as far back as he could remember, looking pensively over just such shimmering textures and slowly twirling the stem of a glass like this one between his thumb and middle finger? He rather thought he had.

He was not in the least abashed or lonely. He had no especial desire to meet or to know any of these people; all he demanded was the right to look on and conjecture, to watch the pageant. The mere stage properties were all he contended for. Nor was he lonely later in the evening, in his lodge at the Metropolitan[②]. He was now entirely rid of his nervous misgivings, of his forced aggressiveness, of the imperative desire to show himself different from his surroundings. He felt now that his surroundings explained him. Nobody questioned the purple[③]; he had only to wear it passively. He had only to

---

① Waltz by Johann Strauss (1825—1899), Austrian composer.
② His box at the Metropolitan Opera House.
③ His assumption of a royal robe.

glance down at his attire to reassure himself that here it would be impossible for anyone to humiliate him.

He found it hard to leave his beautiful sitting room to go to bed that night, and sat long watching the raging storm from his turret window. When he went to sleep it was with the lights turned on in his bedroom; partly because of his old timidity, and partly so that, if he should wake in the night, there would be no wretched moment of doubt, no horrible suspicion of yellow wallpaper, or of Washington and Calvin above his bed.

Sunday morning the city was practically snowbound. Paul breakfasted late, and in the afternoon he fell in with a wild San Francisco boy, a freshman at Yale, who said he had run down for a "little flyer" over Sunday. The young man offered to show Paul the night side of the town, and the two boys went out together after dinner, not returning to the hotel until seven o'clock the next morning. They had started out in the confiding[①] warmth of a champagne friendship, but their parting in the elevator was singularly[②] cool. The freshman pulled himself together to make his train, and Paul went to bed. He awoke at two o'clock in the afternoon, very thirsty and dizzy, and rang for ice-water, coffee, and the Pittsburgh papers.

On the part of the hotel management, Paul excited no suspicion. There was this to be said for him, that he wore his spoils with dignity and in no way made himself conspicuous. Even under the glow of his wine he was never boisterous, though he found the stuff like a magician's wand for wonder-building. His chief greediness lay in his ears and eyes, and his excesses were not offensive ones. His dearest pleasures were the gray winter twilights[③] in his sitting room; his quiet enjoyment of his flowers, his clothes, his wide divan[④], his cigarette, and his sense of power. He could not remember

---

① Unsuspicious; trustful.
② Considerably, remarkably.
③ The time of day immediately following sunset.
④ A long backless sofa, especially one set with pillows against a wall.

a time when he had felt so at peace with himself. The mere release from the necessity of petty[1] lying, lying every day and every day, restored his self-respect. He had never lied for pleasure, even at school; but to be noticed and admired, to assert his difference from other Cordelia Street boys; and he felt a good deal more manly, more honest, even, now that he had no need for boastful pretensions, now that he could, as his actor friends used to say, "dress the part[2]." It was characteristic that remorse did not occur to him. His golden days went by without a shadow, and he made each as perfect as he could.

On the eighth day after his arrival in New York he found the whole affair exploited in the Pittsburgh papers, exploited[3] with a wealth of detail which indicated that local news of a sensational nature was at a low ebb[4]. The firm of Denny & Carson announced that the boy's father had refunded the full amount of the theft and that they had no intention of prosecuting. The Cumberland minister had been interviewed, and expressed his hope of yet reclaiming the motherless lad, and his Sabbath-school teacher declared that she would spare no effort to that end. The rumor had reached Pittsburgh that the boy had been seen in a New York hotel, and his father had gone East to find him and bring him home.

Paul had just come in to dress for dinner; he sank into a chair, weak to the knees, and clasped his head in his hands. It was to be worse than jail, even; the tepid[5] waters of Cordelia Street were to close over him finally and forever. The gray monotony stretched before him in hopeless, unrelieved years; Sabbath school, Young People's Meeting, the yellow-papered room, the damp dishtowels; it all rushed back upon him

---

[1] Small and of little importance.
[2] Smartly dressed.
[3] To use or manipulate to one's advantage.
[4] Decreasing.
[5] Slightly warm, feeling or showing little interest or enthusiasm.

with a sickening vividness. He had the old feeling that the orchestra had suddenly stopped, the sinking sensation that the play was over. The sweat broke out on his face, and he sprang to his feet, looked about him with his white, conscious smile, and winked at himself in the mirror. With something of the old childish belief in miracles with which he had so often gone to class, all his lessons unlearned, Paul dressed and dashed whistling down the corridor to the elevator.

He had no sooner entered the dining room and caught the measure of the music than his remembrance was lightened by his old elastic power of claiming the moment, mounting with it, and finding it all-sufficient. The glare and glitter about him, the mere scenic accessories had again, and for the last time, their old potency. He would show himself that he was game, he would finish the thing splendidly. He doubted, more than ever, the existence of Cordelia Street, and for the first time he drank his wine recklessly. Was he not, after all, one of those fortunate beings born to the purple, was he not still himself and in his own place? He drummed a nervous accompaniment to the *Pagliacci*[①] music and looked about him, telling himself over and over that it had paid.

He reflected drowsily, to the swell of the music and the chill sweetness of his wine, that he might have done it more wisely. He might have caught an outbound steamer and been well out of their clutches before now. But the other side of the world had seemed too far away and too uncertain then; he could not have waited for it; his need had been too sharp. If he had to choose over again, he would do the same thing tomorrow. He looked affectionately about the dining room, now gilded with a soft mist. Ah, it had paid indeed!

Paul was awakened next morning by a painful throbbing in his head and feet. He had thrown himself across the bed without undressing, and had slept with his shoes on. His limbs and hands were lead heavy, and his tongue and throat were parched and

---

① A tragic opera by Ruggiero Leoncavallo (1858—1919).

Chapter 3 Paul's Case

burnt. There came upon him one of those fateful attacks of clear-headedness that never occurred except when he was physically exhausted and his nerves hung loose. He lay still, closed his eyes, and let the tide of things wash over him.

His father was in New York; "stopping at some joint or other," he told himself. The memory of successive summers on the front stoop fell upon him like a weight of black water. He had not a hundred dollars left; and he knew now, more than ever, that money was everything, the wall that stood between all he loathed and all he wanted. The thing was winding itself up; he had thought of that on his first glorious day in New York, and had even provided a way to snap the thread. It lay on his dressing table now; he had got it out last night when he came blindly up from dinner, but the shiny metal hurt his eyes, and he disliked the looks of it.

He rose and moved about with a painful effort, succumbing now and again to attacks of nausea①. It was the old depression exaggerated; all the world had become Cordelia Street. Yet somehow he was not afraid of anything, was absolutely calm; perhaps because he had looked into the dark corner at last and knew. It was bad enough, what he saw there, but somehow not so bad as his long fear of it had been. He saw everything clearly now. He had a feeling that he had made the best of it, that he had lived the sort of life he was meant to live, and for half an hour he sat staring at the revolver. But he told himself that was not the way, so he went downstairs and took a cab to the ferry.

When Paul arrived in Newark he got off the train and took another cab, directing the driver to follow the Pennsylvania tracks out of the town. The snow lay heavy on the roadways and had drifted deep in the open fields. Only here and there the dead grass or dried weed stalks projected, singularly black, above it. Once well into the country, Paul dismissed the carriage and walked, floundering along the tracks, his mind a medley of

---

① Strong aversion; disgust.

irrelevant things. He seemed to hold in his brain an actual picture of everything he had seen that morning. He remembered every feature of both his drivers, of the toothless old woman from whom he had bought the red flowers in his coat, the agent from whom he had got his ticket, and all of his fellow passengers on the ferry. His mind, unable to cope with vital matters near at hand, worked feverishly and deftly at sorting and grouping these images. They made for him a part of the ugliness of the world, of the ache in his head, and the bitter burning on his tongue. He stooped and put a handful of snow into his mouth as he walked, but that, too, seemed hot. When he reached a little hillside, where the tracks ran through a cut some twenty feet below him, he stopped and sat down.

The carnations in his coat were drooping① with the cold, he noticed, their red glory all over. It occurred to him that all the flowers he had seen in the glass cases that first night must have gone the same way, long before this. It was only one splendid breath they had, in spite of their brave mockery② at the winter outside the glass; and it was a losing game in the end, it seemed, this revolt③ against the homilies④ by which the world is run. Paul took one of the blossoms carefully from his coat and scooped a little hole in the snow, where he covered it up. Then he dozed awhile, from his weak condition, seemingly insensible to the cold.

The sound of an approaching train awoke him, and he started to his feet, remembering only his resolution, and afraid lest he should be too late. He stood watching the approaching locomotive⑤, his teeth chattering, his lips drawn away from them in a frightened smile; once or twice he glanced nervously sidewise, as though he

---

① To hang or lean downward with no strength or firmness.
② Showing contempt by laughing.
③ Organized opposition to authority.
④ A sermon on a moral or religious topic.
⑤ A large vehicle that pulls a train.

were being watched. When the right moment came, he jumped. As he fell, the folly[1] of his haste occurred to him with merciless clearness, the vastness of what he had left undone. There flashed through his brain, clearer than ever before, the blue of Adriatic[2] water, the yellow of Algerian[3] sands.

He felt something strike his chest, and that his body was being thrown swiftly through the air, on and on, immeasurably far and fast, while his limbs were gently relaxed. Then, because the picture-making mechanism was crushed[4], the disturbing visions flashed into black, and Paul dropped back into the immense design of things.

Film Comment:

Willa Cather's *Paul's Case*: 54 minutes, color

Starring: Eric Roberts

Screenplay by: Ron Cowen

Directed by: Lamont Johnson

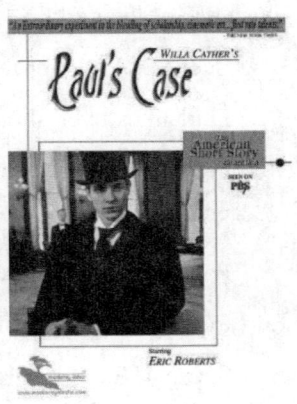

Lost in a world of fantasy, young working-class Paul dreams of escaping his dreary existence in turn-of-the-century Pittsburgh. As fate would have it, Paul gets his chance by stealing some money and subsequently running off to glamorous New York City.

Once there, Paul experiences everything he ever dreamed of…from a luxurious

---

[1] Foolish or senseless behavior.
[2] An arm of the Mediterranean between Slovenia and Croatia and Montenegro and Albania on the east and Italy on the west.
[3] A republic in northwestern Africa on the Mediterranean Sea with a population that is predominantly Sunni Muslim; colonized by France in the 19th century but gained autonomy in the early 1960s.
[4] To compress with violence, out of natural shape or condition.

hotel suite to his first taste of champagne. However, when reality finally comes crashing down around him, Paul realizes the desperate course he must now take.

In a powerful and intense performance, Eric Roberts ("Star 80") plays the title role in Willa Cather's "Paul's Case." As the tortured and tragic young man, Roberts brings to life this classic American story of a sensitive soul pitted against an uncaring materialistic society.

Film Scenes:

Scene 1: Dreamer

Waiting for the school inquisition, Paul still dreams of escaping his dreary existence of the middle-class daily life.

Scene 2: Art lover

Paul likes everything artistic, such as music, painting, theater, play, etc. That is why Paul loses himself in front of a blue Rico.

Scene 3: Want to be like you!

Paul helps with the dinner, and he needs a dime for the car fare to visit Charley Edwards, but he has to ask twice, though his father is not a poor man.

Scene 4: Expelled from school

Paul sleeps in class and talks back to the teachers. The final result of the matter is that the principal goes to his father, and Paul is taken out of school.

Scene 5: The Waldorf Hotel

With the huge amount of money he steals from the firm, Paul registers to live in the Waldorf Hotel, drinking the champagne he has been dreaming for a long time.

Scene 6: End of a dream

Paul would rather commit suicide than go back home with his father, which is to be worse than jail. Paul chooses to jump toward the train to end his life and dream.

Chapter 3 Paul's Case

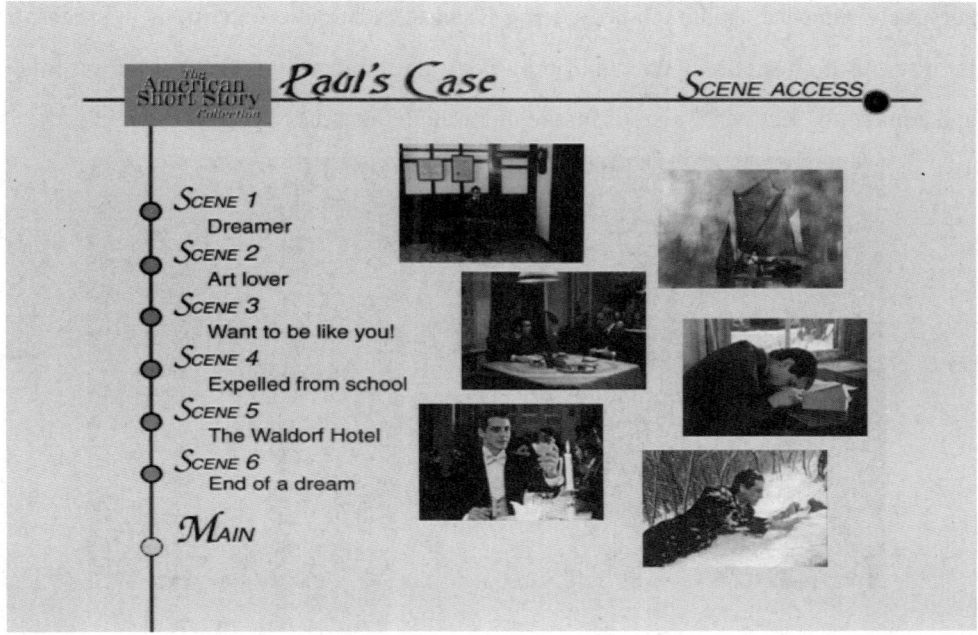

Film Clip:

Committing Suicide

Paul gets off the train, forgetting his suitcase, and then he takes a cab, directing the driver to follow the tracks out of the town. The snow lies heavy on the roadways and has drifted deep in the open fields. Once well into the country, Paul dismisses the carriage and walks, floundering along the tracks. He stoops down and puts a handful of snow into his mouth as he walks. When he reaches a little hillside, where the tracks run through a cut below him, he stops and sits down.

The carnations in his coat are drooping with the cold. Paul takes one of the blossoms carefully from his coat and scoops a little hole in the snow, where he covers it up. Then he dozes awhile, seemingly insensible to the cold at all. The sound of an approaching train awakes him, and Paul starts to his feet. He stands watching the train, his teeth chattering, his lips drawn away in a frightened smile; once or twice he glances nervously sidewise, as though he is being watched. When the right moment comes, he jumps with no hesitation. We could only hear the thundering noise of train on tracks and could only see a thin wisp of smoke up through the trees.

Discussion Questions:

Story Discussion

(1) If you feel that Paul has been unjustly treated by parents, teachers, or society at large, explain the injustice.

(2) If, on the other hand, you feel he suffers from a defect of character, define it.

(3) What is the connection between Paul's fascination with the theater and his crime?

(4) Why is his father's repayment of the stolen money "worse than jail"?

(5) Does Paul repent at the moment of his death? If you think he does not, how do you interpret the end?

Film Appreciation

(1) What's the payment for Paul working as an usher? Where does his money go?

(2) What does Paul say about his mother? What does his father say?

(3) What's Paul's supposition in the basement of their house?

(4) How much does Paul steal? Where does the money go?

(5) How does Paul order food in Waldorf restaurant?

(6) What's the symbolic meaning of flowers in the story and in the film, especially in the play rehearsal?

(7) How does Paul lose himself before a blue Rico in the film?

(8) What are the adapted scenes in the film?

Further Reading and Watching:

The Bohemian Girl

Chapter 4
Bernice Bobs Her Hair

F. Scott Fitzgerald

Author Introduction:

F. Scott Fitzgerald (1896—1940) was born into an upper-middle-class family in St. Paul, Minnesota, and he attended Princeton University until he left in 1917 to enlist in the Army as a second lieutenant.

While stationed at the training camp, he met the beautiful girl Zelda in a country club who was to become his wife. He married Zelda Sayre as the novel *This Side of Paradise* (1920) launched Fitzgerald's career as a writer and provided a steady income suitable to Zelda's needs.

Acting out the glamorous life-style he wrote of in his most popular magazine fiction, the couple traveled with a well-heeled crowd in New York, Paris, and the French Riviera through the 1920s.

Most of their income came from those numerous stories published in magazines such as *The Saturday Evening Post*. Fitzgerald was a spokesman for the so-called Jazz Age, setting a personal as well as literary example for a generation whose first commandment was: Do what you will.

Chapter 4 Bernice Bobs Her Hair

He fell from favor as a writer when the indulgent decade of his triumph went down under the impact of a worldwide Depression. Fitzgerald's alcoholism and financial difficulties, in addition to Zelda's mental illness made for difficult years of their marriage.

Through years of emotional and physical collapse he struggled to repair his life by writing to Hollywood—producing at the same time a series of stories that exposed his humiliations there.

Fitzgerald talks about the Jazz Age in *Echoes of the Jazz Age* this way, "It was an age of miracles, it was an age of art, it was an age of excess, and it was an age of satire."

His major novels include *The Beautiful and Damned* (1922), *The Great Gatsby* (1925), and *Tender Is the Night* (1934), and the unfinished novel *The Last Tycoon* (1941) was published posthumously. His stories, many of which treat themes of youth and promise, and age and despair, were collected in *Flappers and Philosophers* (1921), *Tales of the Jazz Age* (1922), *All the Sad Young Men* (1926), and *Taps at Reveille* (1935).

Story Summary:

The story was based on a detailed memo Fitzgerald wrote to his younger sister, Annabel, advising her how to achieve popularity with boys: "Cultivate deliberate physical grace."

Bernice is of the pre-flapper generation, but her struggles in learning to "fit in" are as modern as today. Bernice starts out as the prototypical "drag." She is taken in town by her know-it-all cousin, Marjorie, who sets out to remake her. Under Marjorie's tutelage, Bernice becomes so adopt in applying the lessons in how to attract and beguile men that she begins to rival Marjorie at her own game. When Marjorie attempts to humiliate Bernice, and actually succeeds in goading her into bobbing her hair, Bernice strikes back in an act of revenge that gives the story a delightful and ironic twist.

We should learn from the twisting irony of the triangular Bernice, Marjorie and Warren, and regard rationally about the female acceptance, rivalry, jealousy, trap, and revenge.

Key Terms:

Flapper: Flappers refer to the rebellious and pioneering young girls, who are popular and fashionable. Bernice and Marjorie belong to the pre-flapper generation.

"Bobbed" Hair: The upper-class girls usually wear a long hair, which is graceful and elegant, so "bobbed" hair is considered rebellious and shocking.

Social Elite: The social elite spend their holiday in dinner, dance and party. These young boys and girls go to the best universities, only worrying about their popularity.

Popularity: The popularity in dancing party lies in the frequency of being cut in by boys, and this is decisive for the reputation of girls.

Jazz Age: During the Jazz Age, it is flourishing in almost every field, including economy and society. And therefore, these young men enjoy their leisure time happily.

Bernice Bobs Her Hair[①]

I

After dark on Saturday night one could stand on the first tee[②] of the golf-course and see the country-club windows as a yellow expanse over a very black and wavy ocean. The waves of this ocean, so to speak, were the heads of many curious caddies[③],

---

① First published in *Saturday Evening Post* on May 1, 1920, and then collected in *Flappers and Philosophers* (1921).
② The starting place for each hole on a golf course.
③ Kids hired to serve as an attendant to a golfer, especially by carrying the golf clubs.

Chapter 4 Bernice Bobs Her Hair

a few of the more ingenious chauffeurs①, the golf professional's deaf sister—and there were usually several stray, diffident waves who might have rolled inside had they so desired. This was the gallery②.

The balcony was inside. It consisted of the circle of wicker chairs that lined the wall of the combination clubroom and ballroom. At these Saturday-night dances it was largely feminine; a great babel③ of middle-aged ladies with sharp eyes and icy hearts behind lorgnettes④ and large bosoms. The main function of the balcony was critical. It occasionally showed grudging admiration, but never approval, for it is well known among ladies over thirty-five that when the younger set dance in the summer-time it is with the very worst intentions in the world, and if they are not bombarded with stony eyes stray couples will dance weird barbaric interludes in the corners, and the more popular, more dangerous, girls will sometimes be kissed in the parked limousines⑤ of unsuspecting dowagers⑥.

But, after all, this critical circle is not close enough to the stage to see the actors' faces and catch the subtler byplay. It can only frown and lean, ask questions and make satisfactory deductions from its set of postulates, such as the one which states that every young man with a large income leads the life of a hunted partridge. It never really appreciates the drama of the shifting, semi-cruel world of adolescence. No; boxes, orchestra-circle, principals, and chorus are represented by the medley of faces and voices that sway to the plaintive African rhythm of Dyer's dance orchestra.

---

① A man paid to drive a privately owned car.
② An area high above the ground at the back or at the sides of a large room or hall.
③ A confusion of sounds or voices. In the *Bible*, a city (now thought to be Babylon) in Shinar where construction of a heaven-reaching tower was interrupted when the builders became unable to understand one another's language.
④ A pair of spectacles or opera glasses mounted on a handle.
⑤ A large luxurious car, usually driven by a chauffeur.
⑥ A widow holding property received from her deceased husband.

From sixteen-year-old Otis Ormonde, who has two more years at Hill School, to G. Reece Stoddard, over whose bureau at home hangs a Harvard law diploma; from little Madeleine Hogue, whose hair still feels strange and uncomfortable on top of her head, to Bessie MacRae, who has been the life of the party a little too long—more than ten years—the medley[①] is not only the center of the stage but contains the only people capable of getting an un-obstructed view of it.

With a flourish and a bang the music stops. The couples exchange artificial, effortless smiles, facetiously repeat "*la*-de-*da*-da dum-*dum*," and then the clatter of young feminine voices soars over the burst of clapping.

A few disappointed stags[②] caught in midfloor as they had been about to cut in subsided listlessly back to the walls, because this was not like the riotous Christmas dances—these summer hops were considered just pleasantly warm and exciting, where even the younger marrieds rose and performed ancient waltzes[③] and terrifying fox trots[④] to the tolerant amusement of their younger brothers and sisters.

Warren McIntyre, who casually attended Yale, being one of the unfortunate stags, felt in his dinner-coat pocket for a cigarette and strolled out onto the wide, semi-dark veranda[⑤], where couples were scattered at tables, filling the lantern-hung night with vague words and hazy laughter. He nodded here and there at the less absorbed and as he passed each couple some half-forgotten fragment of a story played in his mind, for it was not a large city and every one was Who's Who to every one else's past. There, for example, were Jim Strain and Ethel Demorest, who had been privately engaged for

---

① A collection of different tunes or songs that are played one after another as a single piece of music.
② Those who attend a social gathering unaccompanied by a woman.
③ A ballroom dance in triple time with a strong accent on the first beat.
④ A ballroom dance in 2/4 or 4/4 time, encompassing a variety of slow and fast steps.
⑤ A porch or balcony, usually roofed and often partly enclosed, extending along the outside of a building.

three years. Every one knew that as soon as Jim managed to hold a job for more than two months she would marry him. Yet how bored they both looked, and how wearily Ethel regarded Jim sometimes, as if she wondered why she had trained the vines of her affection on such a wind-shaken poplar.

Warren was nineteen and rather pitying with those of his friends who hadn't gone East to college. But, like most boys, he bragged tremendously about the girls of his city when he was away from it. There was Genevieve Ormonde, who regularly made the rounds of dances, house-parties, and football games at Princeton, Yale, Williams, and Cornell; there was black-eyed Roberta Dillon, who was quite as famous to her own generation as Hiram Johnson[①] or Ty Cobb[②]; and, of course, there was Marjorie Harvey, who besides having a fairylike face and a dazzling, bewildering tongue was already justly celebrated for having turned five cart-wheels[③] in succession during the last pump-and-slipper dance[④] at New Haven.

Warren, who had grown up across the street from Marjorie, had long been "crazy about her." Sometimes she seemed to reciprocate[⑤] his feeling with a faint gratitude, but she had tried him by her infallible[⑥] test and informed him gravely that she did not love him. Her test was that when she was away from him she forgot him and had affairs with other boys. Warren found this discouraging, especially as Marjorie had been making little trips all summer, and for the first two or three days after each arrival home he saw

---

① A leading American progressive and isolationist politician from California; he served as the 23rd governor from 1911 to 1917, and as a United States Senator from 1917 to 1945.
② An American Major League Baseball (MLB) center fielder. In 1936, Cobb received the most votes of any player on the inaugural Baseball Hall of Fame ballot.
③ A handspring in which the body turns over sideways with the arms and legs spread like the spokes of a wheel.
④ A dancing party named after Cinderella with the glass slippers and pumpkin coach.
⑤ To act, feel, or give mutually or in return.
⑥ Incapable of failure or error.

great heaps of mail on the Harveys' hall table addressed to her in various masculine handwritings. To make matters worse, all during the month of August she had been visited by her cousin Bernice from Eau Claire[①], and it seemed impossible to see her alone. It was always necessary to hunt round and find someone to take care of Bernice. As August waned this was becoming more and more difficult.

Much as Warren worshipped Marjorie, he had to admit that Cousin Bernice was sorta dopeless. She was pretty, with dark hair and high color, but she was no fun on a party. Every Saturday night he danced a long arduous duty dance with her to please Marjorie, but he had never been anything but bored in her company.

"Warren"—a soft voice at his elbow broke in upon his thoughts, and he turned to see Marjorie, flushed and radiant as usual. She laid a hand on his shoulder and a glow settled almost imperceptibly over him.

"Warren," she whispered, "do something for me—dance with Bernice. She's been stuck with little Otis Ormonde for almost an hour."

Warren's glow faded.

"Why—sure," he answered half-heartedly.

"You don't mind, do you? I'll see that you don't get stuck."

"'Sall right."

Marjorie smiled—that smile that was thanks enough.

"You're an angel, and I'm obliged loads."

With a sigh the angel glanced round the veranda, but Bernice and Otis were not in sight. He wandered back inside, and there in front of the women's dressing-room he found Otis in the center of a group of young men who were convulsed with laughter. Otis was brandishing a piece of timber he had picked up, and discoursing volubly.

"She's gone in to fix her hair," he announced wildly. "I'm waiting to dance another

---

① A city of west-central Wisconsin at the mouth of the Eau Clair River.

hour with her."

Their laughter was renewed.

"Why don't some of you cut in①?" cried Otis resentfully. "She likes more variety."

"Why, Otis," suggested a friend, "you've just barely got used to her."

"Why the two-by-four, Otis?" inquired Warren, smiling.

"The two-by-four? Oh, this? This is a club. When she comes out I'll hit her on the head and knock her in again."

Warren collapsed on a settee② and howled with glee.

"Never mind, Otis," he articulated finally. "I'm relieving you this time."

Otis simulated a sudden fainting attack and handed the stick to Warren.

"If you need it, old man," he said hoarsely.

No matter how beautiful or brilliant a girl may be, the reputation of not being frequently cut in on makes her position at a dance unfortunate. Perhaps boys prefer her company to that of the butterflies with whom they dance a dozen times an evening, but youth in this jazz-nourished generation is temperamentally restless, and the idea of fox-trotting more than one full fox trot with the same girl is distasteful, not to say odious. When it comes to several dances and the intermissions between she can be quite sure that a young man, once relieved, will never tread on her wayward toes again.

Warren danced the next full dance with Bernice, and finally, thankful for the intermission, he led her to a table on the veranda. There was a moment's silence while she did unimpressive things with her fan.

"It's hotter here than in Eau Claire," she said.

Warren stifled a sigh and nodded. It might be for all he knew or cared. He wondered idly whether she was a poor conversationalist because she got no attention or got no attention because she was a poor conversationalist.

---

① To interrupt a dancing couple in order to dance with one of them.
② A long wooden bench with a back.

"You going to be here much longer?" he asked, and then turned rather red. She might suspect his reasons for asking.

"Another week," she answered, and stared at him as if to lunge at his next remark when it left his lips.

Warren fidgeted①. Then with a sudden charitable impulse he decided to try part of his line② on her. He turned and looked at her eyes.

"You've got an awfully kissable mouth," he began quietly.

This was a remark that he sometimes made to girls at college proms③ when they were talking in just such half dark as this. Bernice distinctly jumped. She turned an ungraceful red and became clumsy with her fan. No one had ever made such a remark to her before.

"Fresh!"—the word had slipped out before she realized it, and she bit her lip. Too late she decided to be amused, and offered him a flustered smile.

Warren was annoyed. Though not accustomed to have that remark taken seriously, still it usually provoked a laugh or a paragraph of sentimental banter④. And he hated to be called fresh, except in a joking way. His charitable impulse died and he switched the topic.

"Jim Strain and Ethel Demorest sitting out as usual," he commented.

This was more in Bernice's line, but a faint regret mingled with her relief as the subject changed. Men did not talk to her about kissable mouths, but she knew that they talked in some such way to other girls.

"Oh, yes," she said, and laughed. "I hear they've been mooning round for years

---

① To feel or move restlessly.
② Glib or insincere talk, usually intended to deceive or impress.
③ A formal dance held for a high-school or college class typically at or near the end of the academic year.
④ Teasing or joking talk that is amusing and friendly.

Chapter 4 Bernice Bobs Her Hair

without a red penny. Isn't it silly?"

Warren's disgust increased. Jim Strain was a close friend of his brother's, and anyway he considered it bad form to sneer at people for not having money. But Bernice had had no intention of sneering. She was merely nervous.

II

When Marjorie and Bernice reached home at half after midnight they said good night at the top of the stairs. Though cousins, they were not intimates. As a matter of fact Marjorie had no female intimates—she considered girls stupid. Bernice on the contrary all through this parent-arranged visit had rather longed to exchange those confidences① flavored with giggles and tears that she considered an indispensable factor in all feminine intercourse. But in this respect she found Marjorie rather cold; felt somehow the same difficulty in talking to her that she had in talking to men. Marjorie never giggled, was never frightened, seldom embarrassed, and in fact had very few of the qualities which Bernice considered appropriately and blessedly feminine.

As Bernice busied herself with tooth-brush and paste this night she wondered for the hundredth time why she never had any attention when she was away from home. That her family were the wealthiest in Eau Claire; that her mother entertained tremendously, gave little dinners for her daughter before all dances and bought her a car of her own to drive round in, never occurred to her as factors in her home-town social success. Like most girls she had been brought up on the warm milk prepared by Annie Fellows Johnston② and on novels in which the female was beloved because of certain mysterious womanly qualities, always mentioned but never displayed.

Bernice felt a vague pain that she was not at present engaged in being popular. She

---

① A secret that is confided or entrusted to another.
② An American author of children's fiction who wrote the popular "Little Colonel" series, which was the basis for the 1935 Shirley Temple film *The Little Colonel*.

did not know that had it not been for Marjorie's campaigning she would have danced the entire evening with one man; but she knew that even in Eau Claire other girls with less position and less pulchritude① were given a much bigger rush. She attributed this to something subtly unscrupulous② in those girls. It had never worried her, and if it had her mother would have assured her that the other girls cheapened themselves and that men really respected girls like Bernice.

She turned out the light in her bathroom, and on an impulse decided to go in and chat for a moment with her aunt Josephine, whose light was still on. Her soft slippers bore her noiselessly down the carpeted hall, but hearing voices inside she stopped near the partly opened door. Then she caught her own name, and without any definite intention of eavesdropping③ lingered—and the thread of the conversation going on inside pierced her consciousness sharply as if it had been drawn through with a needle.

"She's absolutely hopeless!" It was Marjorie's voice. "Oh, I know what you're going to say! So many people have told you how pretty and sweet she is, and how she can cook! What of it? She has a bum time. Men don't like her."

"What's a little cheap popularity?"

Mrs. Harvey sounded annoyed.

"It's everything when you're eighteen," said Marjorie emphatically. "I've done my best. I've been polite and I've made men dance with her, but they just won't stand being bored. When I think of that gorgeous coloring wasted on such a ninny④, and think what Martha Carey could do with it—oh!"

"There's no courtesy these days."

Mrs. Harvey's voice implied that modern situations were too much for her. When

---

① Great physical beauty and appeal.
② Devoid of scruples; oblivious to or contemptuous of what is right or honorable.
③ To listen in, to listen without the speaker's knowledge.
④ A fool; a simpleton.

Chapter 4　Bernice Bobs Her Hair

she was a girl all young ladies who belonged to nice families had glorious times.

"Well," said Marjorie, "no girl can permanently bolster up a lame-duck visitor, because these days it's every girl for herself. I've even tried to drop her hints about clothes and things, and she's been furious—given me the funniest looks. She's sensitive enough to know she's not getting away with much, but I'll bet she consoles herself by thinking that she's very virtuous and that I'm too gay and fickle and will come to a bad end. All unpopular girls think that way. Sour grapes①! Sarah Hopkins refers to Genevieve and Roberta and me as gardenia② girls! I'll bet she'd give ten years of her life and her European education to be a gardenia girl and have three or four men in love with her and be cut in on every few feet at dances."

"It seems to me," interrupted Mrs. Harvey rather wearily, "that you ought to be able to do something for Bernice. I know she's not very vivacious."

Marjorie groaned.

"Vivacious! Good grief! I've never heard her say anything to a boy except that it's hot or the floor's crowded or that she's going to school in New York next year. Sometimes she asks them what kind of car they have and tells them the kind she has. Thrilling!"

There was a short silence, and then Mrs. Harvey took up her refrain:

"All I know is that other girls not half so sweet and attractive get partners. Martha Carey, for instance, is stout and loud, and her mother is distinctly common. Roberta Dillon is so thin this year that she looks as though Arizona were the place for her. She's dancing herself to death."

"But, mother," objected Marjorie impatiently, "Martha is cheerful and awfully witty and an awfully slick girl, and Roberta's a marvelous dancer. She's been popular for ages!"

---

① Pretended dislike for something unobtainable.
② A type of large, white or yellow flower with a very pleasant smell.

Mrs. Harvey yawned.

"I think it's that crazy Indian blood in Bernice," continued Marjorie. "Maybe she's a reversion to type①. Indian women all just sat round and never said anything."

"Go to bed, you silly child," laughed Mrs. Harvey. "I wouldn't have told you that if I'd thought you were going to remember it. And I think most of your ideas are perfectly idiotic," she finished sleepily.

There was another silence, while Marjorie considered whether or not convincing her mother was worth the trouble. People over forty can seldom be permanently convinced of anything. At eighteen our convictions are hills from which we look; at forty-five they are caves in which we hide.

Having decided this, Marjorie said good night. When she came out into the hall it was quite empty.

III

While Marjorie was breakfasting late next day Bernice came into the room with a rather formal good morning, sat down opposite, stared intently over and slightly moistened her lips.

"What's on your mind?" inquired Marjorie, rather puzzled.

Bernice paused before she threw her hand-grenade.

"I heard what you said about me to your mother last night."

Marjorie was startled, but she showed only a faintly heightened color and her voice was quite even when she spoke.

"Where were you?"

"In the hall. I didn't mean to listen—at first."

After an involuntary look of contempt Marjorie dropped her eyes and became very

---

① A return to a normal phenotype (usually resulting from a second mutation).

Chapter 4 Bernice Bobs Her Hair

interested in balancing a stray corn-flake on her finger.

"I guess I'd better go back to Eau Claire—if I'm such a nuisance." Bernice's lower lip was trembling violently and she continued on a wavering note: "I've tried to be nice, and—and I've been first neglected and then insulted. No one ever visited me and got such treatment."

Marjorie was silent.

"But I'm in the way, I see. I'm a drag on you. Your friends don't like me." She paused, and then remembered another one of her grievances. "Of course I was furious last week when you tried to hint to me that that dress was unbecoming. Don't you think I know how to dress myself?"

"No," murmured Marjorie less than half-aloud.

"What?"

"I didn't hint anything," said Marjorie succinctly. "I said, as I remember, that it was better to wear a becoming dress three times straight than to alternate it with two frights."

"Do you think that was a very nice thing to say?"

"I wasn't trying to be nice." Then after a pause: "When do you want to go?"

Bernice drew in her breath sharply.

"Oh!" It was a little half-cry.

Marjorie looked up in surprise.

"Didn't you say you were going?"

"Yes, but—"

"Oh, you were only bluffing[①]!"

They stared at each other across the breakfast-table for a moment. Misty waves were passing before Bernice's eyes, while Marjorie's face wore that rather hard

---

① Misleading or deceiving.

expression that she used when slightly intoxicated undergraduates were making love to her.

"So you were bluffing," she repeated as if it were what she might have expected.

Bernice admitted it by bursting into tears. Marjorie's eyes showed boredom.

"You're my cousin," sobbed Bernice. "I'm v-v-visiting you. I was to stay a month, and if I go home my mother will know and she'll wah-wonder—"

Marjorie waited until the shower of broken words collapsed into little sniffles.

"I'll give you my month's allowance," she said coldly, "and you can spend this last week anywhere you want. There's a very nice hotel—"

Bernice's sobs rose to a flute note, and rising of a sudden she fled from the room.

An hour later, while Marjorie was in the library absorbed in composing one of those non-committal, marvelously elusive letters that only a young girl can write, Bernice reappeared, very red-eyed and consciously calm. She cast no glance at Marjorie but took a book at random from the shelf and sat down as if to read. Marjorie seemed absorbed in her letter and continued writing. When the clock showed noon Bernice closed her book with a snap.

"I suppose I'd better get my railroad ticket."

This was not the beginning of the speech she had rehearsed upstairs, but as Marjorie was not getting her cues—wasn't urging her to be reasonable; it's all a mistake—it was the best opening she could muster.

"Just wait till I finish this letter," said Marjorie without looking round. "I want to get it off in the next mail."

After another minute, during which her pen scratched busily, she turned round and relaxed with an air of "at your service." Again Bernice had to speak.

"Do you want me to go home?"

"Well," said Marjorie, considering, "I suppose if you're not having a good time you'd better go. No use being miserable."

Chapter 4　Bernice Bobs Her Hair

"Don't you think common kindness—"

"Oh, please don't quote '*Little Women*'①!" cried Marjorie impatiently. "That's out of style."

"You think so?"

"Heavens, yes! What modern girl could live like those inane females?"

"They were the models for our mothers."

Marjorie laughed.

"Yes, they were—not! Besides, our mothers were all very well in their way, but they know very little about their daughters' problems."

Bernice drew herself up.

"Please don't talk about my mother."

Marjorie laughed.

"I don't think I mentioned her."

Bernice felt that she was being led away from her subject.

"Do you think you've treated me very well?"

"I've done my best. You're rather hard material to work with."

The lids of Bernice's eyes reddened.

"I think you're hard and selfish, and you haven't a feminine quality in you."

"Oh, my Lord!" cried Marjorie in desperation. "You little nut! Girls like you are responsible for all the tiresome colorless marriages; all those ghastly② inefficiencies that pass as feminine qualities. What a blow it must be when a man with imagination marries the beautiful bundle of clothes that he's been building ideals round, and finds that she's just a weak, whining, cowardly mass of affectations!"

Bernice's mouth had slipped half open.

"The womanly woman!" continued Marjorie. "Her whole early life is occupied in

---

① A novel by Louisa May Alcott.
② Extremely unpleasant or bad.

whining criticisms of girls like me who really do have a good time."

Bernice's jaw descended farther as Marjorie's voice rose.

"There's some excuse for an ugly girl whining. If I'd been irretrievably ugly I'd never have forgiven my parents for bringing me into the world. But you're starting life without any handicap—" Marjorie's little fist clinched. "If you expect me to weep with you you'll be disappointed. Go or stay, just as you like." And picking up her letters she left the room.

Bernice claimed a headache and failed to appear at luncheon. They had a matinée date for the afternoon, but the headache persisting, Marjorie made explanation to a not very downcast boy. But when she returned late in the afternoon she found Bernice with a strangely set face waiting for her in her bedroom.

"I've decided," began Bernice without preliminaries, "that maybe you're right about things—possibly not. But if you'll tell me why your friends aren't—aren't interested in me I'll see if I can do what you want me to."

Marjorie was at the mirror shaking down her hair.

"Do you mean it?"

"Yes."

"Without reservations? Will you do exactly what I say?"

"Well, I—"

"Well nothing! Will you do exactly as I say?"

"If they're sensible things."

"They're not! You're no case for sensible things."

"Are you going to make—to recommend—"

"Yes, everything. If I tell you to take boxing-lessons you'll have to do it. Write home and tell your mother you're going to stay another two weeks."

"If you'll tell me—"

"All right—I'll just give you a few examples now. First, you have no ease of

Chapter 4 Bernice Bobs Her Hair

manner. Why? Because you're never sure about your personal appearance. When a girl feels that she's perfectly groomed and dressed she can forget that part of her. That's charm. The more parts of yourself you can afford to forget the more charm you have."

"Don't I look all right?"

"No; for instance, you never take care of your eyebrows. They're black and lustrous, but by leaving them straggly① they're a blemish. They'd be beautiful if you'd take care of them in one-tenth the time you take doing nothing. You're going to brush them so that they'll grow straight."

Bernice raised the brows in question.

"Do you mean to say that men notice eyebrows?"

"Yes—subconsciously. And when you go home you ought to have your teeth straightened a little. It's almost imperceptible, still—"

"But I thought," interrupted Bernice in bewilderment, "that you despised little dainty② feminine things like that."

"I hate dainty minds," answered Marjorie. "But a girl has to be dainty in person. If she looks like a million dollars she can talk about Russia, ping-pong, or the League of Nations③ and get away with it."

"What else?"

"Oh, I'm just beginning! There's your dancing."

"Don't I dance all right?"

"No, you don't—you lean on a man; yes, you do—ever so slightly. I noticed it when we were dancing together yesterday. And you dance standing up straight instead

---

① Growing or spread out in a disorderly or aimless way.
② Overly fastidious; squeamish.
③ A world organization established in 1920 to promote international cooperation and peace. It was first proposed in 1918 by President Woodrow Wilson, although the United States never joined the League. Essentially powerless, it was officially dissolved in 1946.

of bending over a little. Probably some old lady on the side-line once told you that you looked so dignified that way. But except with a very small girl it's much harder on the man, and he's the one that counts."

"Go on." Bernice's brain was reeling.

"Well, you've got to learn to be nice to men who are sad birds. You look as if you'd been insulted whenever you're thrown with any except the most popular boys. Why, Bernice, I'm cut in on every few feet—and who does most of it? Why, those very sad birds. No girl can afford to neglect them. They're the big part of any crowd. Young boys too shy to talk are the very best conversational practice. Clumsy boys are the best dancing practice. If you can follow them and yet look graceful you can follow a baby tank across a barb-wire① sky-scraper."

Bernice sighed profoundly, but Marjorie was not through.

"If you go to a dance and really amuse, say, three sad birds that dance with you; if you talk so well to them that they forget they're stuck with you, you've done something. They'll come back next time, and gradually so many sad birds will dance with you that the attractive boys will see there's no danger of being stuck—then they'll dance with you."

"Yes," agreed Bernice faintly. "I think I begin to see."

"And finally," concluded Marjorie, "poise and charm will just come. You'll wake up some morning knowing you've attained it, and men will know it too."

Bernice rose.

"It's been awfully kind of you—but nobody's ever talked to me like this before, and I feel sort of startled."

Marjorie made no answer but gazed pensively at her own image in the mirror.

"You're a peach to help me," continued Bernice.

---

① Strong wire with barbs at regular intervals used to prevent passage.

Chapter 4 Bernice Bobs Her Hair

Still Marjorie did not answer, and Bernice thought she had seemed too grateful.

"I know you don't like sentiment," she said timidly.

Marjorie turned to her quickly.

"Oh, I wasn't thinking about that. I was considering whether we hadn't better bob your hair."

Bernice collapsed backward upon the bed.

IV

On the following Wednesday evening there was a dinner-dance at the country club. When the guests strolled in Bernice found her place-card with a slight feeling of irritation. Though at her right sat G. Reece Stoddard, a most desirable and distinguished young bachelor, the all-important left held only Charley Paulson. Charley lacked height, beauty, and social shrewdness, and in her new enlightenment Bernice decided that his only qualification to be her partner was that he had never been stuck with her. But this feeling of irritation left with the last of the soup-plates, and Marjorie's specific instruction came to her. Swallowing her pride she turned to Charley Paulson and plunged.

"Do you think I ought to bob my hair, Mr. Charley Paulson?"

Charley looked up in surprise.

"Why?"

"Because I'm considering it. It's such a sure and easy way of attracting attention."

Charley smiled pleasantly. He could not know this had been rehearsed. He replied that he didn't know much about bobbed hair. But Bernice was there to tell him.

"I want to be a society vampire[①], you see," she announced coolly, and went on to inform him that bobbed hair was the necessary prelude. She added that she wanted to

---

① A reanimated corpse that is believed to rise from the grave at night to suck the blood of sleeping people.

ask his advice, because she had heard he was so critical about girls.

Charley, who knew as much about the psychology of women as he did of the mental states of Buddhist contemplatives, felt vaguely flattered.

"So I've decided," she continued, her voice rising slightly, "that early next week I'm going down to the Sevier Hotel barber-shop, sit in the first chair, and get my hair bobbed." She faltered①, noticing that the people near her had paused in their conversation and were listening; but after a confused second Marjorie's coaching told, and she finished her paragraph to the vicinity② at large. "Of course I'm charging admission, but if you'll all come down and encourage me I'll issue passes for the inside seats."

There was a ripple of appreciative laughter, and under cover of it G. Reece Stoddard leaned over quickly and said close to her ear: "I'll take a box right now."

She met his eyes and smiled as if he had said something surpassingly brilliant.

"Do you believe in bobbed hair?" asked G. Reece in the same undertone.

"I think it's unmoral," affirmed Bernice gravely. "But, of course, you've either got to amuse people or feed 'em or shock 'em." Marjorie had culled③ this from Oscar Wilde④. It was greeted with a ripple of laughter from the men and a series of quick, intent looks from the girls. And then as though she had said nothing of wit or moment Bernice turned again to Charley and spoke confidentially in his ear.

"I want to ask you your opinion of several people. I imagine you're a wonderful judge of character."

Charley thrilled faintly—paid her a subtle compliment by overturning her water.

---

① To speak haltingly.
② A surrounding or nearby region.
③ To look for and gather.
④ Irish-born writer. Renowned as a wit in London literary circles, he achieved recognition with *The Picture of Dorian Gray* (1891), a novel. He also wrote plays of lively dialogue, such as *The Importance of Being Earnest* (1895), and poetry, including *The Ballad of Reading Gaol* (1898).

Chapter 4 Bernice Bobs Her Hair

Two hours later, while Warren McIntyre was standing passively in the stag line abstractedly① watching the dancers and wondering whither② and with whom Marjorie had disappeared, an unrelated perception began to creep slowly upon him—a perception that Bernice, cousin to Marjorie, had been cut in on several times in the past five minutes. He closed his eyes, opened them and looked again. Several minutes back she had been dancing with a visiting boy, a matter easily accounted for; a visiting boy would know no better. But now she was dancing with some one else, and there was Charley Paulson headed for her with enthusiastic determination in his eye. Funny—Charley seldom danced with more than three girls an evening.

Warren was distinctly surprised when—the exchange having been effected—the man relieved proved to be none other than G. Reece Stoddard himself. And G. Reece seemed not at all jubilant③ at being relieved. Next time Bernice danced near, Warren regarded her intently. Yes, she was pretty, distinctly pretty; and to-night her face seemed really vivacious. She had that look that no woman, however histrionically proficient, can successfully counterfeit④—she looked as if she were having a good time. He liked the way she had her hair arranged, wondered if it was brilliantine⑤ that made it glisten so. And that dress was becoming—a dark red that set off her shadowy eyes and high coloring. He remembered that he had thought her pretty when she first came to town, before he had realized that she was dull. Too bad she was dull—dull girls unbearable—certainly pretty though.

His thoughts zigzagged back to Marjorie. This disappearance would be like other disappearances. When she reappeared he would demand where she had been—would

---

① In an absentminded or preoccupied manner.
② To where.
③ Extremely happy because of a success.
④ To make a copy with the intent to deceive.
⑤ An oily, perfumed hairdressing.

be told emphatically that it was none of his business. What a pity she was so sure of him! She basked in the knowledge that no other girl in town interested him; she defied him to fall in love with Genevieve or Roberta.

Warren sighed. The way to Marjorie's affections was a labyrinth indeed. He looked up. Bernice was again dancing with the visiting boy. Half unconsciously he took a step out from the stag line in her direction, and hesitated. Then he said to himself that it was charity. He walked toward her—collided suddenly with G. Reece Stoddard.

"Pardon me," said Warren.

But G. Reece had not stopped to apologize. He had again cut in on Bernice.

That night at one o'clock Marjorie, with one hand on the electric-light switch in the hall, turned to take a last look at Bernice's sparkling eyes.

"So it worked?"

"Oh, Marjorie, yes!" cried Bernice.

"I saw you were having a gay time."

"I did! The only trouble was that about midnight I ran short of talk. I had to repeat myself—with different men of course. I hope they won't compare notes."

"Men don't," said Marjorie, yawning, "and it wouldn't matter if they did—they'd think you were even trickier."

She snapped out the light, and as they started up the stairs Bernice grasped the banister thankfully. For the first time in her life she had been danced tired.

"You see," said Marjorie at the top of the stairs, "one man sees another man cut in and he thinks there must be something there. Well, we'll fix up some new stuff tomorrow. Good night."

"Good night."

As Bernice took down her hair she passed the evening before her in review. She had followed instructions exactly. Even when Charley Paulson cut in for the eighth

Chapter 4 Bernice Bobs Her Hair

time she had simulated① delight and had apparently been both interested and flattered. She had not talked about the weather or Eau Claire or automobiles or her school, but had confined her conversation to me, you, and us.

But a few minutes before she fell asleep a rebellious thought was churning drowsily in her brain—after all, it was she who had done it. Marjorie, to be sure, had given her her conversation, but then Marjorie got much of her conversation out of things she read. Bernice had bought the red dress, though she had never valued it highly before Marjorie dug it out of her trunk—and her own voice had said the words, her own lips had smiled, her own feet had danced. Marjorie nice girl—vain, though—nice evening—nice boys—like Warren—Warren—Warren—what's-his-name—Warren—

She fell asleep.

V

To Bernice the next week was a revelation. With the feeling that people really enjoyed looking at her and listening to her came the foundation of self-confidence. Of course there were numerous mistakes at first. She did not know, for instance, that Draycott Deyo was studying for the ministry; she was unaware that he had cut in on her because he thought she was a quiet, reserved girl. Had she known these things she would not have treated him to the line which began "Hello, Shell Shock②!" and continued with the bathtub story—"It takes a frightful lot of energy to fix my hair in the summer—there's so much of it—so I always fix it first and powder my face and put on my hat; then I get into the bathtub, and dress afterward. Don't you think that's the best plan?"

Though Draycott Deyo was in the throes of difficulties concerning baptism by

---

① To pretend.
② Any of various acute, often hysterical neuroses originating in trauma suffered under fire in modern warfare.

immersion and might possibly have seen a connection, it must be admitted that he did not. He considered feminine bathing an immoral subject, and gave her some of his ideas on the depravity of modern society.

But to offset that unfortunate occurrence Bernice had several signal successes to her credit. Little Otis Ormonde pleaded off from a trip East and elected instead to follow her with a puppy-like devotion, to the amusement of his crowd and to the irritation of G. Reece Stoddard, several of whose afternoon calls Otis completely ruined by the disgusting tenderness of the glances he bent on Bernice. He even told her the story of the two-by-four and the dressing-room to show her how frightfully mistaken he and every one else had been in their first judgment of her. Bernice laughed off that incident with a slight sinking sensation.

Of all Bernice's conversation perhaps the best known and most universally approved was the line about the bobbing of her hair.

"Oh, Bernice, when you goin' to get the hair bobbed?"

"Day after to-morrow maybe," she would reply, laughing. "Will you come and see me? Because I'm counting on you, you know."

"Will we? You know! But you better hurry up."

Bernice, whose tonsorial① intentions were strictly dishonorable, would laugh again.

"Pretty soon now. You'd be surprised."

But perhaps the most significant symbol of her success was the gray car of the hypercritical② Warren McIntyre, parked daily in front of the Harvey house. At first the parlor-maid was distinctly startled when he asked for Bernice instead of Marjorie; after a week of it she told the cook that Miss Bernice had gotta holda Miss Marjorie's best fella.

---

① Of or relating to barbering or a barber.
② Excessively or severely critical.

Chapter 4 Bernice Bobs Her Hair

And Miss Bernice had. Perhaps it began with Warren's desire to rouse jealousy in Marjorie; perhaps it was the familiar though unrecognized strain of Marjorie in Bernice's conversation; perhaps it was both of these and something of sincere attraction besides. But somehow the collective mind of the younger set knew within a week that Marjorie's most reliable beau① had made an amazing face-about and was giving an indisputable rush to Marjorie's guest. The question of the moment was how Marjorie would take it. Warren called Bernice on the 'phone twice a day, sent her notes, and they were frequently seen together in his roadster②, obviously engrossed③ in one of those tense, significant conversations as to whether or not he was sincere.

Marjorie on being twitted only laughed. She said she was mighty glad that Warren had at last found some one who appreciated him. So the younger set laughed, too, and guessed that Marjorie didn't care and let it go at that.

One afternoon when there were only three days left of her visit Bernice was waiting in the hall for Warren, with whom she was going to a bridge party. She was in rather a blissful mood, and when Marjorie—also bound for the party—appeared beside her and began casually to adjust her hat in the mirror, Bernice was utterly unprepared for anything in the nature of a clash. Marjorie did her work very coldly and succinctly in three sentences.

"You may as well get Warren out of your head," she said coldly.

"What?" Bernice was utterly astounded.

"You may as well stop making a fool of yourself over Warren McIntyre. He doesn't care a snap of his fingers about you."

For a tense moment they regarded each other—Marjorie scornful, aloof; Bernice

---

① Boyfriend or lover.
② An open automobile having a single seat in the front for two or three people and a rumble seat or luggage compartment in the back.
③ Giving or marked by complete attention to.

astounded, half-angry, half-afraid. Then two cars drove up in front of the house and there was a riotous honking. Both of them gasped faintly, turned, and side by side hurried out.

All through the bridge party Bernice strove in vain to master a rising uneasiness. She had offended Marjorie, the sphinx① of sphinxes. With the most wholesome and innocent intentions in the world she had stolen Marjorie's property. She felt suddenly and horribly guilty. After the bridge game, when they sat in an informal circle and the conversation became general, the storm gradually broke. Little Otis Ormonde inadvertently precipitated it.

"When you going back to kindergarten, Otis?" some one had asked.

"Me? Day Bernice gets her hair bobbed."

"Then your education's over," said Marjorie quickly. "That's only a bluff② of hers. I should think you'd have realized."

"That a fact?" demanded Otis, giving Bernice a reproachful glance.

Bernice's ears burned as she tried to think up an effectual come-back. In the face of this direct attack her imagination was paralyzed.

"There's a lot of bluffs in the world," continued Marjorie quite pleasantly. "I should think you'd be young enough to know that, Otis."

"Well," said Otis, "maybe so. But gee! With a line like Bernice's—"

"Really?" yawned Marjorie. "What's her latest bon mot?"

No one seemed to know. In fact, Bernice, having trifled with her muse's beau, had said nothing memorable of late.

"Was that really all a line?" asked Roberta curiously.

Bernice hesitated. She felt that wit in some form was demanded of her, but under

---

① A winged creature having the head of a woman and the body of a lion, noted for killing those who could not answer its riddle.
② Trickery.

Chapter 4 Bernice Bobs Her Hair

her cousin's suddenly frigid eyes she was completely incapacitated.

"I don't know," she stalled.

"Splush!" said Marjorie. "Admit it!"

Bernice saw that Warren's eyes had left a ukulele[①] he had been tinkering with and were fixed on her questioningly.

"Oh, I don't know!" she repeated steadily. Her cheeks were glowing.

"Splush!" remarked Marjorie again.

"Come through, Bernice," urged Otis. "Tell her where to get off."

Bernice looked round again—she seemed unable to get away from Warren's eyes.

"I like bobbed hair," she said hurriedly, as if he had asked her a question, "and I intend to bob mine."

"When?" demanded Marjorie.

"Any time."

"No time like the present," suggested Roberta.

Otis jumped to his feet.

"Good stuff!" he cried. "We'll have a summer bobbing party. Sevier Hotel barbershop, I think you said."

In an instant all were on their feet. Bernice's heart throbbed violently.

"What?" she gasped.

Out of the group came Marjorie's voice, very clear and contemptuous.

"Don't worry—she'll back out!"

"Come on, Bernice!" cried Otis, starting toward the door.

Four eyes—Warren's and Marjorie's—stared at her, challenged her, defied her. For another second she wavered wildly.

"All right," she said swiftly, "I don't care if I do."

---

① A small four-stringed guitar popularized in Hawaii.

An eternity of minutes later, riding down-town through the late afternoon beside Warren, the others following in Roberta's car close behind, Bernice had all the sensations of Marie Antoinette① bound for the guillotine② in a tumbrel③. Vaguely she wondered why she did not cry out that it was all a mistake. It was all she could do to keep from clutching her hair with both hands to protect it from the suddenly hostile world. Yet she did neither. Even the thought of her mother was no deterrent now. This was the test supreme of her sportsmanship; her right to walk unchallenged in the starry heaven of popular girls.

Warren was moodily silent, and when they came to the hotel he drew up at the curb and nodded to Bernice to precede him out. Roberta's car emptied a laughing crowd into the shop, which presented two bold plate-glass windows to the street.

Bernice stood on the curb and looked at the sign, Sevier Barber-Shop. It was a guillotine indeed, and the hangman④ was the first barber, who, attired in a white coat and smoking a cigarette, leaned nonchalantly against the first chair. He must have heard of her; he must have been waiting all week, smoking eternal cigarettes beside that portentous, too-often-mentioned first chair. Would they blindfold⑤ her? No, but they would tie a white cloth round her neck lest any of her blood—nonsense—hair—should get on her clothes.

"All right, Bernice," said Warren quickly.

With her chin in the air she crossed the sidewalk, pushed open the swinging screen-door, and giving not a glance to the uproarious, riotous row that occupied the

---

① Marie Antoinette (1755—1793), Queen of France. Her husband was King Louis XVI.
② A device consisting of a heavy blade held aloft between upright guides and dropped to behead the victim below.
③ A crude cart used to carry condemned prisoners to their place of execution, as during the French Revolution.
④ A man whose job is to execute people by hanging them.
⑤ To cover the eyes of (someone) to prevent him from seeing.

Chapter 4 Bernice Bobs Her Hair

waiting bench, went up to the first barber.

"I want you to bob my hair."

The first barber's mouth slid somewhat open. His cigarette dropped to the floor.

"Huh?"

"My hair—bob it!"

Refusing further preliminaries, Bernice took her seat on high. A man in the chair next to her turned on his side and gave her a glance, half lather, half amazement. One barber started and spoiled little Willy Schuneman's monthly haircut. Mr. O'Reilly in the last chair grunted and swore musically in ancient Gaelic as a razor bit into his cheek. Two bootblacks[①] became wide-eyed and rushed for her feet. No, Bernice didn't care for a shine.

Outside a passer-by stopped and stared; a couple joined him; half a dozen small boys' noses sprang into life, flattened against the glass; and snatches of conversation borne on the summer breeze drifted in through the screen-door.

"Lookada long hair on a kid!"

"Where'd yuh get 'at stuff? 'At's a bearded lady he just finished shavin'."

But Bernice saw nothing, heard nothing. Her only living sense told her that this man in the white coat had removed one tortoise-shell comb and then another; that his fingers were fumbling clumsily with unfamiliar hairpins; that this hair, this wonderful hair of hers, was going—she would never again feel its long voluptuous pull as it hung in a dark-brown glory down her back. For a second she was near breaking down, and then the picture before her swam mechanically into her vision—Marjorie's mouth curling in a faint ironic smile as if to say:

"Give up and get down! You tried to buck me and I called your bluff. You see you haven't got a prayer."

---

① Kids who clean and polish shoes for a living.

And some last energy rose up in Bernice, for she clinched her hands under the white cloth, and there was a curious narrowing of her eyes that Marjorie remarked on to some one long afterward.

Twenty minutes later the barber swung her round to face the mirror, and she flinched at the full extent of the damage that had been wrought. Her hair was not curly, and now it lay in lank lifeless blocks on both sides of her suddenly pale face. It was ugly as sin—she had known it would be ugly as sin. Her face's chief charm had been a Madonna①-like simplicity. Now that was gone and she was—well, frightfully mediocre—not stagy; only ridiculous, like a Greenwich Villager who had left her spectacles at home.

As she climbed down from the chair she tried to smile—failed miserably. She saw two of the girls exchange glances; noticed Marjorie's mouth curved in attenuated mockery—and that Warren's eyes were suddenly very cold.

"You see"—her words fell into an awkward pause—"I've done it."

"Yes, you've—done it," admitted Warren.

"Do you like it?"

There was a half-hearted "Sure" from two or three voices, another awkward pause, and then Marjorie turned swiftly and with serpent-like intensity to Warren.

"Would you mind running me down to the cleaners?" she asked. "I've simply got to get a dress there before supper. Roberta's driving right home and she can take the others."

Warren stared abstractedly at some infinite speck② out the window. Then for an instant his eyes rested coldly on Bernice before they turned to Marjorie.

"Be glad to," he said slowly.

---

① Virgin Mary.
② A small spot, mark, or discoloration.

VI

Bernice did not fully realize the outrageous① trap that had been set for her until she met her aunt's amazed glance just before dinner.

"Why, Bernice!"

"I've bobbed it, Aunt Josephine."

"Why, child!"

"Do you like it?"

"Why, Ber-nice!"

"I suppose I've shocked you."

"No, but what'll Mrs. Deyo think tomorrow night? Bernice, you should have waited until after the Deyos' dance—you should have waited if you wanted to do that."

"It was sudden, Aunt Josephine. Anyway, why does it matter to Mrs. Deyo particularly?"

"Why, child," cried Mrs. Harvey, "in her paper on 'The Foibles② of the Younger Generation' that she read at the last meeting of the Thursday Club she devoted fifteen minutes to bobbed hair. It's her pet abomination③. And the dance is for you and Marjorie!"

"I'm sorry."

"Oh, Bernice, what'll your mother say? She'll think I let you do it."

"I'm sorry."

Dinner was an agony. She had made a hasty attempt with a curling-iron, and burned her finger and much hair. She could see that her aunt was both worried and grieved, and her uncle kept saying, "Well, I'll be darned!" over and over in a hurt and faintly hostile tone. And Marjorie sat very quietly, intrenched behind a faint smile, a

---

① Unacceptable or very shocking.
② Minor weakness or failing of character.
③ Hate coupled with disgust.

faintly mocking smile.

Somehow she got through the evening. Three boys called; Marjorie disappeared with one of them, and Bernice made a listless unsuccessful attempt to entertain the two others—sighed thankfully as she climbed the stairs to her room at half past ten. What a day!

When she had undressed for the night the door opened and Marjorie came in.

"Bernice," she said, "I'm awfully sorry about the Deyo dance. I'll give you my word of honor I'd forgotten all about it."

"'Sall right," said Bernice shortly. Standing before the mirror she passed her comb slowly through her short hair.

"I'll take you down-town to-morrow," continued Marjorie, "and the hairdresser'll fix it so you'll look slick①. I didn't imagine you'd go through with it. I'm really mighty sorry."

"Oh, 'sall right!"

"Still it's your last night, so I suppose it won't matter much."

Then Bernice winced as Marjorie tossed her own hair over her shoulders and began to twist it slowly into two long blond braids until in her cream-colored negligée she looked like a delicate painting of some Saxon princess. Fascinated, Bernice watched the braids grow. Heavy and luxurious they were, moving under the supple fingers like restive snakes—and to Bernice remained this relic and the curling-iron and a to-morrow full of eyes. She could see G. Reece Stoddard, who liked her, assuming his Harvard manner and telling his dinner partner that Bernice shouldn't have been allowed to go to the movies so much; she could see Draycott Deyo exchanging glances with his mother and then being conscientiously charitable to her. But then perhaps by to-morrow Mrs. Deyo would have heard the news; would send round an icy little note

---

① Smooth, glossy, and slippery.

Chapter 4 Bernice Bobs Her Hair

requesting that she fail to appear—and behind her back they would all laugh and know that Marjorie had made a fool of her; that her chance at beauty had been sacrificed to the jealous whim of a selfish girl. She sat down suddenly before the mirror, biting the inside of her cheek.

"I like it," she said with an effort. "I think it'll be becoming."

Marjorie smiled.

"It looks all right. For heaven's sake, don't let it worry you!"

"I won't."

"Good night, Bernice."

But as the door closed something snapped within Bernice. She sprang dynamically to her feet, clinching her hands, then swiftly and noiselessly crossed over to her bed and from underneath it dragged out her suitcase. Into it she tossed toilet articles and a change of clothing. Then she turned to her trunk and quickly dumped in two drawerfuls of lingerie① and summer dresses. She moved quietly, but with deadly efficiency, and in three-quarters of an hour her trunk was locked and strapped and she was fully dressed in a becoming new traveling suit that Marjorie had helped her pick out.

Sitting down at her desk she wrote a short note to Mrs. Harvey, in which she briefly outlined her reasons for going. She sealed it, addressed it, and laid it on her pillow. She glanced at her watch. The train left at one, and she knew that if she walked down to the Marborough Hotel two blocks away she could easily get a taxicab.

Suddenly she drew in her breath sharply and an expression flashed into her eyes that a practiced character reader might have connected vaguely with the set look she had worn in the barber's chair—somehow a development of it. It was quite a new look for Bernice and it carried consequences.

She went stealthily to the bureau, picked up an article that lay there, and turning

---

① Women's underclothes.

out all the lights stood quietly until her eyes became accustomed to the darkness. Softly she pushed open the door to Marjorie's room. She heard the quiet, even① breathing of an untroubled conscience asleep.

She was by the bedside now, very deliberate and calm. She acted swiftly. Bending over she found one of the braids of Marjorie's hair, followed it up with her hand to the point nearest the head, and then holding it a little slack so that the sleeper would feel no pull, she reached down with the shears② and severed③ it. With the pigtail in her hand she held her breath. Marjorie had muttered something in her sleep. Bernice deftly amputated④ the other braid, paused for an instant, and then flitted swiftly and silently back to her own room.

Down-stairs she opened the big front door, closed it carefully behind her, and feeling oddly happy and exuberant stepped off the porch into the moonlight, swinging her heavy grip like a shopping-bag. After a minute's brisk walk she discovered that her left hand still held the two blond braids. She laughed unexpectedly—had to shut her mouth hard to keep from emitting an absolute peal. She was passing Warren's house now, and on the impulse she set down her baggage, and swinging the braids like pieces of rope flung them at the wooden porch, where they landed with a slight thud. She laughed again, no longer restraining herself.

"Huh!" she giggled wildly. "Scalp⑤ the selfish thing!"

Then picking up her suitcase she set off at a half-run down the moonlit street.

---

① Being level or straight or regular and without variation.
② Large scissors with strong blades.
③ To cut off from a whole.
④ To remove surgically.
⑤ The skin that covers the top of the head, taken as trophy of victory for American Indians. Remove the scalp of, when used as a verb.

Chapter 4 Bernice Bobs Her Hair

Film Comment:

F. Scott Fitzgerald's *Bernice Bobs Her Hair*: 48 minutes, color

Starring: Shelley Duvall & Bud Cort

Screenplay by: Joan Micklin Silver

Directed by: Joan Micklin Silver

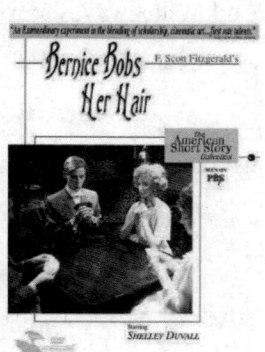

It's the hot summer of 1919. Visiting her cousin Marjorie (Veronica Cartwright), sweet-but-dull Bernice (Shelley Duvall) is transformed into a smooth-talking man-trap by her vampish kin. However, the "make-over" works too well, Bernice becomes the belle of the ball, captivating every boy's interest…even Marjorie's boyfriend Warren (Bud Cort).

The now worldly Bernice has the last laugh…a clever and ironic twist. One of the best screen translations of F. Scott Fitzgerald's literary work, "Bernice Bobs Her Hair" also includes the delightful supporting role performances of Dennis Christopher ("Breaking Away") and Polly Holliday ("Alice").

Film Scenes:

Scene 1: the cousin

Bernice and Marjorie are cousins. Bernice is visiting Marjorie, but proves to be a burden, for she is pretty but dull, not popular among boys.

Scene 2: transformation

With Marjorie's lecture on dance, clothes, manners, etc., Bernice learns very fast and transforms a lot, attracting the boys' attention.

Scene 3: jealousy

Bernice soon outdoes Marjorie in her field, and even gets hold of Warren, the previous admirer of Marjorie, leading to her jealousy.

Scene 4: Bernice bobs her hair

Out of jealousy, Marjorie sets a trap for Bernice, and forces her to bob her hair. And in this way, she wins Warren back.

Scene 5: revenge

As a revenge, Bernice takes a pair of scissors and cuts off the hair of Marjorie. And this is a double revenge, for she throws the braids into Warren's car.

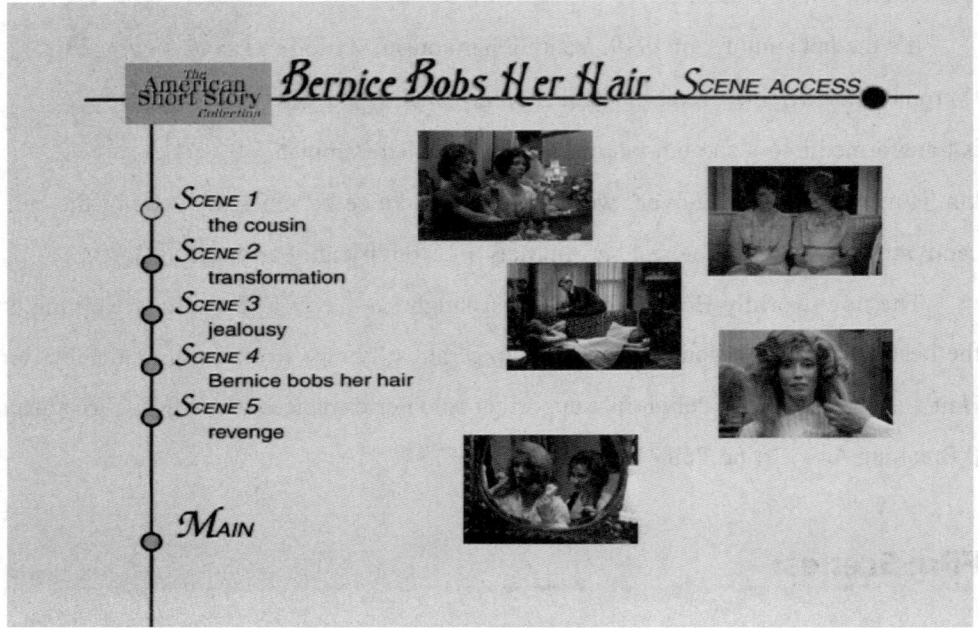

Film Clip:

The Scalping

After an absent-minded talk with Marjorie, Bernice starts to toss toilet articles, a change of clothing, two drawerfuls of women's underclothes and summer dresses into her suitcase. And then, Bernice writes a short note to Mrs. Harvey, in which she briefly outlines her reasons for going. She seals the letter, addresses it, and lays it on her pillow. Pretty soon, Bernice is fully dressed in a becoming new traveling suit that Marjorie has helped her pick out, getting ready for the leaving.

Suddenly Bernice draws in her breath sharply, and an expression flashes into her eyes, a development of the curious narrowing of her eyes. This new look of Bernice does carry consequences. She goes stealthily to the bureau, picking up a pair of scissors. Softly pushing open the door to Marjorie's room and coming to her bedside, Bernice deliberately and swiftly cuts off the two braids of Marjorie one after another. Although Marjorie mutters something in her sleep, she doesn't wake up.

Downstairs Bernice opens the big front door, and steps off the porch into the moonlight street, swinging her heavy grip like a shopping-bag. After a minute's brisk walk, she discovers that her left hand still holds the two blond braids of Marjorie. Bernice laughs unexpectedly, and when passing by Warren's roadster, she swings the braids onto the car's front seat. Fulfilling the double revenge against both Marjorie and Warren, the gratified Bernice walks away.

Discussion Questions:

Story Discussion

(1) What's the role of country club among the upper-class people in the story?

(2) How do the young ladies catch and maintain the masculine attention? How is it different for the young men?

(3) Bernice learns very fast and soon outdoes her teacher, Marjorie. How does she

make that possible?

(4) What do you think of the rivalry, trap and even revenge between girls?

(5) What does the long hair mean for young girls? Can you see the twisting irony in the story ending?

Film Appreciation

(1) What's Bernice's reaction to Warren's line?

(2) What does Marjorie's lecturing include?

(3) Is the sentence "Scalp the selfish thing" still there? Why (not)?

(4) How much is the gardenia flower Warren bought?

(5) What's the brand of Warren's car?

(6) What's the color of Bernice's hair?

(7) What are the examples of close up, low angle shot and high angle shot in the film?

(8) Does Marjorie give Bernice a chance to back up?

(9) What are the adapted scenes of the film?

Further Reading and Watching:

Babylon Revisited

Unit Three: Narration

Chapter 5: I'm a Fool

Chapter 6: Soldier's Home

Chapter 5
I'm a Fool

Sherwood Anderson

Author Introduction:

Sherwood Anderson (1876—1941) was born in Camden, Ohio, and spent most of his childhood in small Midwestern towns. After some intermittent schooling, Anderson enlisted in the Army for service in Cuba during the Spanish-American War. Self-educated, he rose to become a successful copywriter and business owner in Cleveland and Elyria, Ohio.

A few years later, in the spirit of rebellion against industrial and commercial civilization which was to color his writing thereafter, Anderson had a nervous breakdown that led him to abandon his business and family to become a writer. Going to Chicago, he was eventually married three more times.

In the ferment of a literary renaissance, Anderson made friends with writers and began to publish his own poetry and fiction. He became famous with the appearance of his most enduring work *Winesburg, Ohio* (1919), the stories of which show life and desire frustrated by the provincialism of the Midwest. It is a collection of 23 inter-related stories of small-town life, featuring George Willard, a reporter for the local newspaper, who has ambitions to become a famous writer.

Sherwood lived in many places around the United States, but he spent nearly half of his life in Ohio. Though his boyhood home of Clyde, Ohio, served as the primary model of his fictional town Winesburg, elements of his other Ohio "homes" helped complete the portrait. Sherwood also lived in the Ohio cities of Cleveland, Elyria and Springfield.

Characteristic of Anderson's work is a tone of melancholy reminiscence in which he projects remembered realities on the screen of a philosophic imagination. Anderson might be most remembered for his influential effect on the next generation of young writers, as he inspired and helped gain publication for William Faulkner and Ernest Hemingway.

His autobiography, *A Story-Teller's Story* (1924), is partly fictional, as most of his fiction is partly autobiographical. His novels include *Windy McPherson's Son* (1916), *Poor White* (1920), *Many Marriages* (1923), and *Dark Laughter* (1925). His later collections of stories are *The Triumph of the Egg* (1921), *Horses and Men* (1923), and *Death in the Woods and Other Stories* (1933).

Story Summary:

The story puts forward the conflict between life in the stable and life in the grandstand. And the biggest irony is that "She wasn't stuck on me because of the lie about my father being rich and all that."

Andy ("I") is a young boy, making it on his own as a "swipe" on the Ohio racetrack circuit in the 1900s. One day, as a spectator in the grandstand, he meets a beautiful young lady—his feminine ideal comes to life—to whom he tells some monumental lies about his wealth and his position in an attempt to win her. When she reveals a fondness for him and a desire to keep in touch, Andy is trapped—hopelessly enmeshed in the web of his own falsehoods. Like a typical human, after he makes his mistake, he finds something and someone to blame it on. Andy, the young "fool" in the story, is therefore a good example of an actual 19-year-old boy trying to impress a girl.

We should learn from the "fool" Andy, who tells a monumental lie to impress his feminine ideal Lucy, but remorsefully falls into the trap of his own falsehood.

Key Terms:

Contemporary: Andy tells a monumental lie to impress Lucy, but it ends in making himself a fool, and the story has its contemporary significance.

Loneliness: Andy works as a swipe, taking care of racing horse. And he works with Burt, a black man. Having very few friends, Andy feels lonely and unconfident.

Material Possession: Mr. Mathers has a lot of money and owns some coal mines, the representative of the wealthy, but at the same time he is also a hypocrite.

Deceit: Facing his feminine ideal and the girl in dream, Andy attempts to win her by telling a lie about his father, but falls into the trap of his own falsehood.

Realism: Andy tells the story with Lucy to make himself look like a fool, and he also finds the Windsor guy to blame for his own mistake, which is typically a young boy in reality.

I'm a Fool[1]

It was a hard jolt[2] for me, one of the most bitterest I ever had to face. And it all came about through my own foolishness, too. Even yet sometimes, when I think of it, I

---

[1] First published in the little literary magazine *Dial* in 1922, and later collected in *Horses and Men* (1923).
[2] An unpleasant surprise or shock.

want to cry or swear or kick myself. Perhaps, even now, after all this time, there will be a kind of satisfaction in making myself look cheap by telling of it.

It began at three o'clock one October afternoon as I sat in the grandstand① at the fall trotting and pacing meet② at Sandusky, Ohio.

To tell the truth, I felt a little foolish that I should be sitting in the grandstand at all. During the summer before I had left my home town with Harry Whitehead and, with a nigger named Burt, had taken a job as swipe③ with one of the two horses Harry was campaigning through the fall race meets that year. Mother cried and my sister Mildred, who wanted to get a job as a school teacher in our town that fall, stormed and scolded about the house all during the week before I left. They both thought it something disgraceful that one of our family should take a place as a swipe with race horses. I've an idea Mildred thought my taking the place would stand in the way of her getting the job she'd been working so long for.

But after all I had to work, and there was no other work to be got. A big lumbering④ fellow of nineteen couldn't just hang around the house and I had got too big to mow people's lawns and sell newspapers. Little chaps who could get next to people's sympathies by their sizes were always getting jobs away from me. There was one fellow who kept saying to everyone who wanted a lawn mowed or a cistern⑤ cleaned, that he was saving money to work his way through college, and I used to lay awake nights thinking up ways to injure him without being found out. I kept thinking of wagons running over him and bricks falling on his head as he walked along the street. But never mind him.

---

① A roofed stand for spectators at a stadium or racetrack.
② The racing in the story is harness racing, in which the horse draws a light two-wheeled vehicle seating the driver.
③ A horse trainer.
④ Awkward in movement, slow and laborious because of weight.
⑤ A container for storing rain water.

Chapter 5 I'm a Fool

　　I got the place with Harry and I liked Burt fine. We got along splendid together. He was a big nigger with a lazy sprawling body and soft, kind eyes, and when it came to a fight he could hit like Jack Johnson[①]. He had Bucephalus[②], a big black pacing stallion[③] that could do 2.09 or 2.10, if he had to, and I had a little gelding[④] named Doctor Fritz that never lost a race all fall when Harry wanted him to win.

　　We set out from home late in July in a box car with the two horses and after that, until late November, we kept moving along to the race meets and the fairs. It was a peachy time for me, I'll say that. Sometimes now I think that boys who are raised regular in houses, and never have a fine nigger like Burt for best friend, and go to high schools and college, and never steal anything, or get drunk a little, or learn to swear from fellows who know how, or come walking up in front of a grandstand in their shirt sleeves and with dirty horsey pants on when the races are going on and the grandstand is full of people all dressed up—What's the use of talking about it? Such fellows don't know nothing at all. They've never had no opportunity.

　　But I did. Burt taught me how to rub down a horse and put the bandage on after a race and steam a horse out[⑤] and a lot of valuable things for any man to know. He could wrap a bandage on a horse's leg so smooth that if it had been the same color you would think it was his skin, and I guess he'd have been a big driver, too, and got to the top like Murphy and Walter Cox and the others if he hadn't been black.

　　Gee whizz, it was fun. You got to a county seat town, maybe say on a Saturday or Sunday, and the fair began the next Tuesday and lasted until Friday afternoon. Doctor Fritz would be, say in the 2.25 trot on Tuesday afternoon and on Thursday afternoon

---

① World heavyweight boxing champion, 1908—1915, black.
② Alexander the Great's war horse.
③ An adult male horse that has not been castrated, especially one kept for breeding.
④ A castrated animal, especially a male horse.
⑤ To walk a horse slowly after a race so that the sweat gradually steams out.

Bucephalus would knock 'em cold in the "free-for-all" pace. It left you a lot of time to hang around and listen to horse talk, and see Burt knock some yap cold that got too gay, and you'd find out about horses and men and pick up a lot of stuff you could use all the rest of your life, if you had some sense and salted down what you heard and felt and saw.

And then at the end of the week when the race meet was over, and Harry had run home to tend up to his livery stable business, you and Burt hitched the two horses to carts and drove slow and steady across country, to the place for the next meeting, so as to not overheat the horses, etc., etc., you know.

Gee whizz, Gosh amighty, the nice hickorynut and beechnut and oaks and other kind of trees along the roads, all brown and red, the good smells, and Burt singing a song that was called Deep River①, and the country girls at the windows of houses and everything. You can stick your colleges up your nose for all me. I guess I know where I got my education.

Why, one of those little burgs of towns you come to on the way, say now on a Saturday afternoon, and Burt says, "let's lay up here." And you did.

And you took the horses to a livery stable and fed them, and you got your good clothes out of a box and put them on.

And the town was full of farmers gaping, because they could see you were race-horse people, and the kids maybe never see a nigger before and was afraid and run away when the two of us walked down their main street.

And that was before prohibition② and all that foolishness, and so you went into a saloon, the two of you, and all the yaps come and stood around, and there was always someone pretended he was horsey and knew things and spoke up and began asking

---

① An old song of African-Americans.
② The period (1920—1933) during which the 18th Amendment forbidding the manufacture and sale of alcoholic beverages was in force in the United States.

Chapter 5 I'm a Fool

questions, and all you did was to lie and lie all you could about that horses you had, and I said I owned them, and then some fellow said "will you have a drink of whisky" and Burt knocked his eye out the way he could say, offhand-like, "Oh well, all right, I'm agreeable to a little nip. I'll split a quart① with you." Gee whizz.

But that isn't what I want to tell my story about. We got home late in November and I promised mother I'd quit the race horses for good. There's a lot of things you've got to promise a mother because she don't know any better.

And so, there not being any work in our town any more than when I left there to go to the races, I went off to Sandusky and got a pretty good place taking care of horses for a man who owned a teaming and delivery and storage and coal and real estate business there. It was a pretty good place with good eats, and a day off each week, and sleeping on a cot② in a big barn, and mostly just shoveling in hay and oats to a lot of big good-enough skates of horses, that couldn't have trotted a race with a load. I wasn't dissatisfied and I could send money home.

And then, as I started to tell you, the fall races come to Sandusky and I got the day off and I went. I left the job at noon and had on my good clothes and my new brown derby hat③, I'd just bought the Saturday before, and a stand-up collar.

First of all I went downtown and walked about with the dudes④. I've always thought to myself, "put up a good front" and so I did it. I had forty dollars in my pocket and so I went into the West House, a big hotel, and walked up to the cigar stand. "Give me three twenty-five cent cigars," I said. There was a lot of horsemen and strangers and

---

① A unit of volume or capacity in the U.S. Customary System, used in liquid measure, equal to ¼ gallon or 32 ounces (0.946 liter).
② A narrow bed, usually made of canvas fitted over a frame which can be folded up.
③ A stiff-felt hat with a round crown and a narrow, curved brim.
④ Those who are very fancy or sharp in dress and demeanor.

dressed-up people from other towns standing around in the lobby and in the bar, and I mingled amongst them. In the bar there was a fellow with a cane and a Windsor tie[①] on, that it made me sick to look at him. I like a man to be a man and dress up, but not to go put on that kind of airs. So I pushed him aside, kind of rough, and had me a drink of whisky. And then he looked at me, as though he thought maybe he'd get gay, but he changed his mind and didn't say anything. And then I had another drink of whisky, just to show him something, and went out and had a hack[②] out to the races, all to myself, and when I got there I bought myself the best seat I could get up in the grandstand, but didn't go in for any of these boxes. That's putting on too many airs.

And so there I was, sitting up in the grandstand as gay as you please and looking down on the swipes coming out with their horses, and with their dirty horsey pants on and the horse blankets swung over their shoulders, same as I had been doing all the year before. I liked one thing about the same as the other, sitting up there and feeling grand and being down there and looking up at the yaps and feeling grander and more important, too. One thing's about as good as another, if you take it just right. I've often said that.

Well, right in front of me, in the grandstand that day, there was a fellow with a couple of girls and they was about my age. The young fellow was a nice guy all right. He was the kind maybe that goes to college and then comes to be a lawyer or maybe a newspaper editor or something like that, but he wasn't stuck on himself. There are some of that kind are all right and he was one of the ones.

He had his sister with him and another girl and the sister looked around over his shoulder, accidental at first, not intending to start anything—she wasn't that kind—and her eyes and mine happened to meet.

You know how it is. Gee, she was a peach! She had on a soft dress, kind of a blue

---

① A wide silk necktie tied in a loose bow.
② A carriage or hackney for hire.

Chapter 5 I'm a Fool

stuff and it looked carelessly made, but was well sewed and made and everything. I knew that much. I blushed when she looked right at me and so did she. She was the nicest girl I've ever seen in my life. She wasn't stuck on herself and she could talk proper grammar without being like a school teacher or something like that. What I mean is, she was O.K. I think maybe her father was well-to-do, but not rich to make her chesty① because she was his daughter, as some are. Maybe he owned a drugstore or a drygoods store in their home town, or something like that. She never told me and I never asked.

My own people are all O.K. too, when you come to that. My grandfather was Welsh and over in the old country, in Wales he was— But never mind that.

The first heat of the first race come off and the young fellow setting there with the two girls left them and went down to make a bet. I knew what he was up to, but he didn't talk big and noisy and let everyone around know he was a sport, as some do. He wasn't that kind. Well, he come back and I heard him tell the two girls what horse he'd bet on, and when the heat was trotted they all half got to their feet and acted in the excited, sweaty way people do when they've got money down on a race, and the horse they bet on is up there pretty close at the end, and they think maybe he'll come on with a rush, but he never does because he hasn't got the old juice in him, come right down to it.

And then, pretty soon, the horses came out for the 2.18 pace and there was a horse in it I knew. He was a horse Bob French had in his string but Bob didn't own him. He was a horse owned by a Mr. Mathers down at Marietta, Ohio.

This Mr. Mathers had a lot of money and owned some coal miners or something, and he had a swell place out in the country, and he was stuck on race horses, but was a

---

① Arrogant or proud; conceited.

Presbyterian① or something, and I think more than likely his wife was one, too, maybe a stiffer one than himself. So he never raced his horses himself, and the story round the Ohio race tracks was that when one of his horses got ready to go to the races he turned him over to Bob French and pretended to his wife he was sold.

So Bob had the horses and he did pretty much as he pleased and you can't blame Bob, at least, I never did. Sometimes he was out to win and sometimes he wasn't. I never cared much about that when I was swiping a horse. What I did want to know was that my horse had the speed and could go out in front, if you wanted him to.

And, as I'm telling you, there was Bob in his race with one of Mr. Mathers' horses, was named "About Ben Ahem"② or something like that, and was fast as a steak. He was a gelding and had a mark of 2.21, but could step in .08 or .09.

Because when Burt and I were out, as I've told you, the year before, there was a nigger, Burt knew, worked for Mr. Mathers and we went out there one day when we didn't have no race on at the Marietta Fair and our boss Harry was gone home.

And so everyone was gone to the fair but just this one nigger and he took us all through Mr. Mathers' swell house and he and Burt tapped a bottle of wine Mr. Mathers had hid in his bedroom, back in a closet, without his wife knowing, and he showed us this Ahem horse. Burt was always stuck on being a driver but didn't have much chance to get to the top, being a nigger, and he and the other nigger gulped that whole bottle of wine and Burt got a little lit up.

So the nigger let Burt take this About Ben Ahem and step him a mile in a track Mr. Mathers had all to himself, right there on the farm. And Mr. Mathers had one child, a daughter, kinda sick and not very good-looking, and she came home and we had to hustle and get About Ben Ahem stuck back in the barn.

---

① A follower of Calvinism as taught in the Protestant Church.
② Abou Ben Adhem is the title character of a well-known poem by Leigh Hunt, and here it is possibly the misspelling of the title character's name for the race horse.

Chapter 5 I'm a Fool

I'm only telling you to get everything straight. At Sandusky, that afternoon I was at the fair, this young fellow with two girls was fussed, being with the girls and losing his bet. You know how a fellow is that way. One of them was his girl and the other his sister I had figured that out.

"Gee whizz," I says to myself, "I'm going to give him the dope[①]."

He was mighty nice when I touched him on the shoulder. He and the girls were nice to me right from the start and clear to the end. I'm not blaming them.

And so he leaned back and I give him the dope on About Ben Ahem. "Don't bet a cent on this first heat because he'll go like an oxen hitched to a plow, but when the first heat is over go right down and lay on your pile." That's what I told him.

Well, I never saw a fellow treat anyone sweller. There was a fat man sitting beside the little girl, that had looked at me twice by this time, and I at her, and both blushing, and what did he do but have the nerve to turn and ask the fat man to get up and change places with me so I could set with his crowd.

Gee whizz, craps amighty. There I was. What a chump[②] I was to go and get gay up there in the West House bar, and just because that dude was standing there with a cane and that kind of a necktie on, to go and get all balled up and drink that whisky, just to show off.

Of course she would know, me setting right beside her and letting her smell of my breath. I could have kicked myself right down out of that grandstand and all around that race track and made a faster record than most of the skates of horses they had there that year.

Because that girl wasn't any mutt of a girl. What wouldn't I have give right

---

① Factual information, especially of a private nature.
② A stupid or foolish person; a dolt.

then for a stick of chewing gum to chew, or a lozenger①, or some liquorice②, or most anything. I was glad I had those twenty-five cent cigars in my pocket and right away I give that fellow one and lit one myself. Then that fat man got up and we changed places and there I was, plunked right down beside her.

They introduced themselves and the fellow's best girl, he had with him, was named Miss Elinor Woodbury, and her father was a manufacturer of barrels③ from a place called Tiffin, Ohio. And the fellow himself was named Wilbur Wessen and his sister was Miss Lucy Wessen.

I suppose it was their having such swell names got me off my trolley④. A fellow, just because he has been a swipe with a race horse, and works taking care of horses for a man in the teaming, delivery, and storage business, isn't any better or worse than anyone else. I've often thought that, and said it too.

But you know how a fellow is. There's something in that kind of nice clothes, and the kind of nice eyes she had, and the way she had looked at me, awhile before, over her brother's shoulder, and me looking back at her, and both of us blushing.

I couldn't show her up for a boob⑤, could I?

I made a fool of myself, that's what I did. I said my name was Walter Mathers from Marietta, Ohio, and then I told all three of them the smashingest⑥ lie you ever heard. What I said was that my father owned the horse About Ben Ahem and that he had let him out to this Bob French for racing purposes, because our family was proud and had never gone into racing that way, in our own name, I mean. Then I had got started and they were all leaning over and listening, and Miss Lucy Wessen's eyes were

---

① A misspelling of lozenge, a hard medicinal candy for soothing your throat.
② A black candy flavored with the dried root of the licorice plant.
③ A large, round container for liquids or food.
④ To lose wits.
⑤ A stupid or foolish person.
⑥ Extraordinarily impressive or fine; wonderful.

Chapter 5 I'm a Fool

shining, and I went the whole log.

I told about our place down at Marietta, and about the big stables and the grand brick house we had on a hill, up above the Ohio River, but I knew enough not to do it in no bragging way. What I did was to start things and then let them drag the rest out of me. I acted just as reluctant to tell as I could. Our family hasn't got any barrel factory, and, since I've known us, we've always been pretty poor, but not asking anything of anyone at that, and my grandfather, over in Wales—but never mind that.

We set there talking like we had known each other for years and years, and I went and told them that my father had been expecting maybe this Bob French wasn't on the square, and had sent me up to Sandusky on the sly① to find out what I could.

And I buffed it through I had found out all about the 2.18 pace, in which About Ben Ahem was to start.

I said he would lose the first heat by pacing like a lame cow and then he would come back and skin 'em alive after that. And to back up what I said I took thirty dollars out of my pocket and handed it to Mr. Wilbur Wessen and asked him, would he mind, after the first heat, to go down and place it on About Ben Ahem for whatever odds he could get. What I said was that I didn't want Bob French to see me and none of the swipes.

Sure enough the first heat come off and About Ben Ahem went off his stride, up the back stretch, and looked like a wooden horse or a sick one, and come in to be last. Then this Wilbur Wessen went down to the betting place and when that Miss Woodbury was looking the other way once, Lucy Wessen kinda, with her shoulder you know, kinda touched me. Not just tucking down, I don't mean. You know how a woman can do. They get close, but not getting gay either. You know what they do. Gee whizz.

---

① Secretly.

And then they give me a jolt. What they had done, when I didn't know, was to get together, and they had decided Wilber Wessen would bet fifty dollars, and the two girls had gone and put in ten dollars each, of their own money, too. I was sick then, but I was sicker later.

About the gelding, About Ben Ahem, and their winning their money, I wasn't worried a lot about that. It come out O.K. Ahem stepped the next three heats like a bushel of spoiled eggs going to market before they could be found out, and Wilber Wessen had got nine to two for the money. There was something else eating at me.

Because Wilbur come back, after he had bet the money, and after that he spent most of his time talking to that Miss Woodbury, and Lucy Wessen and I was left alone together like on a desert island. Gee, if I'd only been on the square or if there had been any way of getting myself on the square. There ain't any Walter Mathers, like I said to her and them, and there hasn't ever been one, but if there was, I bet I'd go to Marietta, Ohio, and shoot him tomorrow.

There I was, big boob that I am. Pretty soon the race was over, and Wilbur had gone down and collected our money, and we had a hack downtown, and he stood us a swell supper at the West House, and a bottle of champagne beside.

And I was with that girl and she wasn't saying much, and I wasn't saying much either. One thing I know. She wasn't stuck on me because of the lie about my father being rich and all that. There's a way you know... Craps amighty. There's a kind of girl, you see just once in your life, and if you don't get busy and make hay, then you're gone for good and all, and might as well go jump off a bridge. They give you a look from inside of them somewhere, and it ain't no vamping[①], and what it means is—you want that girl to be your wife, and you want nice things around her like flowers and swell clothes, and you want her to have the kids you're going to have, and you want

---

① A seductive woman who uses her sex appeal to exploit men.

Chapter 5 I'm a Fool

good music played and no ragtime①. Gee whizz.

There's a place over near Sandusky, across a kind of bay, and it's called Cedar Point. And after we had supper we went over to it in a launch, all by ourselves. Wilbur and Miss Lucy and that Miss Woodbury had to catch a ten o'clock train back to Tiffin, Ohio, because, when you're out with girls like that you can't get careless and miss any trains and stay out all night, like you can with some kinds of Janes.

And Wilbur blowed himself to the launch and it cost him fifteen cold plunks, but I wouldn't never have knew if I hadn't listened. He wasn't no tin horn kind of a sport.

Over at the Cedar Point place, we didn't stay around where there was a gang of common kind of cattle at all.

There was big dance halls and dining places for yaps, and there was a beach you could walk along and get where it was dark, and we went there.

She didn't talk hardly at all and neither did I, and I was thinking how glad I was my mother was all right, and always made us kids learn to eat with a fork at table, and not swill soup, and not be noisy and rough like a gang you see around a race track that way.

Then Wilbur and his girl went away up the beach and Lucy and I sat down in a dark place, where there was some roots of old trees, the water had washed up, and after that the time, till we had to go back in the launch② and they had to catch their trains, wasn't nothing at all. It went like winking your eye.

Here's how it was. The place we were setting in was dark, like I said, and there was the roots from that old stump③ sticking up like arms, and there was a watery smell,

---

① A style of jazz characterized by elaborately syncopated rhythm in the melody and a steadily accented accompaniment.
② A motor-driven boat.
③ The part of a tree trunk left protruding from the ground after the tree has fallen or has been felled.

and the night was like—as if you could put your hand out and feel it—so warm and soft and dark and sweet like an orange.

I most cried and I most swore and I most jumped up and danced, I was so mad and happy and sad.

When Wilbur come back from being alone with his girl, and she saw him coming, Lucy she says, "we got to go to the train now," and she was most crying too, but she never knew nothing I knew, and she couldn't be so all busted① up. And then, before Wilbur and Miss Woodbury got up to where we was, she put her face up and kissed me quick and put her head up against me and she was all quivering and—Gee whizz.

Sometimes I hope I have cancer and die. I guess you know what I mean. We went in the launch across the bay to the train like that, and it was dark, too. She whispered and said it was like she and I could get out of the boat and walk on the water, and it sounded foolish, but I knew what she meant.

And then quick we were right at the depot②, and there was a big gang of yaps, the kind that goes to the fairs, and crowded and milling around like cattle, and how could I tell her? "It won't be long because you'll write and I'll write to you." That's all she said.

I got a chance like a hay barn afire. A swell chance I got.

And maybe she would write to me, down at Marietta that way, and the letter would come back, and stamped on the front of it by the U.S.A. "there ain't any such guy," or something like that, whatever they stamp on a letter that way.

And me trying to pass myself off for a bigbug and a swell—to her, as decent a little body as God ever made. Craps amighty—a swell chance I got!

And then the train come in, and she got on it, and Wilbur Wessen he come and

---

① Suddenly and violently broken open, especially from internal pressure.
② A railroad or bus station.

shook hands with me, and that Miss Woodbury was nice too and bowed to me, and I at her, and the train went and I busted out and cried like a kid.

Gee, I could have run after that train and made Dan Patch① look like a freight train after a wreck but, socks amighty, what was the use? Did you ever see such a fool?

I'll bet you what—if I had an arm broke right now or a train had run over my foot—I wouldn't go to no doctor at all. I'd go set down and let her hurt and hurt—that's what I'd do.

I'll bet you what—if I hadn't a drunk that booze② I'd a never been such a boob as to go tell such a lie—that couldn't never be made straight to a lady like her.

I wish I had that fellow right here that had on a Windsor tie and carried a cane. I'd smash him for fair. Gosh darn his eyes. He's a big fool—that's what he is.

And if I'm not another you just go find me one and I'll quit working and be a bum and give him my job. I don't care nothing for working, and earning money, and saving it for no such boob as myself.

Film Comment:

Sherwood Anderson's *I'm a Fool*: 38 minutes, color

Starring: Ron Howard & Amy Irving

Screenplay by: Ron Cowen

Directed by: Dan McCann

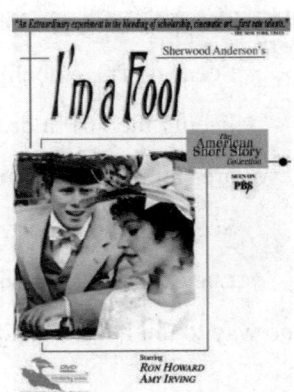

Traveling from town to town during the summer of 1919, young Andy (Ron Howard) has left his Ohio home in search of adventure and romance as a horse trainer on the country fair racing circuit.

---

① One of the fastest harness horses in history.
② Heavy drinking.

More than a little "wet behind the ears," Andy learns a bittersweet lesson about life when he meets Lucy (Amy Irving), the girl of his dreams, at the race track one day. Ashamed of his occupation, Andy leads Lucy to believe he's wealthy. Soon one lie leads to another until there is no way to tell Lucy the truth.

The irony of the story is that Lucy and Andy have fallen deeply in love. As Andy dejectedly admits on his way out of town, all is lost because "I'm a Fool."

Film Scenes:

Scene 1: The journey

Andy works as a swipe, taking care of race horses. He travels from town to town with Burt over the whole horse racing season.

Scene 2: Walter L. Mathers Farm

Andy travels to the farm of the wealthy Walter L. Mathers, Windy Acres Farm, getting to know about the horse About Ben Ahem.

Scene 3: At the race track

With a brand-new derby hat and the formal suit, Andy comes to the race track. Drinking two cups of whisky at the bar, he feels a little dizzy.

Scene 4: The embellishment

Facing the girl in dream, Andy tells a monumental lie about his father, and Lucy's eyes are shining. Only one lie leads to another, and Andy falls into his own trap.

Scene 5: The goodbye

Lucy falls in love with Andy and reveals a desire to keep in touch, but Andy has no way to tell her the truth. The goodbye becomes farewell, making himself a fool.

Chapter 5 I'm a Fool

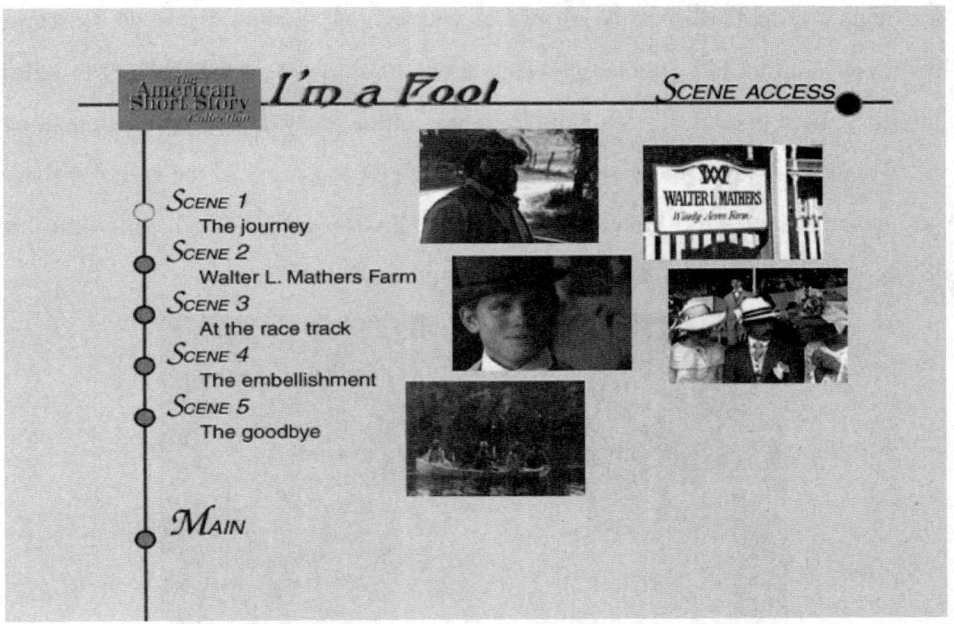

Film Clip:

The West House Hotel

Formally dressed with the brand-new suit and a derby hat, Andy walks up to the cigar stand of the West House hotel, buying two 10-cent cigars, leaving 5 cents for a tip. Coming upstairs into the lobby and the bar, Andy intends to have a drink of whisky, raising his finger, but getting no attention from the bartender. He has to call out to ask for a cup of whisky with no water. Then a dude with a cane and a Windsor tie on comes around, "May I trouble you for a light?" Seemingly he is asking for a light from Andy, but actually the dude is showing off his Havana cigar, much superior to that of Andy's. Being despised, Andy could only retaliate by drinking a whisky, and then another. Going downstairs, Andy throws his previously-bought cigars into the dustbin and buys another four 25-cent Havana cigars, going off to the horse racing.

Obviously, Andy is still inexperienced in smoking and drinking. He buys some cheap cigars at first. He has two drinks of whisky, just to show the dude something, which makes him a little lighted up. This is one important reason for Andy to tell the lie to Lucy, hard to control his tongue for being a little dizzy. However, when making a fool of himself, Andy could always find someone else to blame. At the end of the story, Andy calls himself a fool, but also blames the Windsor-tie guy for having him drink two cups of whisky and tell a monumental lie to Lucy.

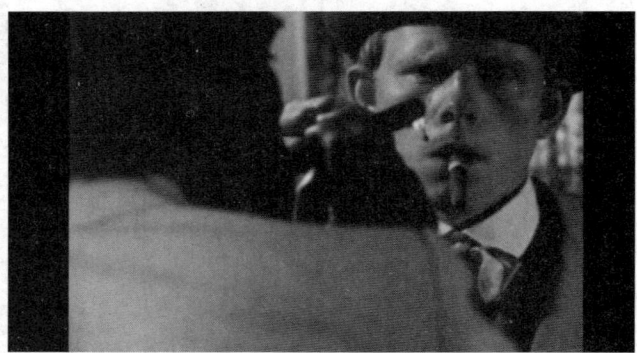

Discussion Questions:

Story Discussion

(1) What did Andy get from the wandering year as a horse swipe? What's the opinion from his family?

(2) Why did Andy lie to Lucy? What are the consequences of such a big lie?

(3) Do you really think Andy "a Fool"? Put in his position, what would you do?

(4) Can you see the irony that Lucy and Andy have really fallen in love?

(5) What does Andy learn from the lesson of being "a Fool"? How can the story apply to the modern young men?

Film Appreciation

(1) What's the name of the farm of Mr. Mathers?

(2) What's Andy's dream about life/girl when talking in the barn?

(3) What's the music when Andy coming to the West House hotel?

(4) What's the price of a piece of Havana Cigar?

(5) Why does Andy drink two cups of whiskey in the bar?

(6) Why does Andy lie? Does he hesitate when start lying?

(7) Has Andy tried telling Lucy the truth?

(8) Where is the passage of ideal girl in the film?

(9) How does the film rearrange timeline in an orderly manner?

Further Reading and Watching:

Death in the Woods

Chapter 6
Soldier's Home

Ernest Hemingway

Author Introduction:

Ernest Hemingway (1899—1961) was born in Oak Park, Illinois, the son of a doctor, who gave him an enduring enthusiasm for the outdoor life. As a boy, Hemingway spent most of his summers in the woods of upper Michigan that became the setting for some of his best-known stories.

Toward the end of the First World War, he volunteered for service as an ambulance driver with the Italian Army and was seriously wounded in the fighting on the Austrian front. Recovering from his wounds, he went to Paris as a correspondent for the *Toronto Star* and there met, among other writers, Ezra Pound and Gertrude Stein.

They encouraged him in the invention of his own style, and Hemingway won swift acclaim for his early stories, *In Our Time* (1925), and for his first novel, *The Sun Also Rises* (1926), which portrays the "Lost Generation" of postwar American expatriate community in France and Spain. Hemingway used the sentence "You are all a lost generation" (attributing it to Gertrude Stein) as an epigraph for the novel.

Later, he became a celebrity, often photographed as a marlin fisherman or a lion hunter. A fan of bullfighting, he wrote one nonfiction book on the subject, *Death in the Afternoon* (1932). The Hemingway hero and his code of conduct—living with "grace under pressure"—were as widely emulated and admired as the style of his short stories and novels.

During the Spanish Civil War he went to Spain as a war correspondent and wrote one of his best novels, *For Whom the Bell Tolls* (1940), about that conflict. Afterwards, he followed the American Army in Europe as a correspondent before returning to peacetime life at his home in Cuba, where he wrote *The Old Man and the Sea* (1952).

Hemingway talks about the iceberg theory in *Death in the Afternoon*, "If a writer of prose knows enough of what he is writing about he may omit things that he knows and the reader, if the writer is writing truly enough, will have a feeling of those things as strongly as though the writer had stated them. The dignity of movement of an iceberg is due to only one-eighth of it being above water. A good writer does not need to reveal every detail of a character or action."

Hemingway got the Nobel Prize for literature in 1954. It was awarded "for his mastery of the art of narrative, most recently demonstrated in *The Old Man and the Sea*, and for the influence that he has exerted on contemporary style." In 1961, mentally distressed and physically ailing, Hemingway killed himself with his favorite shotgun.

His other novels include *A Farewell to Arms* (1929), *To Have and Have Not* (1937), and *Across the River and Into the Trees* (1950). In *A Movable Feast* (1964) he recreates the Paris of his earlier years. His later collections of stories are *Men without Women* (1927) and *Winner Take Nothing* (1933).

Story Summary:

The story lies in the hardest part of the war—coming home.

Harold Krebs is a soldier returned. Quietly and without ceremony he comes home after the First World War. No longer does he fit into the life he left. Despite gentle pressure from family and friends, he cannot get hold of his own future. Between the non-changed hero and his past there is a desperate incompatibility. A climatic scene between mother and son foreshadows Krebs' decision to find himself again in a new place, away from the old and familiar, which, for all time, he has outgrown.

We should learn from the veteran Harold, who has lost his aim, ambition, belief, hope and capacity to live, and cannot fit into the society which he has outgrown.

Key Terms:

Unexpressive: Coming back from the war, Harold is mentally hurt. Still in the process of recovery, he doesn't want to talk at all and seldom talks indeed.

Conformance: Before going to the war, Harold attends a Methodist college and conforms to the society, wearing exactly the same height and style collar.

Society: After several years of absence, Harold finds that he cannot fit into the society he left, which he has outgrown.

Psychological: Harold doesn't want to talk and he doesn't talk much, but we can get his psychological activities from his wandering life rhythm.

Lost Generation: Harold is a typical member of the Lost Generation, having no aims in life and having lost their ambition and belief.

Soldier's Home[1]

Krebs went to the war from a Methodist[2] college in Kansas. There is a picture which shows him among his fraternity[3] brothers, all of them wearing exactly the same height and style collar. He enlisted in the Marines in 1917 and did not return to the United States until the second division[4] returned from the Rhine[5] in the summer of 1919.

There is a picture which shows him on the Rhone[6] with two German girls and another corporal. Krebs and the corporal look too big for their uniforms. The German girls are not beautiful. The Rhine does not show in the picture.

By the time Krebs returned to his home town in Oklahoma the greeting of heroes was over. He came back much too late. The men from the town who had been drafted[7] had all been welcomed elaborately on their return. There had been a great deal of hysteria[8]. Now the reaction had set in. People seemed to think it was rather ridiculous for Krebs to be getting back so late, years after the war was over.

At first Krebs, who had been at Belleau Wood, Soissons, the Champagne, St. Mihiel and in the Argonne[9] did not want to talk about the war at all. Later he felt the need to talk but no one wanted to hear about it. His town had heard too many atrocity[10]

---

[1] First published in *In Our Time* (1925).
[2] Protestant Christians who follow the teachings of John Wesley and who have their own branch of the Christian church and their own form of worship.
[3] A society of male university or college students.
[4] A group of military units which fight as a single unit.
[5] A river of Western Europe flowing through Germany and the Netherlands to the North Sea.
[6] A river rising in Switzerland, flowing through France and into the Mediterranean Sea.
[7] Ordered to serve in the armed forces.
[8] A state of uncontrolled excitement, anger, or panic.
[9] These places are in the areas of northern and northwestern France. All are the major battlegrounds during the First World War.
[10] A very cruel, shocking action.

stories to be thrilled by actualities. Krebs found that to be listened to at all he had to lie and after he had done this twice he, too, had a reaction against the war and against talking about it. A distaste for everything that had happened to him in the war set in because of the lies he had told. All of the times that had been able to make him feel cool and clear inside himself when he thought of them; the times so long back when he had done the one thing, the only thing for a man to do, easily and naturally, when he might have done something else, now lost their cool, valuable quality and then were lost themselves.

His lies were quite unimportant lies and consisted in attributing to himself things other men had seen, done or heard of, and stating as facts certain apocryphal① incidents familiar to all soldiers. Even his lies were not sensational at the pool② room. His acquaintances, who had heard detailed accounts of German women found chained to machine guns in the Argonne and who could not comprehend, or were barred by their patriotism from interest in, any German machine gunners who were not chained, were not thrilled by his stories.

Krebs acquired the nausea③ in regard to experience that is the result of untruth or exaggeration, and when he occasionally met another man who had really been a soldier and they talked a few minutes in the dressing room at a dance he fell into the easy pose of the old soldier among other soldiers: that he had been badly, sickeningly frightened all the time. In this way he lost everything.

During this time, it was late summer, he was sleeping late in bed, getting up to walk down town to the library to get a book, eating lunch at home, reading on the front porch until he became bored and then walking down through the town to spend the

---

① Being of questionable authenticity.
② Any of several games played on a six-pocket billiard table usually with 15 object balls and a cue ball.
③ Disgust so strong making you feel sick.

Chapter 6 Soldier's Home

hottest hours of the day in the cool dark of the pool room. He loved to play pool.

In the evening he practiced on his clarinet, strolled down town, read and went to bed. He was still a hero to his two young sisters. His mother would have given him breakfast in bed if he had wanted it. She often came in when he was in bed and asked him to tell her about the war, but her attention always wandered. His father was non-committal.

Before Krebs went away to the war he had never been allowed to drive the family motor car. His father was in the real estate business and always wanted the car to be at his command when he required it to take clients out into the country to show them a piece of farm property. The car always stood outside the First National Bank building where his father had an office on the second floor. Now, after the war, it was still the same car.

Nothing was changed in the town except that the young girls had grown up. But they lived in such a complicated world of already defined alliances① and shifting feuds② that Krebs did not feel the energy or the courage to break into it. He liked to look at them, though. There were so many good-looking young girls. Most of them had their hair cut short. When he went away only little girls wore their hair like that or girls that were fast③. They all wore sweaters and shirt waists④ with round Dutch collars. It was a pattern. He liked to look at them from the front porch as they walked on the other side of the street. He liked to watch them walking under the shade of the trees. He liked the round Dutch collars above their sweaters. He liked their silk stockings and flat shoes. He liked their bobbed hair and the way they walked.

When he was in town their appeal to him was not very strong. He did not like

---

① A connection based on kinship or marriage or common interest.
② A bitter quarrel between two parties.
③ Unrestrained by convention or morality.
④ A woman's dress with a tailored bodice resembling a shirt.

them when he saw them in the Greek's ice cream parlor. He did not want them themselves really. They were too complicated. There was something else. Vaguely he wanted a girl but he did not want to have to work to get her. He would have liked to have a girl but he did not want to have to spend a long time getting her. He did not want to get into the intrigue① and the politics. He did not want to have to do any courting. He did not want to tell any more lies. It wasn't worth it.

  He did not want any consequences. He did not want any consequences ever again. He wanted to live along without consequences. Besides he did not really need a girl. The army had taught him that. It was all right to pose② as though you had to have a girl. Nearly everybody did that. But it wasn't true. You did not need a girl. That was the funny thing. First a fellow boasted how girls mean nothing to him, that he never thought of them, that they could not touch him. Then a fellow boasted that he could not get along without girls, that he had to have them all the time, that he could not go to sleep without them.

  That was all a lie. It was all a lie both ways. You did not need a girl unless you thought about them. He learned that in the army. Then sooner or later you always got one. When you were really ripe for a girl you always got one. You did not have to think about it. Sooner or later it could come. He had learned that in the army.

  Now he would have liked a girl if she had come to him and not wanted to talk. But here at home it was all too complicated. He knew he could never get through it all again. It was not worth the trouble. That was the thing about French girls and German girls. There was not all this talking. You couldn't talk much and you did not need to talk. It was simple and you were friends. He thought about France and then he began to think about Germany. On the whole he had liked Germany better. He did not want to leave Germany. He did not want to come home. Still, he had come home. He sat on the

---

① Trickery.
② To behave affectedly or unnaturally in order to impress others.

Chapter 6 Soldier's Home

front porch.

He liked the girls that were walking along the other side of the street. He liked the look of them much better than the French girls or the German girls. But the world they were in was not the world he was in. He would like to have one of them. But it was not worth it. They were such a nice pattern. He liked the pattern. It was exciting. But he would not go through all the talking. He did not want one badly enough. He liked to look at them all, though. It was not worth it. Not now when things were getting good again.

He sat there on the porch reading a book on the war. It was a history and he was reading about all the engagements he had been in. It was the most interesting reading he had ever done. He wished there were more maps. He looked forward with a good feeling to reading all the really good histories when they would come out with good detail maps. Now he was really learning about the war. He had been a good soldier. That made a difference.

One morning after he had been home about a month his mother came into his bedroom and sat on the bed. She smoothed her apron.

"I had a talk with your father last night, Harold," she said, "and he is willing for you to take the car out in the evenings."

"Yeah?" said Krebs, who was not fully awake. "Take the car out? Yeah?"

"Yes. Your father has felt for some time that you should be able to take the car out in the evenings whenever you wished but we only talked it over last night."

"I'll bet you made him," Krebs said.

"No. It was your father's suggestion that we talk the matter over."

"Yeah. I'll bet you made him," Krebs sat up in bed.

"Will you come down to breakfast, Harold?" his mother said.

"As soon as I get my clothes on," Krebs said.

His mother went out of the room and he could hear her frying something downstairs while he washed, shaved and dressed to go down into the dining-room for breakfast. While he was eating breakfast, his sister brought in the mail.

"Well, Hare," she said. "You old sleepy-head. What do you ever get up for?"

Krebs looked at her. He liked her. She was his best sister.

"Have you got the paper?" he asked.

She handed him *The Kansas City Star* and he shucked off its brown wrapper and opened it to the sporting page. He folded *The Star* open and propped it against the water pitcher[①] with his cereal dish to steady it, so he could read while he ate.

"Harold," his mother stood in the kitchen doorway, "Harold, please don't muss up the paper. Your father can't read his *Star* if it's been mussed."

"I won't muss it," Krebs said.

His sister sat down at the table and watched him while he read.

"We're playing indoor over at school this afternoon," she said. "I'm going to pitch."

"Good," said Krebs. "How's the old wing?"

"I can pitch better than lots of the boys. I tell them all you taught me. The other girls aren't much good."

"Yeah?" said Krebs.

"I tell them all you're my beau[②]. Aren't you my beau, Hare?"

"You bet."

"Couldn't your brother really be your beau just because he's your brother?"

"I don't know."

"Sure you know. Couldn't you be my beau, Hare, if I was old enough and if you wanted to?"

---

① A container for liquids, usually having a handle and a lip or spout for pouring; this word also has another meaning: the player who throws the ball from the mound to the batter.

② The boyfriend of a woman or girl.

Chapter 6　Soldier's Home

"Sure. You're my girl now."

"Am I really your girl?"

"Sure."

"Do you love me?"

"Uh, huh."

"Do you love me always?"

"Sure."

"Will you come over and watch me play indoor?"

"Maybe."

"Aw, Hare, you don't love me. If you loved me, you'd want to come over and watch me play indoor."

Krebs's mother came into the dining-room from the kitchen. She carried a plate with two fried eggs and some crisp bacon on it and a plate of buckwheat cakes.

"You run along, Helen," she said. "I want to talk to Harold."

She put the eggs and bacon down in front of him and brought in a jug of maple syrup[①] for the buckwheat cakes. Then she sat down across the table from Krebs.

"I wish you'd put down the paper a minute, Harold," she said.

Krebs took down the paper and folded it.

"Have you decided what you are going to do yet, Harold?" his mother said, taking off her glasses.

"No," said Krebs.

"Don't you think it's about time?" His mother did not say this in a mean way. She seemed worried.

"I hadn't thought about it," Krebs said.

"God has some work for every one to do," his mother said. "There can be no idle

---

① The juice of a fruit or plant boiled with sugar until thick and sticky.

hands in His Kingdom."

"I'm not in His Kingdom," Krebs said.

"We are all of us in His Kingdom."

Krebs felt embarrassed and resentful as always.

"I've worried about you too much, Harold," his mother went on. "I know the temptations you must have been exposed to. I know how weak men are. I know what your own dear grandfather, my own father, told us about the Civil War and I have prayed for you. I pray for you all day long, Harold."

Krebs looked at the bacon fat hardening on his plate.

"Your father is worried, too," his mother went on. "He thinks you have lost your ambition, that you haven't got a definite aim in life. Charley Simmons, who is just your age, has a good job and is going to be married. The boys are all settling down; they're all determined to get somewhere; you can see that boys like Charley Simmons are on their way to being really a credit to the community."

Krebs said nothing.

"Don't look that way, Harold," his mother said. "You know we love you and I want to tell you for your own good how matters stand. Your father does not want to hamper① your freedom. He thinks you should be allowed to drive the car. If you want to take some of the nice girls out riding with you, we are only too pleased. We want you to enjoy yourself. But you are going to have to settle down to work, Harold. Your father doesn't care what you start in at. All work is honorable as he says. But you've got to make a start at something. He asked me to speak to you this morning and then you can stop in and see him at his office."

"Is that all?" Krebs said.

"Yes. Don't you love your mother, dear boy?"

---

① To prevent the free movement, action, or progress of.

Chapter 6　Soldier's Home

"No," Krebs said.

His mother looked at him across the table. Her eyes were shiny. She started crying.

"I don't love anybody," Krebs said.

It wasn't any good. He couldn't tell her, he couldn't make her see it. It was silly to have said it. He had only hurt her. He went over and took hold of her arm. She was crying with her head in her hands.

"I didn't mean it," he said. "I was just angry at something. I didn't mean I didn't love you."

His mother went on crying. Krebs put his arm on her shoulder.

"Can't you believe me, mother?"

His mother shook her head.

"Please, please, mother. Please believe me."

"All right," his mother said chokily. She looked up at him. "I believe you, Harold."

Krebs kissed her hair. She put her face up to him.

"I'm your mother," she said. "I held you next to my heart when you were a tiny baby."

Krebs felt sick and vaguely nauseated[①].

"I know, Mummy," he said. "I'll try and be a good boy for you."

"Would you kneel and pray with me, Harold?" his mother asked.

They knelt down beside the dining-room table and Krebs's mother prayed.

"Now, you pray, Harold," she said.

"I can't," Krebs said.

"Try, Harold."

"I can't."

---

①　Feeling about to vomit.

"Do you want me to pray for you?"

"Yes."

So his mother prayed for him and then they stood up and Krebs kissed his mother and went out of the house. He had tried so to keep his life from being complicated. Still, none of it had touched him. He had felt sorry for his mother and she had made him lie. He would go to Kansas City and get a job and she would feel all right about it. There would be one more scene maybe before he got away. He would not go down to his father's office. He would miss that one. He wanted his life to go smoothly. It had just gotten going that way. Well, that was all over now, anyway. He would go over to the schoolyard and watch Helen play indoor baseball.

Film Comment:

Ernest Hemingway's *Soldier's Home*: 42 minutes, color

Starring: Richard Backus & Nancy Marchand

Screenplay by: Robert Geller

Directed by: Robert Young

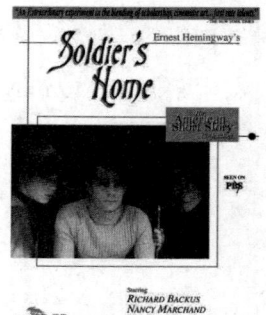

Harold Krebs (Richard Backus) went off to fight the First World War, "the war to end all wars." Then he came home… and found himself wishing it had never ended. To Ernest Hemingway, the hardest part of the war was coming home. This is the essence of "Soldier's Home"—a story with many similarities to the experience of those Vietnam veterans.

Harold finds he doesn't fit in anymore. He's outgrown his old life and now needs peace and quiet to work things out for himself. Yet he's pressured by his mother (Nancy Marchand), loving but misunderstanding, to rejoin a community in which he feels alien.

Chapter 6 Soldier's Home

An intense and personal character study from the giant of American Literature, Harold discovers going home is never easy—and maybe it isn't even possible.

Film Scenes:

Scene 1: Coming home

When Harold comes back home alone by himself, the greeting of heroes has been over. He comes back too late, quietly and without ceremony.

Scene 2: Old friends

Harold wanders aimlessly in the town, without much talking, and he likes spending the hottest hours in the pool room, where he meets with some old friends.

Scene 3: Socializing

Harold attends some social gathering. He wants a hometown girl, like Roselle, but he doesn't want to do any courting, because it is too complicated.

Scene 4: The conversation

The mother starts a conversation with Harold about his future work, but Harold doesn't want to continue the topic. He decides to find himself again in a new place.

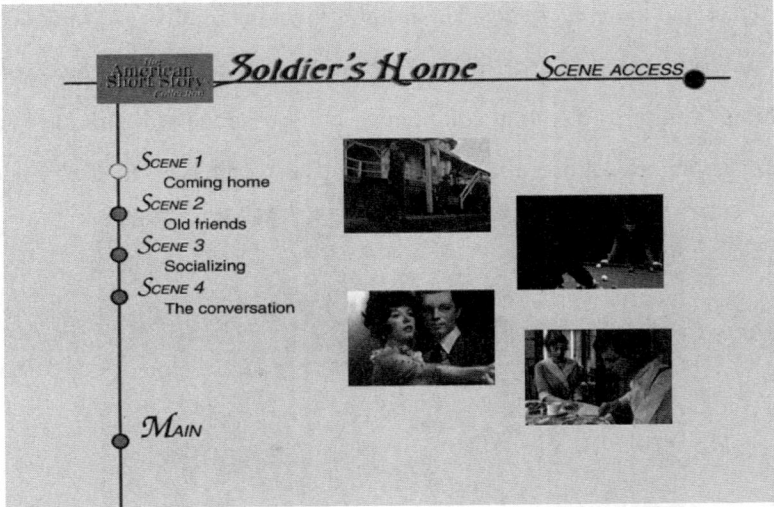

Film Clip:

Life back at Home

Harold gets up early, hearing the sound of milk bottles of milkmen, and seeing some group of people going to work, taking their lunch box with them. Taking a walk, Harold meets with a neighbor of old man, who is greeting him warmly and obviously wants to have a lasting talk. But Harold simply says goodbye, making the old man not pleased. Seeing some girls with short hair, Harold looks attentively and then walks by with no talk. Passing by a barber's shop, Harold sees some acquaintances of the barber and customer, still without any talk. Going over a clothes store, Harold watches the sales girl from feet to face, welcomed by a smiling face, but still no talk. Meeting with a lady pushing a baby carriage, Harold walks with them for a while, facing a big smile of the baby, but no talk again. And finally, Harold comes to the car of his father, the same car parked in front of the window office of his father.

Harold's life back in town is quite a leisure, a very slow pace of life. All of these show that Harold couldn't find himself fit in anymore, and coming back after the war, Harold has lost his goal, direction, ambition, aim, hope, youth, love, and belief, just wandering here and there every day. He has outgrown his old life and now needs peace and quiet to work things out for himself. Harold needs to make some changes soon and gets himself fit in to the alien community. Otherwise, he will still have to wander everywhere, having no definite aim in life, typically a member of the Lost Generation.

Discussion Questions:

Story Discussion

(1) What war does Harold go to fight for? Why does he come home so late?

(2) Harold couldn't find himself fit in anymore. Has he or the community changed? Or both changed?

(3) Where does the pressure come from? What's the conflict between his mother and him?

(4) Harold has to make a decision for his future. What kind of life is waiting for the homecoming soldier?

(5) The author thinks that the hardest part of the war is coming home. Do you agree with that or not?

Film Appreciation

(1) What are the two pictures at the beginning of the film? Who makes the welcome sign?

(2) What's Harold's daily life back in town? What's the difference if compared with the story?

(3) What are Harold's attitudes toward the female: French/German girls (memory); hometown girls (Roselle); little sister (Margie); his mother (pressure)?

(4) How does Harold change his religious belief?

(5) Who is the model boy for Harold? What's his job?

(6) How is Harold different from the wounded soldier Bill?

(7) What do you think of the father-mother relationship?

(8) Why does Harold come back home so late?

Further Reading and Watching:

The Snows of Kilimanjaro

Unit Four: Setting

Chapter 7: The Greatest Man in the World

Chapter 8: Barn Burning

Chapter 7
The Greatest Man in the World

James Thurber

Author Introduction:

James Thurber (1894—1961) was born in Columbus, Ohio, and attended Ohio State University. The accidental loss of an eye in boyhood kept him from military service in the First World War, but he worked briefly for the Department of State as a code clerk, first in Washington, D.C., and then at the Embassy of the United States, Paris, France.

After the war, he returned home to write for the *Columbus Dispatch*, and to compose and direct musical comedies for a theatrical group at Ohio State University. In 1924, he traveled to Paris as a correspondent to sample the world of the expatriates, where he wrote for the *Chicago Tribune* and other newspapers.

Thurber was back in New York, by 1926, submitting his humorous pieces to *The New Yorker* in its early days. With the help of E. B. White, his friend and fellow *New Yorker* contributor, he worked briefly as its managing editor and then contributed regularly to its "Talk of the Town" department until the 1950s.

Thurber had drawn before he began to write. Thurber's cartoons included seals, sea lions, strange tigers, harried men, determined women, and, most of all, dogs. Thurber's dogs became something like a national comic institution, and they dotted the pages of a whole series of books. *The New Yorker* printed several series of his cartoons as well as fables, essays, comment, and short stories through the many years of his association with the magazine. Many of his short stories are humorous fictional memoirs from his life, but he also wrote darker materials.

Despite his failing eyesight, Thurber continues writing humor and satire until his death, including "The Secret Life of Walter Mitty," which is regarded as one of the best short stories written in the 20th century. Walter Mitty Syndrome later even becomes a clinical condition. His carefully wrought style faithfully embodies the richness of the American vernacular.

Most of his books contain mixed offerings of stories, essays, fables, and cartoons. Among them are *Fables for Our Time* (1940), *My World—and Welcome to It* (1942), *The Thurber Carnival* (1945), and *Thurber Country* (1953).

Story Summary:

The story simply asks such a question, "What would happen if a hero turned out to be a 'crumb'?"

It is 1937—Admiral Byrd has flown over the North and South Poles. Lucky Lindbergh has flown solo from New York to Paris. But what if our next aviation hero turns out to be a slob, author James Thurber wonders. Enter Pal Smurch, a foul-mouthed, gin-guzzling mechanic who becomes the first man to fly solo around the world. Here is a hero in a new mold who the press and even the President try to make into the Byrd-Lindbergh model. It doesn't work. Smurch scratches himself and bellows, "When do the parties start? Where's the broad? Where's the dough?" Smurch has to go. He simply can't be allowed to besmirch his officially created public image.

Chapter 7 The Greatest Man in the World

We should learn from the tragic death of Jack, who is unworthy of the title, and the natural-born hooligan won't be allowed to affect the public image of the national hero.

Key Terms:

Truth: It is the responsibility of the media to reveal the truth to the public. Yet, the media sometimes cover the truth and make up the report instead.

Politics and the Media: In most cases, politics will guide the media, while the media serve politics, even sacrificing the truth of report.

Image: The image of the national hero, the greatest man in the world, is officially created. It couldn't be affected by a natural-born hooligan.

Satire: Jack is unworthy of the title hero, and he simply cannot live in this world. This is a satire against the media, the politics and the authorities.

Hero: Both heroic deed and heroic character are indispensable to make a hero, and it is the insufficiency of character that finally leads to Jack's tragic ending.

The Greatest Man in the World[1]

Looking back on it now, from the vantage point of 1950, one can only marvel that it hadn't happened long before it did. The United States of America had been, ever since Kitty Hawk[2], blindly constructing the elaborate petard[3] by which, sooner or later, it must be hoist. It was inevitable that some day there would come roaring

---

[1] First published in *The Middle-Aged Man on the Flying Trapeze* (1931).
[2] The site of the first sustained airplane flights, in 1903 by Orville and Wilbur Wright.
[3] A case containing explosives to break down a door, gate, or wall. Thurber alludes to the expression "Hoist with one's own petard," which means to get caught in one's own trap.

out of the skies a national hero of insufficient intelligence, background, and character successfully to endure the mounting orgies of glory prepared for aviators who stayed up a long time or flew a great distance. Both Lindbergh[1] and Byrd[2], fortunately for national decorum and international amity, had been gentlemen; so had our other famous aviators. They wore their laurels[3] gracefully, withstood the awful weather of publicity[4], married excellent women, usually of fine family, and quietly retired to private life and the enjoyment of their varying fortunes. No untoward incidents, on a world-wide scale, marred the perfection of their conductor on the perilous heights of fame. The exception to the rule was, however, bound to occur and it did, in July, 1937, when Jack ("Pal") Smurch, erstwhile mechanic's helper in a small garage in Westfield, Iowa, flew a second-hand, single-motored Bresthaven Dragon-Fly III monoplane[5] all the way around the world, without stopping.

Never before in the history of aviation had such a flight as Smurch's ever been dreamed of. No one had even taken seriously the weird floating auxiliary gas tanks, invention of the mad New Hampshire professor of astronomy, Dr. Charles Lewis Gresham, upon which Smurch placed full reliance. When the garage worker, a slightly built, surly, unprepossessing young man of twenty-two, appeared at Roosevelt Field[6] in early July, 1937, slowly chewing a great quid of scrap tobacco, and announced, "Nobody ain't seen no flyin' yet," the newspapers touched briefly and satirically upon his projected twenty-five-thousand-mile flight. Aeronautical and automotive experts

---

[1] American aviator Charles Augustus Lindbergh (1902—1974) made the first solo, nonstop transatlantic flight in 1927.

[2] American explorers Richard Evelyn Byrd (1888—1957) and Floyd Bennett were the first men to fly over the North Pole in 1926.

[3] A wreath of laurel foliage worn on the head as an emblem of victory.

[4] Information or actions that are intended to attract the public's attention.

[5] An aeroplane with only one pair of wings.

[6] The starting point for Charles Augustus Lindbergh's 1927 transatlantic flight.

Chapter 7 The Greatest Man in the World

dismissed the idea curtly, implying that it was a hoax, a publicity stunt. The rusty, battered, second-hand plane wouldn't go. The Gresham auxiliary tanks wouldn't work. It was simply a cheap joke.

　　Smurch, however, after calling on a girl in Brooklyn who worked in the flap-folding department of a large paper-box factory, a girl whom he later described as his "sweet patootie①," climbed nonchalantly into his ridiculous plane at dawn of the memorable seventh of July, 1937, spit a curve of tobacco juice into the still air, and took off, carrying with him only a gallon of bootleg② gin and six pounds of salami③.

　　When the garage boy thundered out over the ocean the papers were forced to record, in all seriousness, that a mad, unknown young man—his name was variously misspelled—had actually set out upon a preposterous attempt to span the world in a rickety, one-engined contraption, trusting to the long-distance refueling device of a crazy schoolmaster. When, nine days later, without having stopped once, the tiny plane appeared above San Francisco Bay, headed for New York, spluttering and choking, to be sure, but still magnificently and miraculously aloft, the headlines, which long since had crowded everything else off the front page—even the shooting of the Governor of Illinois by the Vileti gang—swelled to unprecedented size, and the news stories began to run to twenty-five and thirty columns. It was noticeable, however, that the accounts of the epoch-making flight touched rather lightly upon the aviator himself. This was not because facts about the hero as a man were too meager, but because they were too complete.

　　Reporters, who had been rushed out to Iowa when Smurch's plane was first sighted over the little French coast town of Serly-le-Mer, to dig up the story of the

---

① Slang for sweet heart, possibly coming from sweet potato.
② Produced, sold, or transported illegally.
③ A type of strong-flavored sausage, usually thinly sliced and eaten cold.

great man's life, had promptly discovered that the story of his life could not be printed. His mother, a sullen short-order cook in a shack restaurant on the edge of a tourists' camping ground near Westfield, met all inquiries as to her son with an angry "Ah, the hell with him; I hope he drowns." His father appeared to be in jail somewhere for stealing spotlights and lap robes from tourists' automobiles; his young brother, a weak-minded lad, had but recently escaped from the Preston, Iowa, Reformatory[①] and was already wanted in several Western towns for the theft of money-order blanks from post offices. These alarming discoveries were still piling up at the very time that Pal Smurch, the greatest hero of the twentieth century, blear-eyed, dead for sleep, half-starved, was piloting his crazy junk-heap high above the region in which the lamentable story of his private life was being unearthed, headed for New York and a greater glory than any man of his time had ever known.

The necessity for printing some account in the papers of the young man's career and personality had led to a remarkable predicament[②]. It was of course impossible to reveal the facts, for a tremendous popular feeling in favor of the young hero had sprung up, like a grass fire, when he was halfway across Europe on his flight around the globe. He was, therefore, described as a modest chap, taciturn, blond, popular with his friends, popular with girls. The only available snapshot[③] of Smurch, taken at the wheels of a phony automobile in a cheap photo studio at an amusement park, was touched up so that the little vulgarian looked quite handsome. His twisted leer[④] was smoothed into a pleasant smile. The truth was, in this way, kept from the youth's ecstatic compatriots; they did not dream that the Smurch family was despised and feared by its neighbors in the obscure Iowa town, nor that the hero himself, because of numerous unsavory

---

① A penal institution for the discipline, reformation, and training of young or first offenders.
② Embarrassment.
③ A photograph that is taken quickly and casually.
④ A desirous, sly, or knowing look.

Chapter 7 The Greatest Man in the World

exploits, had come to be regarded in Westfield as a nuisance and a menace. He had, the reporters discovered, once knifed the principal of his high school—not mortally, to be sure, but he had knifed him; and on another occasion, surprised in the act of stealing an altar-cloth① from a church, he had bashed the sacristan② over the head with a pot of Easter lilies; for each of these offences he had served a sentence in the reformatory.

Inwardly, the authorities, both in New York and in Washington, prayed that an understanding Providence might, however awful such a thing seemed, bring disaster to the rusty, battered plane and its illustrious pilot, whose unheard-of flight had aroused the civilized world to hosannas③ of hysterical praise. The authorities were convinced that the character of the renowned aviator was such that the limelight of adulation was bound to reveal him to all the world as a congenital hooligan④ mentally and morally unequipped to cope with his own prodigious fame. "I trust," said the Secretary of State, at one of many secret Cabinet meetings called to consider the national dilemma, "I trust that his mother's prayer will be answered," by which he referred to Mrs. Emma Smurch's wish that her son might be drowned. It was, however, too late for that—Smurch had leaped the Atlantic and then the Pacific as if they were millponds. At three minutes after two o'clock on the afternoon of July 17, 1937, the garage boy brought his idiotic plane into Roosevelt Field for a perfect three-point landing.

It had, of course, been out of the question to arrange a modest little reception for the greatest flier in the history of the world. He was received at Roosevelt Field with such elaborate and pretentious ceremonies as rocked the world. Fortunately, however,

---

① The cloth used for covering an altar, often applied to the frontal.
② Person in charge of the ceremonial equipment in a church.
③ A shout of fervent and worshipful praise, often used to express praise or adoration to God.
④ A cruel and brutal fellow who behaves in a noisy and violent way in a public place.

the worn and spent hero promptly swooned①, had to be removed bodily from his plane, and was spirited from the field without having opened his mouth once. Thus he did not jeopardize the dignity of this first reception, a reception illumined by the presence of the Secretaries of War and the Navy, Mayor Michael J. Moriarity of New York, the Premier of Canada, governors Fanniman, Groves, McFeely, and Critchfield, and a brilliant array of European diplomats. Smurch did not, in fact, come to in time to take part in the gigantic hullabaloo arranged at City Hall for the next day. He was rushed to a secluded nursing home and confined to bed. It was nine days before he was able to get up, or to be more exact, before he was permitted to get up. Meanwhile the greatest minds in the country, in solemn assembly, had arranged a secret conference of city, state, and government officials, which Smurch was to attend for the purpose of being instructed in the ethics and behavior of heroism.

On the day that the little mechanic was finally allowed to get up and dress and, for the first time in two weeks, took a great chew of tobacco, he was permitted to receive the newspapermen—this by way of testing him out. Smurch did not wait for questions. "Youse guys," he said—and the *Times*② man winced—"youse guys can tell the cock-eyed world dat I put it over on Lindbergh, see? Yeh—an' made an ass o' them two frogs." The "two frogs" was a reference to a pair of gallant French fliers who, in attempting a flight only halfway round the world, had, two weeks before, unhappily been lost at sea. The *Times* man was bold enough, at this point to sketch out for Smurch the accepted formula for interviews in cases of this kind; he explained that there should be no arrogant statements belittling the achievements of other heroes, particularly heroes of foreign nations. "Ah, the hell with that," said Smurch. "I did it, see? I did it, an' I'm talkin' about it." And he did talk about it.

None of this extraordinary interview was, of course, printed. On the contrary, the

---

① Fainted.
② *New York Times*.

Chapter 7 The Greatest Man in the World

newspapers, already under the disciplined direction of a secret directorate created for the occasion and composed of statesmen and editors, gave out to a panting and restless world that "Jacky," as he had been arbitrarily nicknamed, would consent to say only that he was very happy and that anyone could have done what he did. "My achievement has been, I fear, slightly exaggerated," the *Times* man's article had him protest, with a modest smile. These newspaper stories were kept from the hero, a restriction which did not serve to abate the rising malevolence of his temper. The situation was, indeed, extremely grave, for Pal Smurch was, as he kept insisting, "rarin' to go." He could not much longer be kept from a nation clamorous to lionize him. It was the most desperate crisis the United States of America had faced since the sinking of the *Lusitania*①.

On the afternoon of the twenty-seventh of July, Smurch was spirited away to a conference-room in which were gathered mayors, governors, government officials, behaviorist psychologists, and editors. He gave them each a limp, moist paw and a brief unlovely grin. "Hah ya?" he said. When Smurch was seated, the Mayor of New York arose and, with obvious pessimism, attempted to explain what he must say and how he must act when presented to the world, ending his talk with a high tribute② to the hero's courage and integrity. The Mayor was followed by Governor Fanniman of New York, who after a touching declaration of faith, introduced Cameron Spottiswood, Second Secretary of the American Embassy③ in Paris, the gentleman selected to coach Smurch in the amenities④ of public ceremonies. Sitting in a chair, with a soiled yellow tie in his hand and his shirt open at the throat, unshaved, smoking a rolled cigarette, Jack Smurch listened with a leer on his lips. "I get ya, I get ya," he cut in, nastily. "Ya want

---

① British luxury liner that was bombed by a German submarine on May 7, 1915. Of the 1,195 people who died, 128 were Americans.
② Something that you say, do, or make to show your admiration and respect for someone.
③ The diplomatic rank in the system of professional and social status used in the world of diplomacy and international relations.
④ Social courtesies; pleasantries.

me to ack like a softy, huh? Ya want me to ack like that—baby-faced Lindbergh, huh? Well, nuts to that, see?" Everyone took in his breath sharply; it was a sigh and a hiss. "Mr. Lindbergh," began a United States Senator, purple with rage, "and Mr. Byrd—" Smurch, who was paring his nails with a jackknife, cut in again. "Byrd!" he exclaimed. "Aw fa God's sake, dat big—" Somebody shut off his blasphemies① with a sharp word. A newcomer had entered the room. Everyone stood up, except Smurch, who, still busy with his nails, did not even glance up. "Mr. Smurch," said someone sternly, "the President of the United States!" It had been thought that the presence of the Chief Executive might have a chastening② effect upon the young hero, and the former had been, thanks to the remarkable cooperation of the press, secretly brought to the obscure conference-room.

A great, painful silence fell. Smurch looked up, waved a hand at the President. "How ya comin'?" he asked, and began rolling a fresh cigarette. The silence deepened. Someone coughed in a strained way. "Geez, it's hot, ain't it?" said Smurch. He loosened two more shirt buttons, revealing a hairy chest and the tattooed word "Sadie" enclosed in a stenciled heart. The great and important men in the room, faced by the most serious crisis in recent American history, exchanged worried frowns. Nobody seemed to know how to proceed. "Come awn, come awn," said Smurch. "Let's get the hell out here! When do I start cuttin' in on de parties, huh? And what's they goin' to be *in* it?" he rubbed a thumb and forefinger together meaningly. "Money!" exclaimed a state senator, shocked, pale. "Yeh, money," said Pal, flipping③ his cigarette out of a window. "An' big money." He began rolling a fresh cigarette. "Big money," he repeated, frowning over the rice paper. He tilted back in his chair, and leered at each gentleman, separately, the leer of an animal that knows its power, the leer of a leopard loose in a bird-and-

---

① Blasphemous language (expressing disrespect for God or for something sacred).
② A chastening experience makes you regret that you have behaved badly or stupidly.
③ To throw or toss with a light motion.

Chapter 7　The Greatest Man in the World

god shop. "Aw fa God's sake, let's get some place where it's cooler," he said. "I have cooped up plenty for three weeks!"

Smurch stood up and walked over to an open window, where he stood staring down into the street, nine floors below. The faint shouting of newsboys floated up to him. He made out his name. "Hot dog!" he cried, grinning, ecstatic. He leaned out over the sill. "You tell 'em, babies!" he shouted down. "Hot diggity dog!" In the tense little knot of men standing behind him, a quick, mad impulse flared up. An unspoken word of appeal, of command, seemed to ring through the room. Yet it was deadly silent. Charles K. L. Brand, secretary to the Mayor of New York City, happened to be standing nearest Smurch; he looked inquiringly at the President of the United States. The President, pale, grim, nodded shortly. Brand, a tall, powerfully built man, once a tackle[①] at Rutgers[②], stepped forward, seized the greatest man in the world by his left shoulder and the seat of his pants, and pushed him out the window.

"My God, he's fallen out the window!" cried a quick-witted editor.

"Get me out of here!" cried the President. Several men sprang to his side and he was hurriedly escorted out of a door toward a side-entrance of the building. The editor of the Associated Press[③] took charge, being used to such things. Crisply he ordered certain men to leave, others to stay; quickly he outlined a story which all the papers were to agree on, sent two men to the street to handle that end of the tragedy, commanded a Senator[④] to sob and two Congressmen[⑤] to go to pieces nervously. In a word, he skillfully set the stage for the gigantic task that was to follow, the task of breaking to a grief-stricken world the sad story of the untimely, accidental death of its

---

① Either of the two line players on a team positioned between the guard and the end.
② Rutgers University is a public research university with campuses in New Brunswick, Newark, and Camden, New Jersey.
③ The national news agency of America.
④ A member of a political Senate, for example, in the United States or Australia.
⑤ A male member of the U.S. Congress, especially of the House of Representatives.

most illustrious and spectacular figure.

The funeral was, as you know, the most elaborate, the finest, the solemnest, and the saddest ever held in the United States of America. The monument in Arlington Cemetery[①], with its clean white shaft of marble and the simple device of a tiny plane carved on its base, is a place for pilgrims, in deep reverence, to visit. The nations of the world paid lofty tributes to little Jacky Smurch, America's greatest hero. At a given hour there were two minutes of silence throughout the nation. Even the inhabitants of the small, bewildered town of Westfield, Iowa, observed this touching ceremony; agents of the Department of Justice[②] saw to that. One of them was especially assigned to stand grimly in the doorway of a little shack restaurant on the edge of the tourists' camping ground just outside the town. There, under his stern scrutiny[③], Mrs. Emma Smurch bowed her head above two hamburger steaks sizzling on her grill—bowed her head and turned away, so that the Secret Service man could not see the twisted, strangely familiar, leer on her lips.

Film Comment:

James Thurber's *The Greatest Man in the World*: 51 minutes, color

Starring: Brad Davis & Carol Kane

Screenplay by: Jeff Wanshel

Directed by: Ralph Rosenblum

---

① Located in northern Virginia across the Potomac River from Washington, D.C.; it is the place where American war dead and other notables, including William Howard Taft and John F. Kennedy, are buried.

② The United States federal department responsible for enforcing federal laws (including the enforcement of all civil rights legislation); created in 1870.

③ The act of examining something closely (as for mistakes).

Chapter 7   The Greatest Man in the World

Only the off-beat humor of writing great, James Thurber could bring to life a "hero" like Jack Smurch, played by Brad Davis ("Midnight Express"). Fortified with only a gallon of gin and a salami, Smurch bests even Lindberg with the first non-stop, around the world flight. During the four days he's airborne, this unknown kid becomes a world hero.

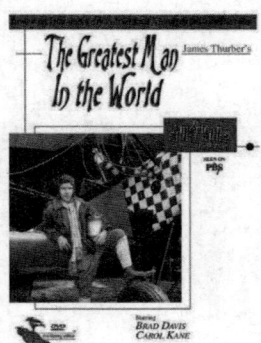

But, on the ground a young reporter, anxious to tell the world about their new idol, learns Smurch is bad news. An arrogant, illiterate lout with a police record, Smurch's only interests are "parties, broads and dough." But, the reporter is silenced and Smurch is locked up until the press and politicos can make him into their kind of American hero at any cost.

Film Scenes:

Scene 1: the flight

When Jack starts his non-stop twenty-five-thousand-mile flight, the newspapers touch it briefly and satirically, calling it simply a cheap joke.

Scene 2: Jack's life

The two journalists come to interview Jack's mother, father, principal and sweet patootie, illustrating Jack's life for the news report.

Scene 3: the lies

The reporters discover that the story of Jack's life could not be printed. They have to tell the lies and make up the story to keep the truth from the public.

Scene 4: the cover up

Coming back from the glorious flight, Jack is hidden within a secluded nursing house, under the cover up, for he is not ready to cope with his own prodigious fame.

Scene 5: the assassination

Jack Smurch refuses to be coached, and desires to be remembered, heading to his death directly and ending in the tragic assassination.

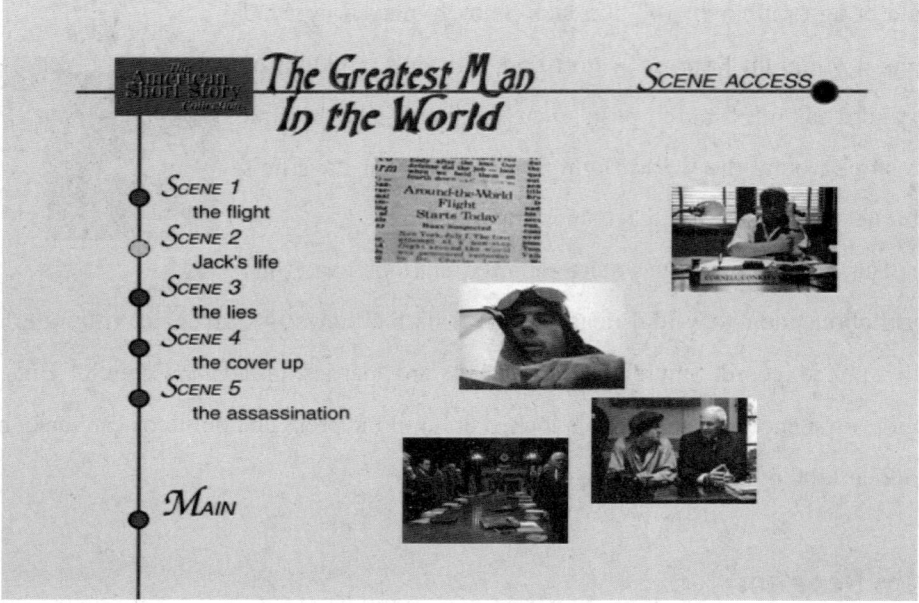

Film Clip:

The Assassination

The guards escort Jack Smurch walking into the conference room. The Secretary of the State introduces to Jack the officials and diplomats there, but he behaves very rudely before these important people. The Secretary of the State further explains the following arrangement for Jack, what he must say and how he must act when presented to the world, but he shows much disdain towards that.

Jack refuses to be coached, "acting like a softy," and he goes further to despise the character of Lindbergh and Byrd. He simply rejects any learning about the rituals of public ceremonies. Before the authorities, Jack feels no pressure at all and behaves as usual, "raring to go." He boasts that he has escaped once, and he could escape again. This makes sense, for the Secretary of the State adds that he has escaped from the

Chapter 7   The Greatest Man in the World

reformatory school for six times. This is supposedly the last straw on the camel.

Jack Smurch just bellows out for parties, girls, and money, a big money. The President of the United States also secretly comes to the conference room and intends to chasten upon the young hero. Everyone stands up, but Smurch, still busy with his nail, does not even glance up, showing no appropriate respect at all to the Chief Executive. When reminded the arrival of the President, Jack just sits down in a chair and raises his finger, "How ya comin'?"

Smurch stands up and walks over to an open window, staring down into the street and making out his name. Jack cries, grinning, ecstatic, and he leans out over the sill, shouting down to the news boy. In the tense little knot of men standing behind him, a quick, mad impulse flares up. An unspoken word of appeal, of command, seems to ring through the room. The President, pale, grim, flips his cigarette shortly. The Secretary of the State receives the order and nods his head. Brand, a tall, powerfully built man, steps forward, seizes the greatest man in the world by his left shoulder and the seat of his pants, and pushes him out of the window.

Jack Smurch simply cannot live in this world, and he can't be allowed to besmirch his officially created public image. The authorities could silence Jack Smurch at any cost. As a national hero of insufficient intelligence, background, and character, Jack refuses to be coached, and desires to be remembered, heading to his death directly. It is the insufficiency of his character and the cruelty of the authorities that lead to Jack's tragic ending.

Discussion Questions:

Story Discussion

(1) What makes Pal Smurch a national hero, the greatest man in the world?

(2) What are the differences between Smurch and the other flying heroes, such as Byrd and Lindbergh?

(3) How is Smurch's story different from the reports of newspapers? What are the relations between media and politics?

(4) Why cannot Smurch live in this world? What can we learn from his death?

(5) What do you think of Mrs. Smurch? Did she finally realize something about her son's death?

Film Appreciation

(1) What's the contrast of the two reporters? Who is always trying to reveal the truth?

(2) Who do the two reporters interview? What's special about the interview of Jack's father?

(3) How does the newspaper make up the story of Jack's life?

(4) What's Jack doing in the secluded nursing home?

(5) How does the authorities try out Jack? Does Jack pass the trial?

(6) How does Jack escape from the secluded nursing home? Why is he found so soon?

(7) How does Jack get assassinated?

(8) What's the reaction of everybody on the funeral of Jack?

(9) What's the function of film language and adapted scenes?

Further Reading and Watching:

The Secret Life of Walter Mitty

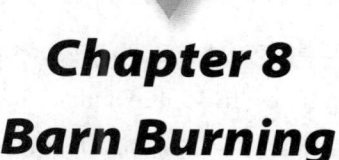

Chapter 8
Barn Burning

William Faulkner

Author Introduction:

William Faulkner (1897—1962) was born in New Albany, but soon moved to Oxford, Mississippi. He attended the University of Mississippi in Oxford before and after his service in the Royal Canadian Air Force in the First World War.

Thereafter he lived in Oxford most of his life, though he had to write Hollywood scripts and teach at the University of Virginia to support himself. It was in New Orleans that his literary career began, and there he became acquainted with various members of the literary community, most notably Sherwood Anderson, who encouraged him to turn from poetry to fiction and helped him get his first novel published.

Beginning with *Sartoris* (1929), most of his novels and short stories were set in the fictional Yoknapatawpha County, which was based on, and nearly geographically identical to, Lafayette County, of which his hometown Oxford is the county seat. Faulkner states in *Lion in the Garden*: "Beginning with *Sartoris* I discovered that my own little postage stamp of native soil was worth writing about and that I would never live long enough to exhaust it, and by sublimating the actual into apocryphal I would have complete liberty to use whatever talent I might have to its absolute top."

Faulkner traced the fortunes of several families in this fictional county, including the aristocratic Compsons and Sartorises and the white-trash, dollar-grabbing Snopeses, from the civil war to modern times. In 1938, Faulkner began writing "Barn Burning," which would be published in *Harper's Magazine* the following year. But Faulkner was not finished with the story. He had in mind a trilogy about the Snopes family, a lower-class rural laboring white family, who had little regard for southern tradition, heritage, or lineage. The Snopes, often regarded as Faulkner's metaphor for the rising "redneck" middle class in the South, more interested in avaricious commercial gain than honor or pride, were to be led in the trilogy by the enterprising Flem Snopes, who had appeared only briefly as the eldest son of Abner Snopes.

Faulkner made frequent use of "stream of consciousness" in his writing, the literary technique that records the multifarious thoughts and feelings of a character without regard to logical argument or narrative sequence. The writer attempts by the stream of consciousness to reflect all the forces, external and internal, influencing the psychology of a character at a single moment. Faulkner's influence on the fellow Southern writers has been profound, and in 1950 he was awarded the Nobel Prize for literature.

His major novels include *The Sound and the Fury* (1929), *As I Lay Dying* (1930), *Sanctuary* (1931), *Light in August* (1932), *Absalom, Absalom!* (1936), *Wild Palms* (1936), and *The Hamlet* (1940). His books of short stories include *These Thirteen* (1931), *Go Down, Moses* (1942), and the *Collected Stories of William Faulkner* (1950).

Story Summary:

The story mainly concerns about the conflict between loyalty to one's family and loyalty to honor and justice.

Chapter 8 Barn Burning

Abner Snopes, a proud, poor Southern tenant farmer in the late 19th century believes his employer has treated him unfairly. Abner will get revenge by burning his employer's barn. Abner's son, Sarty, wants his father's acceptance and love, but is horrified by the fire. Abner senses this and lectures his son on loyalty and the value of taking justice into your own hands. The burning can't be pinned on Snopes, but he and his family are told to move on. In a new job with a rich Major de Spain, Snopes once again is offended. So he tracks dirt on his employer's rug. The Major demands $100 compensation. Sarty sees the fire beginning to rage in his father's cold eyes. Sarty agonizes. He hesitates. Then he warns the Major to look after his barn and thus betrays his father.

We should learn from the dilemma of young Sarty, who is torn between the loyalty to blood and to justice, and initiates into manhood through the betrayal against his father.

Key Terms:

Authority: For the little young boy Sarty, almost everybody around him, including his father, the Justice of Peace and the landlord, is the authority, superior to him.

Revenge: For the proud father Abner, he believes that his employer has treated him unfairly, so he will get revenge by burning the barn of his employer.

Betrayal: Sarty wants his father's acceptance and love, but dislikes his father's barn burning. He warns the Major to look after his barn and thus betrays his father.

Loyalty: Sarty is torn between the loyalty to one's family and blood and loyalty to honor and justice, gradually initiating into manhood.

Obligation: As a tenant farmer, the Snopes family have an obligation to work for the landlord, fulfilling the contract they have signed.

Sharecropper: Sharecropper refers to tenant farmers. They rent the farming land, plant crops, raise stock, and pay to the landlord at gathering time.

Post Civil War South: The Snopes, more interested in avaricious commercial gain than honor or pride, are rising and developing into the redneck middle class in Post Civil War South.

Barn Burning[①]

The store in which the justice of the Peace's court[②] was sitting smelled of cheese. The boy, crouched on his nail keg[③] at the back of the crowded room, knew he smelled cheese, and more: from where he sat he could see the ranked shelves close-packed with the solid, squat, dynamic shapes of tin cans whose labels his stomach read, not from the lettering which meant nothing to his mind but from the scarlet devils and the silver curve of fish—this, the cheese which he knew he smelled and the hermetic meat[④] which his intestines believed he smelled coming in intermittent gusts momentary and brief between the other constant one, the smell and sense just a little of fear because mostly of despair and grief, the old fierce pull of blood. He could not see the table where the Justice sat and before which his father and his father's enemy (*our enemy* he thought in that despair; *ourn! mine and hisn both! He's my father!*) stood, but he could hear them, the two of them that is, because his father had said no word yet:

"But what proof have you, Mr. Harris?"

"I told you. The hog[⑤] got into my corn. I caught it up and sent it back to him. He

---

① First published in *Harper's Magazine* in 1939, later collected in Faulkner's *Collected Stories* (1950), and then reprinted in the *Selected Short Stories of William Faulkner* (1961).
② A local magistrate with limited powers.
③ A small barrel used for storing something such as beer or other alcoholic drinks.
④ Canned meat; *completely sealed, completely airtight.*
⑤ Pig.

Chapter 8　Barn Burning

had no fence that would hold it. I told him so, warned him. The next time I put the hog in my pen①. When he came to get it I gave him enough wire to patch up his pen. The next time I put the hog up and kept it. I rode down to his house and saw the wire I gave him still rolled on to the spool in his yard. I told him he could have the hog when he paid me a dollar pound fee. That evening a nigger came with the dollar and got the hog. He was a strange nigger. He said, 'He say to tell you wood and hay kin burn.' I said, 'What?' 'That whut he say to tell you,' the nigger said. 'Wood and hay kin burn.' That night my barn burned. I got the stock out but I lost the barn."

"Where is the nigger? Have you got him?"

"He was a strange nigger, I tell you. I don't know what became of him."

"But that's not proof. Don't you see that's not proof?"

"Get that boy up here. He knows." For a moment the boy thought too that the man meant his older brother until Harris said, "Not him. The little one. The boy." and, crouching, small for his age, small and wiry like his father, in patched and faded jeans even too small for him, with straight, uncombed, brown hair and eyes gray and wild as storm scud, he saw the men between himself and the table part and become a lane② of grim faces, at the end of which he saw the justice, a shabby, collarless, graying man in spectacles, beckoning him, he felt no floor under his bare feet; he seemed to walk beneath the palpable weight of the grim turning faces. His father, stiff in his black Sunday coat donned③ not for the trial but for the moving, did not even look at him. *He aims for me to lie*, he thought, again with that frantic grief and despair. *And I will have to do hit.*

"What's your name, boy?" the Justice said.

---

① A fenced enclosure for animals.
② A narrow road, especially in the country.
③ To put on, dress.

"Colonel Sartoris Snopes[①]," the boy whispered.

"Hey?" the Justice said. "Talk louder. Colonel Sartoris? I reckon anybody named for Colonel Sartoris in this country can't help but tell the truth, can they?" The boy said nothing. *Enemy! Enemy!* he thought; for a moment he could not even see, could not see that the justice's face was kindly nor discern that his voice was troubled when he spoke to the man named Harris: "Do you want me to question this boy?" But he could hear, and during those subsequent long seconds while there was absolutely no sound in the crowded little room save that of quiet and intent breathing it was as if he had swung outward at the end of a grape vine, over a ravine, and at the top of the swing had been caught in a prolonged instant of mesmerized gravity, weightless in time.

"No!" Harris said violently, explosively. "Damnation! Send him out of here!" Now time, the fluid world, rushed beneath him again, the voices coming to him again through the smell of cheese and sealed meat, the fear and despair and the old grief of blood:

"This case is closed. I can't find against you, Snopes, but I can give you advice. Leave this county and don't come back to it."

His father spoke for the first time, his voice cold and harsh, level, without emphasis: "I aim to. I don't figure to stay in a country among people who ..." he said something unprintable and vile, addressed to no one.

"That'll do," the justice said. "Take your wagon and get out of this county before dark. Case dismissed."

His father turned, and he followed the stiff black coat, the wiry figure walking a little stiffly from where a Confederate provost's man's[②] musket[③] ball had taken him

---

① The Snopes family figures in many Faulkner stories and novels; Colonel Sartoris is a major personage among Faulkner's fictional inhabitants of Yoknapatawpha County.
② Military policeman.
③ An early type of gun with a long barrel, which was used before rifles were invented.

Chapter 8 Barn Burning

in the heel on a stolen horse thirty years ago, followed the two backs now, since his older brother had appeared from somewhere in the crowd, no taller than the father but thicker, chewing tobacco steadily, between the two lines of grim-faced men and out of the store and across the worn gallery and down the sagging① steps and among the dogs and half-grown boys in the mild May dust, where as he passed a voice hissed:

"Barn burner!"

Again he could not see, whirling; there was a face in a red haze, moonlike, bigger than the full moon, the owner of it half again his size, he leaping in the red haze toward the face, feeling no blow, feeling no shock when his head struck the earth, scrabbling up and leaping again, feeling no blow this time either and tasting no blood, scrabbling up to see the other boy in full flight and himself already leaping into pursuit as his father's hand jerked him back, the harsh, cold voice speaking above him: "Go get in the wagon."

It stood in a grove of locusts and mulberries across the road. His two hulking sisters in their Sunday dresses and his mother and her sister in calico and sunbonnets were already in it, sitting on and among the sorry residue② of the dozen and more movings which even the boy could remember—the battered stove, the broken beds and chairs, the clock inlaid with mother-of-pearl③, which would not run, stopped at some fourteen minutes past two o'clock of a dead and forgotten day and time, which had been his mother's dowry. She was crying, though when she saw him she drew her sleeve across her face and began to descend from the wagon. "Get back," the father said.

"He's hurt. I got to get some water and wash his …"

"Get back in the wagon," his father said, he got in too, over the tail-gate. His father

---

① Hanging down (as from exhaustion or weakness).
② The remainder of estate.
③ The shiny layer on the inside of some shells, used to make buttons or to decorate things.

mounted to the seat where the older brother already sat and struck the gaunt mules two savage blows with the peeled willow, but without heat. It was not even sadistic; it was exactly that same quality which in later years would cause his descendants to overrun the engine before putting a motor car into motion, striking and reining back in the same movement. The wagon went on, the store with its quiet crowd of grimly watching men dropped behind; a curve in the road hid it. *Forever* he thought. *Maybe he's done satisfied now, now that he has* ... stopping himself, not to say it aloud even to himself. His mother's hand touched his shoulder.

"Does hit hurt?" she said.

"Naw," he said. "Hit don't hurt. Lemme be."

"Can't you wipe some of the blood off before hit dries?"

"I'll wash to-night," he said. "Lemme be, I tell you."

The wagon went on. He did not know where they were going. None of them ever did or ever asked, because it was always somewhere, always a house of sorts waiting for them a day or two days or even three days away. Likely, his father had already arranged to make a crop on another farm before he ... Again he had to stop himself. He (the father) always did. There was something about his wolflike independence and even courage, when the advantage was at least neutral, which impressed strangers, as if they got from his latent ravening[①] ferocity not so much a sense of dependability as a feeling that his ferocious conviction in the rightness of his own actions would be of advantage to all whose interest lay with his.

That night they camped, in a grove of oaks and beeches where a spring ran. The nights were still cool and they had a fire against it, of a rail lifted from a nearby fence and cut into lengths—a small fire, neat, niggard[②] almost, a shrewd fire; such fires were his father's habit and custom always, even in freezing weather. Older, the boy

---

① Greedily predacious; voracious or rapacious.
② Thrifty.

might have remarked this and wondered why not a big one; why should not a man who had not only seen the waste and extravagance[①] of war, but who had in his blood an inherent voracious prodigality[②] with material not his own, have burned everything in sight? Then he might have gone a step farther and thought that that was the reason: that niggard blaze was the living fruit of nights passed during those four years in the woods hiding from all men, blue or gray[③], with his strings of horses (captured horses, he called them). And older still, he might have divined the true reason: that the element of fire spoke to some deep mainspring of his father's being, as the element of steel or of powder spoke to other men, as the one weapon for the preservation of integrity, else breath were not worth the breathing, and hence to be regarded with respect and used with discretion[④].

But, he did not think this now and he had seen those same niggard blazes all his life. He merely ate his supper beside it and was already half asleep over his iron plate when his father called him, and once more he followed the stiff back, the stiff and ruthless limp, up the slope and on to the starlit road where, turning, he could see his father against the stars but without face or depth—a shape black, flat, and bloodless as though cut from tin in the iron folds of the frockcoat which had not been made for him, the voice harsh like tin and without heat like tin:

"You were fixing to tell them. You would have told him." He didn't answer. His father struck him with the flat of his hand on the side of the head, hard but without heat, exactly as he had struck the two mules at the store, exactly as he would strike either of them with any stick in order to kill a horse fly, his voice still without heat or anger: "You're getting to be a man. You got to learn. You got to learn to stick to your own

---

① Excessive spending.
② Excessive spending.
③ The color of Union and Confederate Civil War (1861—1865) uniforms, respectively.
④ The trait of judging wisely and objectively.

blood or you ain't going to have any blood to stick to you. Do you think either of them, any man there this morning, would? Don't you know all they wanted was a chance to get at me because they knew I had them beat? Eh?" Later, twenty years later, he was to tell himself, "If I had said they wanted only truth, justice, he would have hit me again." But now he said nothing. He was not crying. He just stood there. "Answer me," his father said.

"Yes," he whispered. His father turned.

"Get on to bed. We'll be there tomorrow."

Tomorrow they were there. In the early afternoon the wagon stopped before a paintless two-room house identical almost with the dozen others it had stopped before even in the boy's ten years, and again, as on the other dozen occasions, his mother and aunt got down and began to unload the wagon, although his two sisters and his father and brother had not moved.

"Likely hit ain't fitten for hawgs," one of the sisters said.

"Nevertheless, fit it will and you'll hog it and like it," his father said. "Get out of them chairs and help your Ma unload."

The two sisters got down, big, bovine, in a flutter of cheap ribbons; one of them drew from the jumbled wagon bed a battered lantern, the other a worn broom. His father handed the reins to the older son and began to climb stiffly over the wheel. "When they get unloaded, take the team to the barn and feed them." Then he said, and at first, the boy thought he was still speaking to his brother: "Come with me."

"Me?" he said.

"Yes," his father said. "You."

"Abner," his mother said. His father paused and looked back—the harsh level state beneath the shaggy, graying, irascible brows.

"I reckon I'll have a word with the man that aims to begin tomorrow owning me body and soul for the next eight months."

Chapter 8 Barn Burning

They went back up the road. A week ago—or before last night, that is—he would have asked where they were going, but not now. His father had struck him before last night but never before had he paused afterward to explain why, it was as if the blow and the following calm, outrageous voice still rang, repercussed, divulging nothing to him save the terrible handicap of being young, the light weight of his few years, just heavy enough to prevent his soaring free of the world as it seemed to be ordered but not heavy enough to keep him footed solid in it, to resist it and try to change the course of its events.

Presently he could see the grove of oaks and cedars and the other flowering trees and shrubs where the house would be, though not the house yet. They walked beside a fence massed with honeysuckle and Cherokee roses① and came to a gate swinging open between two brick pillars, and now, beyond a sweep of drive, he saw the house for the first time and at that instant he forgot his father and the terror and despair both, and even when he remembered his father again (who had not stopped) the terror and despair did not return. Because, for all the twelve movings, they had sojourned② until now in a poor country, a land of small farms and fields and houses, and he had never seen a house like this before. *Hit's big as a courthouse* he thought quietly, with a surge of peace and joy whose reason he could not have thought into words, being too young for that: *They are safe from him. People whose lives are a part of this peace and dignity are beyond his touch, he no more to them than a buzzing wasp*③: *capable of stinging for a little moment but that's all; the spell of this peace and dignity rendering even the barns and stable and cribs which belong to it impervious to the puny flames he might*

---

① A prickly, climbing, evergreen rose, native to China and naturalized in the southeast United States, having showy, white, fragrant flowers.
② To reside temporarily.
③ An insect with wings and yellow and black stripes across its body, which has a painful sting like a bee but does not produce honey.

contrive ... this, the peace and joy, ebbing for an instant as he looked again at the stiff black back, the stiff and implacable[①] limp of the figure which was not dwarfed[②] by the house, for the reason that it had never looked big anywhere and which now, against the serene columned backdrop, had more than ever that impervious quality of something cut ruthlessly from tin, depthless, as though, sidewise to the sun, it would cast no shadow. Watching him, the boy remarked the absolutely undeviating course which his father held and saw the stiff foot come squarely down in a pile of fresh droppings[③] where a horse had stood in the drive and which his father could have avoided by a simple change of stride. But it ebbed only for a moment, though he could not have thought this into words either, walking on in the spell of the house, which he could ever want but without envy, without sorrow, certainly never with that ravening and jealous rage which unknown to him walked in the ironlike black coat before him: *Maybe he will feel it too, Maybe it will even change him now from what maybe he couldn't help but be.*

    They crossed the portico. Now he could hear his father's stiff foot as it came down on the boards with clocklike finality, a sound out of all proportion to the displacement of the body it bore and which was not dwarfed either by the white door before it, as though it had attained to a sort of vicious and ravening minimum not to be dwarfed by anything—the flat, wide, black hat, the formal coat of broadcloth which had once been black but which had now that friction-glazed greenish cast of the bodies of old house flies, the lifted sleeve which was too large, the lifted hand like a curled claw. The door opened so promptly that the boy knew the Negro must have been watching them all the time, an old man with neat grizzled hair, in a linen jacket, who stood barring the door with his body, saying, "Wipe yo foots, white man, fo you come in here, Major ain't

---

①   Having very strong feelings of hostility or disapproval that nobody can change.
②   To make appear small by comparison.
③   The excrement of animals, especially from large animals such as cattle and horses.

Chapter 8 Barn Burning

home nohow."

"Get out of my way, nigger," his father said, without heat too, flinging the door back and the Negro also and entering, his hat still on his head. And now the boy saw the prints of the stiff foot on the doorjamb and saw them appear on the pale rug behind the machinelike deliberation of the foot which seemed to bear (or transmit) twice the weight which the body compassed. The Negro was shouting "Miss Lula! Miss Lula!" somewhere behind them, then the boy, deluged as though by a warm wave by a suave turn of carpeted stair and a pendant glitter of chandeliers① and a mute gleam of gold frames, heard the swift feet and saw her too, a lady—perhaps he had never seen her like before either—in a gray, smooth gown with lace at the throat and an apron tied at the waist and the sleeves turned back, wiping cake or biscuit dough from her hands with a towel as she came up the hall, looking not at his father at all but at the tracks on the blond rug with an expression of incredulous amazement.

"I tried," the Negro cried. "I tole him to …"

"Will you please go away?" she said in a shaking voice. "Major de Spain is not at home. Will you please go away?"

His father had not spoken again. He did not speak again. He did not even look at her. He just stood stiff in the center of the rug, in his hat, the shaggy iron-gray brows twitching slightly above the pebble-colored eyes as he appeared to examine the house with brief deliberation. Then with the same deliberation he turned; the boy watched him pivot② on the good leg and saw the stiff foot drag round the arc of the turning, leaving a final long and fading smear③. His father never looked at it, he never once looked down at the rug. The Negro held the door. It closed behind them, upon the hysteric and

---

① A branched, decorative lighting fixture that holds a number of bulbs or candles and is suspended from a ceiling.
② To balance or turn on a central point.
③ A dirty or oily mark.

indistinguishable woman-wail. His father stopped at the top of the steps and scraped① his boot clean on the edge of it. At the gate he stopped again. He stood for a moment, planted stiffly on the stiff foot, looking back at the house. "Pretty and white, ain't it?" he said. "That's sweat. Nigger sweat. Maybe it ain't white enough yet to suit him. Maybe he wants to mix some white sweat with it."

Two hours later the boy was chopping wood behind the house within which his mother and aunt and the two sisters (the mother and aunt, not the two girls, he knew that; even at this distance and muffled by walls the flat loud voices of the two girls emanated an incorrigible idle inertia) were setting up the stove to prepare a meal, when he heard the hooves and saw the linen-clad man on a fine sorrel② mare, whom he recognized even before he saw the rolled rug in front of the Negro youth following on a fat boy carriage horse—a suffused, angry face vanishing, still at full gallop, beyond the corner of the house where his father and brother were sitting in the two tilted chairs; and a moment later, almost before he could have put the axe down, he heard the hooves again and watched the sorrel mare go back out of the yard, already galloping again. Then his father began to shout one of the sisters' names, who presently emerged backward from the kitchen door dragging the rolled rug along the ground by one end while the other sister walked behind it.

"If you ain't going to tote, go on and set up the wash pot," the first said.

"You, Sarty!" the second shouted. "Set up the wash pot!" His father appeared at the door, framed against that shabbiness, as he had been against that other bland perfection, impervious to either, the mother's anxious face at his shoulder.

"Go on," the father said. "Pick it up." The two sisters stooped③, broad, lethargic④;

---

① To scratch repeatedly.
② A brownish orange to light brown.
③ To bend your body forward and downward.
④ Not having much energy or enthusiasm.

stooping, they presented an incredible expanse of pale cloth and a flutter of tawdry ribbons.

"If I thought enough of a rug to have to git hit all the way from France I wouldn't keep hit where folks coming in would have to tromp on hit," the first said. They raised the rug,

"Abner," the mother said. "Let me do it."

"You go back and git dinner," his father said. "I'll tend to this."

From the woodpile through the rest of the afternoon the boy watched them, the rug spread flat in the dust beside the bubbling wash-pot, the two sisters stooping over it with that profound and lethargic reluctance, while the father stood over them in turn, implacable and grim, driving them though never raising his voice again. He could smell the harsh homemade lye① they were using; he saw his mother come to the door once and look toward them with an expression not anxious now but very like despair; he saw his father turn, and he fell to with the axe and saw from the corner of his eye his father raise from the ground a flattish fragment of field stone and examine it and return to the pot, and this time his mother actually spoke: "Abner. Abner. Please don't. Please, Abner."

Then he was done too. It was dusk; the whippoorwills② had already begun. He could smell coffee from the room where they would presently eat the cold food remaining from the mid-afternoon meal, though when he entered the house he realized they were having coffee again probably because there was a fire on the hearth, before which the rug now lay spread over the backs of the two chairs. The tracks of his father's foot were gone. Where they had been were now long, water-cloudy scoriations

---

① A caustic, unsuitable for cleaning fine fabrics.
② An insect-eating nocturnal North American bird of the goatsucker family, having spotted brown feathers that blend with its woodland habitat.

resembling the sporadic course of a Lilliputian① mowing machine.

It still hung there while they ate the cold food and then went to bed, scattered without order or claim up and down the two rooms, his mother in one bed, where his father would later lie, the older brother in the other, himself, the aunt, and the two sisters on pallets on the floor. But his father was not in bed yet. The last thing the boy remembered was the depthless, harsh silhouette of the hat and coat bending over the rug and it seemed to him that he had not even closed his eyes when the silhouette was standing over him, the fire almost dead behind it, the stiff foot prodding him awake. "Catch up the mule," his father said.

When he returned with the mule his father was standing in the black door, the rolled rug over his shoulder. "Ain't you going to ride?" he said.

"No, Give me your foot."

He bent his knee into his father's hand, the wiry, surprising power flowed smoothly, rising, he rising with it, on to the mule's bare back (they had owned a saddle once; the boy could remember it though not when or where) and with the same effortlessness his father swung the rug up in front of him. Now in the starlight they retraced the afternoon's path, up the dusty road rife with honeysuckle, through the gate and up the black tunnel of the drive to the lightless house, where he sat on the mule and felt the rough warp of the rug drag across his thighs and vanish.

"Don't you want me to help?" he whispered. His father did not answer and now he heard again that stiff foot striking the hollow portico with that wooden and clock like deliberation, that outrageous overstatement of the weight it carried. The rug, hunched, not flung (the boy could tell that even in the darkness) from his father's shoulder struck the angle of wall and floor with a sound unbelievably loud, thunderous, then the foot again, unhurried and enormous; a light came on in the house and the boy sat, tense,

---

① A very small person or being; after the Lilliputians, a people in *Gulliver's Travels* (1726) by Jonathan Swift.

breathing steadily and quietly and just a little fast, though the foot itself did not increase its beat at all, descending the steps now; now the boy could see him.

"Don't you want to ride now?" he whispered. "We kin both ride now," the light within the house altering now, flaring up and sinking. *He's coming down the stairs now*, he thought. He had already ridden the mule up beside the horse block; presently his father was up behind him and he doubled the reins over and slashed the mule across the neck, but before the animal could begin to trot the hard, thin arm came round him, the hard, knotted hand jerking the mule back to a walk.

In the first red rays of the sun they were in the lot, putting plow gear on the mules. This time the sorrel mare was in the lot before he heard it at all, the rider collarless and even bareheaded, trembling, speaking in a shaking voice as the woman in the house had done, his father merely looking up once before stooping again to the hame he was buckling, so that the man on the mare spoke to his stooping back:

"You must realize you have ruined that rug. Wasn't there anybody here, any of your women ..." he ceased, shaking, the boy watching him, the older brother leaning now in the stable door, chewing, blinking slowly and steadily at nothing apparently. "It cost a hundred dollars. But you never had a hundred dollars. You never will. So I'm going to charge you twenty bushels[①] of corn against your crop. I'll add it in your contract and when you come to the commissary[②] you can sign it. That won't keep Mrs. de Spain quiet but maybe it will teach you to wipe your feet off before you enter her house again."

Then he was gone. The boy looked at his father, who still had not spoken or even looked up again, who was now adjusting the logger-head in the hame.

---

① A unit of volume that is used for measuring agricultural produce such as corn or beans, which is equivalent in volume to eight gallons.
② A shop that provides food and equipment in a place such as a military base or a prison.

"Pap," he said. His father looked at him—the inscrutable[①] face, the shaggy brows beneath which the gray eyes glinted coldly. Suddenly the boy went toward him, fast, stopping also, suddenly. "You done the best you could!" he cried. "If he wanted hit done different why didn't he wait and tell you how? He won't git no twenty bushels! He won't git none! We'll gether hit and hide hit! I kin watch …"

"Did you put the cutter back in that straight stock like I told you?"

"No, sir," he said.

"Then go do it."

That was Wednesday. During the rest of that week he worked steadily, at what was within his scope and some which was beyond it, with an industry that did not need to be driven nor even commanded twice; he had this from his mother, with the difference that some at least of what he did he liked to do, such as splitting wood with the half-size axe which his mother and aunt had earned; or saved money somehow, to present him with at Christmas. In company with the two older women (and on one afternoon, even one of the sisters), he built pens for the shoat[②] and the cow which were a part of his father's contract with the landlord, and one afternoon, his father being absent, gone somewhere on one of the mules, he went to the field.

They were running a middle buster[③] now, his brother holding the plow straight while he handled the reins, and walking beside the straining mule, the rich black sod shearing cool and damp against his bare ankles, he thought *Maybe this is the end of it. Maybe even that twenty bushels that seems hard to have to pay for just a rug will be a cheap price for him to stop forever and always from being what he used to be*; thinking, dreaming now, so that his brother had to speak sharply to him to mind the mule: *Maybe he even won't collect the twenty bushels. Maybe it will all add up and balance and*

---

① Hard to predict.
② A young pig just after weaning.
③ A double moldboard plow that throws a ridge of earth both ways.

Chapter 8 Barn Burning

vanish—corn, rug, fire; the terror and grief the being pulled two ways like between two teams of horses—gone, done with for ever and ever.

Then it was Saturday; he looked up from beneath the mule he was harnessing and saw his father in the black coat and hat. "Not that," his father said. "The wagon gear." And then, two hours later, sitting in the wagon bed behind his father and brother on the seat, the wagon accomplished a final curve, and he saw the weathered paintless store with its tattered tobacco- and patent-medicine posters and the tethered wagons and saddle animals below the gallery. He mounted the gnawed steps behind his father and brother, and there again was the lane of quiet, watching faces for the three of them to walk through. He saw the man in spectacles sitting at the plank table and he did not need to be told this was a Justice of the Peace; he sent one glare of fierce, exultant, partisan defiance① at the man in collar and cravat now, whom he had seen but twice before in his life, and that on a galloping horse, who now wore on his face an expression riot of rage but of amazed unbelief which the boy could not have known was at the incredible circumstance of being sued by one of his own tenants, and came and stood against his father and cried at the Justice: "He ain't done it! He ain't burnt ..."

"Go back to the wagon," his father said.

"Burnt?" the Justice said. "Do I understand this rug was burned too?"

"Does anybody here claim it was?" his father said. "Go back to the wagon." But he did not, he merely retreated to the rear of the room, crowded as that other had been, but not to sit down this time, instead, to stand pressing among the motionless bodies, listening to the voices:

"And you claim twenty bushels of corn is too high for the damage you did to the rug?"

"He brought the rug to me and said he wanted the tracks washed out of it. I

---

① Intentionally contemptuous behavior or attitude.

washed the tracks out and took the rug back to him."

"But you didn't carry the rug back to him in the same condition it was in before you made the tracks on it."

His father did not answer, and now for perhaps half a minute there was no sound at all save that of breathing, the faint, steady suspiration of complete and intent listening.

"You decline to answer that, Mr. Snopes?" Again his father did not answer. "I'm going to find against you, Mr. Snopes. I'm going to find that you were responsible for the injury to Major de Spain's rug and hold you liable① for it. But twenty bushels of corn seems a little high for a man in your circumstances to have to pay. Major de Spain claims it cost a hundred dollars. October corn will be worth about fifty cents. I figure that if Major de Spain can stand a ninety-five dollar loss on something he paid cash for, you can stand a five-dollar loss you haven't earned yet. I hold you in damages to Major de Spain to the amount of ten bushels of corn over and above your contract with him, to be paid to him out of your crop at gathering time. Court adjourned②."

It had taken no time hardly, the morning was but half begun. He thought they would return home and perhaps back to the field, since they were late, far behind all other farmers. But instead his father passed on behind the wagon, merely indicating with his hand for the older brother to follow with it, and crossed the road toward the blacksmith shop opposite, pressing on after his father, overtaking him, speaking, whispering up at the harsh, calm face beneath the weathered hat: "He won't git no ten bushels neither. He won't git one. We'll..." until his father glanced for an instant down at him, the face absolutely calm, the grizzled eyebrows tangled above the cold eyes, the voice almost pleasant, almost gentle:

"You think so? Well, we'll wait till October anyway."

The matter of the wagon—the setting of a spoke or two and the tightening of

---

① Legally responsible.
② Ended.

Chapter 8 Barn Burning

the tires—did not take long either, the business of the tires accomplished by driving the wagon into the spring branch behind the shop and letting it stand there, the mules nuzzling into the water from time to time, and the boy on the seat with the idle reins, looking up the slope and through the sooty tunnel of the shed where the slow hammer rang and where his father sat on an upended cypress bolt, easily, either talking or listening, still sitting there when the boy brought the dripping wagon up out of the branch and halted it before the door.

"Take them on to the shade and hitch," his father said. He did so and returned. His father and the smith and a third man squatting on his heels inside the door were talking, about crops and animals; the boy, squatting too in the ammoniac dust and hoof parings and scales of rust, heard his father tell a long and unhurried story out of the time before the birth of the older brother even when he had been a professional horsetrader. And then his father came up beside him where he stood before a tattered last year's circus poster on the other side of the store, gazing rapt and quiet it the scarlet horses, the incredible poisings and convolutions of tulle and tights and painted leers of comedians, and said, "It's time to eat."

But not at home. Squatting beside his brother against the front wall, he watched his father emerge from the store and produce from a paper sack a segment of cheese and divide it carefully and deliberately into three with his pocket knife and produce crackers from the same sack. They all three squatted on the gallery and ate, slowly, without talking; then in the store again, they drank from a tin dipper tepid water smelling of the cedar bucket and of living beech trees. And still they did not go home. It was as a horse lot this time, a tall rail fence upon and along which men stood and sat and out of which one by one horses were led, to be walked and trotted and then cantered back and forth along the road while the slow swapping and buying went on and the sun began to slant westward, they—the three of them—watching and listening, the older brother with his muddy eyes and his steady, inevitable tobacco, the father commenting now and then on certain of the animals, to no one in particular.

It was after sundown when they reached home. They ate supper by lamplight, then, sitting on the doorstep, the boy watched the night fully accomplish, listening to the whippoorwills and the frogs, when he heard his mother's voice: "Abner! No! No! Oh, God. Oh, God. Abner!" and he rose, whirled, and saw the altered light through the door where a candle stub now burned in a bottle neck on the table and his father, still in the hat and coat, at once formal and burlesque as though dressed carefully for some shabby and ceremonial violence, emptying the reservoir of the lamp back into the five-gallon kerosene can from which it had been filled, while the mother tugged at his arm until he shifted the lamp to the other hand and flung her back, not savagely or viciously, just hard, into the wall, her hands flung out against the wall for balance, her mouth open and in her face the same quality of hopeless despair as had been in her voice. Then his father saw him standing in the door. "Go to the barn and get that can of oil we were oiling the wagon with," he said. The boy did not move. Then he could speak.

"What …" he cried. "What are you …"

"Go get that oil," his father said. "Go."

Then he was moving, running, outside the house, toward the stable: this the old habit, the old blood which he had not been permitted to choose for himself, which had been bequeathed him willy nilly and which had run for so long (and who knew where, battening① on what of outrage and savagery and lust) before it came to him. *I could keep on*, he thought. *I could run on and on and never look back, never need to see his face again. Only I can't, I can't*, the rusted can in his hand now, the liquid sploshing in it as he ran back to the house and into it, into the sound of his mother's weeping in the next room, and handed the can to his father.

"Ain't you going to even send a nigger?" he cried. "At least you sent a nigger

---

① To thrive, especially at the expense of someone else.

Chapter 8 Barn Burning

before!"

This time his father didn't strike him, The hand came even faster than the blow had, the same hand which had set the can on the table with almost excruciating[①] care flashing from the can toward him too quick for him to follow it, gripping him by the back of his shirt and on to tiptoe before he had seen it quit the can, the face stooping at him in breathless and frozen ferocity, the cold, dead voice speaking over him to the older brother who leaned against the table, chewing with that steady, curious, sidewise motion of cows:

"Empty the can into the big one and go on. I'll catch up with you."

"Better tie him up to the bedpost," the brother said.

"Do like I told you," the father said. Then the boy was moving, his bunched shirt and the hard, bony hand between his shoulder-blades, his toes just touching the floor, across the room and into the other one, past the sisters sitting with spread heavy thighs in the two chairs over the cold hearth, and to where his mother and aunt sat side by side on the bed, the aunt's arms about his mother's shoulders.

"Hold him," the father said. The aunt made a startled movement. "Not you," the father said. "Lennie. Take hold of him. I want to see you do it." His mother took him by the wrist. "You'll hold him better than that. If he gets loose don't you know what he is going to do? He will go up yonder." He jerked his head toward the road. "Maybe I'd better tie him."

"I'll hold him," his mother whispered.

"See you do then." Then his father was gone, the stiff foot heavy and measured upon the boards, ceasing at last.

Then he began to struggle. His mother caught him in both arms, he jerking and wrenching at them. He would be stronger in the end, he knew that. But he had no time

---

① Intensely painful; agonizing.

to wait for it. "Lemme go!" he cried. "I don't want to have to hit you!"

"Let him go!" the aunt said. "If he don't go, before God, I am going up there myself!"

"Don't you see I can't?" his mother cried. "Sarty! Sarty! No! No! Help me, Lizzie!"

Then he was free. His aunt grasped at him but it was too late. He whirled[①], running, his mother stumbled forward on to her knees behind him, crying to the nearer sister: "Catch him, Net! Catch him!" But that was too late too, the sister (the sisters were twins, born at the same time, yet either of them now gave the impression of being, encompassing as much living meat and volume and weight as any other two of the family) not yet having begun to rise from the chair, her head, face, alone merely turned, presenting to him in the flying instant an astonishing expanse of young female features untroubled by any surprise even, wearing only an expression of bovine interest. Then he was out of the room, out of the house, in the mild dust of the starlit road and the heavy rifeness of honeysuckle, the pale ribbon unspooling with terrific slowness under his running feet, reaching the gate at last and turning in, running, his heart and lungs drumming, on up the drive toward the lighted house, the lighted door. He did not knock, he burst in, sobbing for breath, incapable for the moment of speech; he saw the astonished face of the Negro in the linen jacket without knowing when the Negro had appeared.

"De Spain!" he cried, panted. "Where's …" then he saw the white man too emerging from a white door down the hall. "Barn!" he cried. "Barn!"

"What?" the white man said. "Barn?"

"Yes!" the boy cried. "Barn!"

"Catch him!" the white man shouted.

---

① To move around or turn around very quickly.

Chapter 8　Barn Burning

But it was too late this time too. The Negro grasped his shirt, but the entire sleeve, rotten with washing, carried away, and he was out that door too and in the drive again, and had actually never ceased to run even while he was screaming into the white man's face.

Behind him the white man was shouting, "My horse! Fetch my horse!" and he thought for an instant of cutting across the park and climbing the fence into the road, but he did not know the park nor how high the vine-massed fence might be and he dared not risk it. So he ran on down the drive, blood and breath roaring; presently he was in the road again though he could not see it. He could not hear either: the galloping mare was almost upon him before he heard her, and even then he held his course, as if the very urgency of his wild grief and need must in a moment more find him wings, waiting until the ultimate instant to hurl himself aside and into the weed-choked roadside ditch as the horse thundered past and on, for an instant in furious silhouette[①] against the stars, the tranquil early summer night sky which, even before the shape of the horse and rider vanished, stained abruptly and violently upward: a long, swirling roar incredible and soundless, blotting the stars, and he springing up and into the road again, running again, knowing it was too late yet still running even after he heard the shot and, an instant later, two shots, pausing now without knowing he had ceased to run, crying "Pap! Pap!", running again before he knew he had begun to run, stumbling, tripping over something and scrabbling[②] up again without ceasing to run, looking backward over his shoulder at the glare as he got up, running on among the invisible trees, panting, sobbing, "Father! Father!"

At midnight he was sitting on the crest of a hill. He did not know it was midnight and he did not know how far he had come. But there was no glare behind him now and he sat now, his back toward what he had called home for four days anyhow, his

---

① An outline of a solid object (as cast by its shadow).
② To feel searchingly.

face toward the dark woods which he would enter when breath was strong again, small, shaking steadily in the chill darkness, hugging himself into the remainder of his thin, rotten shirt, the grief and despair now no longer terror and fear but just grief and despair. *Father. My father*, he thought. "He was brave!" he cried suddenly, aloud but not loud, no more than a whisper: "He was! He was in the war! He was in Colonel Sartoris' cav'ry!" not knowing that his father had gone to that war a private[①] in the fine old European sense, wearing no uniform, admitting the authority of and giving fidelity to no man or army or flag, going to war as Malbrouck[②] himself did; for booty—it meant nothing and less than nothing to him if it were enemy booty[③] or his own.

The slow constellations[④] wheeled on. It would be dawn and then sun-up after a while and he would be hungry. But that would be to-morrow and now he was only cold, and walking would cure that. His breathing was easier now, and he decided to get up and go on, and then he found that he had been asleep because he knew it was almost dawn, the night almost over. He could tell that from the whippoorwills. They were everywhere now among the dark trees below him, constant and inflectioned[⑤] and ceaseless, so that, as the instant for giving over to the day birds drew nearer and nearer, there was no interval at all between them. He got up. He was a little stiff, but walking would cure that too as it would the cold, and soon there would be the sun. He went on down the hill, toward the dark woods within which the liquid silver voices of the birds, called unceasing—the rapid and urgent beating of the urgent and quiring heart of the late spring night. He did not look back.

---

① A soldier of the lowest rank in an army or the marines.
② The reference is to the chief character in a popular and pervasive 18th-century nursery ditty about a legendary warrior. Originally this warrior figure may have derived from the character and exploits of John Churchill, duke of Marlborough (1650—1722).
③ A collection of valuable things stolen from a place, especially by soldiers after a battle.
④ A group of stars which form a pattern and have a name.
⑤ An inflection in someone's voice is a change in its tone or pitch as they are speaking.

Chapter 8 Barn Burning

Film Comment:

William Faulkner's *Barn Burning*: 41 minutes, color

Starring: Tommy Lee Jones & Diane Kagan

Screenplay by: Horton Foote

Directed by: Peter Werner

Abner Snopes (Tommy Lee Jones, Academy Award Winner) is a Southern tenant farmer whose unrelenting and violent nature proves to be his undoing in William Faulkner's "Barn Burning."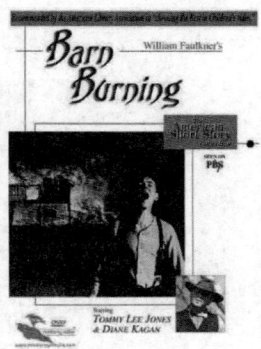

Snopes sets his employer's barn on fire when he thinks he's been treated unfairly. His son, Sarty, is horrified. Snopes escapes justice for lack of proof, but he and his family are told to move on. No sooner do they move than Snopes is offended by his new rich employer. Torn between trying to win his father's acceptance and his aversion to what his father will do, Sarty must make a decision and act quickly.

Adapted by Academy Award winning screenwriter Horton Foote, Faulkner's complex world of class divisions and hostile family relationships comes to life through a boy's attempt to liberate himself from hatred and poverty.

Film Scenes:

Scene 1: departure

The Justice can't find against Abner for barn burning, but can give him advice: leave this county. The father has already got prepared for the departure.

Scene 2: the rug

The father mars the rug with deliberation, though he never looks at the rug. The possible motivation is the greedy and jealous rage against the landlord.

Scene 3: the hearing

The father sues Major de Spain to the court. The Justice finds against the father and finds him responsible for the injury to the rug and holds him liable for it.

Scene 4: barn burning

The father takes a revenge and chooses to burn the barn of Major de Spain. Sarty gives the warning to the Major and thus betrays his father.

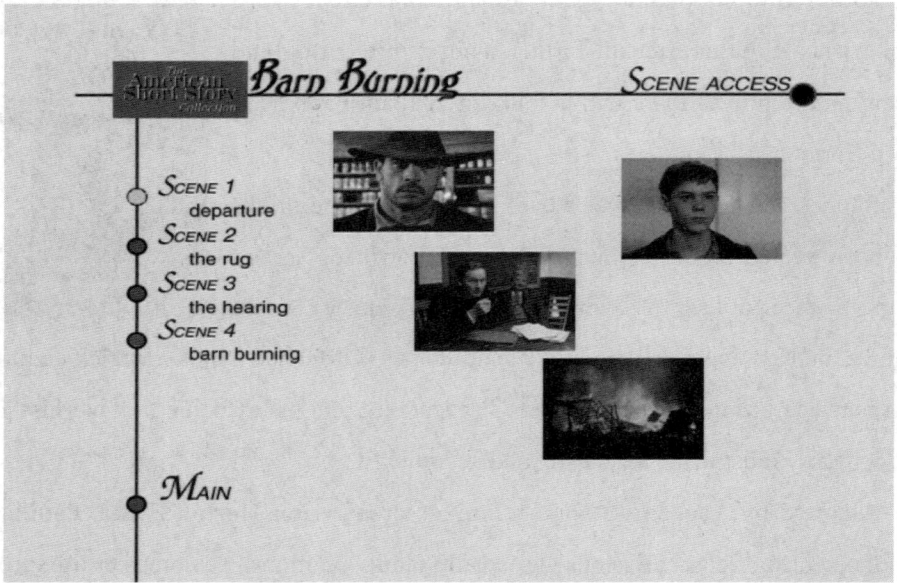

Film Clip:

Marring de Spain's Rug

Sarty follows his father to the house of Major de Spain, who is going to own him for the next eight months. The moment Sarty sees the house for the first time, he forgets his father and the terror and despair. For all the previous twelve movings, the family has stayed in a poor country, a land of small farms and fields and houses. Sarty has never seen a grand house like this before. It is as big as a courthouse, and he pauses to have a look.

Chapter 8 Barn Burning

The father continues his walk: he holds the absolutely undeviating course and the stiff foot comes squarely down in a pile of fresh horse droppings. The father could have avoided by a simple change of stride, but he doesn't change at all. Sarty walks on in the spell of the house, without envy and without sorrow, but his father is walking with a greedy and jealous rage, feeling no spell of the house at all.

Coming into the house with his dirty boots, the father pays no attention to the warning of the Negro butler. The hostess recognizes the father but asks him to go away, since Major de Spain is not at home. This shows that the father has been to the house before, and Abner has already settled the next employment before the burning of Mr. Harris' barn and before the sentence of the Justice of Peace's court.

Ignoring the woman's cry about the dirty rug, the father just stands stiff in the center of the rug, seeming to examine the house with brief deliberation. Then with the same deliberation the father turns, pivoting on the good leg, and the stiff foot drags round the arc of the turning, leaving a final long and fading mark on the rug. His father never looks at the rug, and he never once looks down at the rug, leaving the woman wailing and complaining behind.

Coming out of the house, the father cleans his boots on the edge of steps. At the gate the father stops again, planted stiffly on the stiff foot. Looking back at the house, the father speaks out the possible motivation for marring the rug: the house of Major de Spain is pretty and white. But that's sweat. Whose sweat? Nigger sweat. Maybe the house isn't white enough yet to suit him. Maybe he wants to mix some white sweat with nigger sweat. Whose sweat? The sweat of the white Snopes family.

This is the central image of the story. The marring of the rug leads to the following sequences of cleaning the rug, ruining the rug, suing de Spain, and the Justice of Peace's sentence. Not satisfied with the sentence and taking revenge for the insult, the father decides to burn the barn of Major de Spain, while the boy chooses to give a warning, thus betraying the father and leaving the family, torn between loyalty to blood and kin and loyalty to honor and justices, and gradually initiating into manhood.

Discussion Questions:

Story Discussion

(1) By what values does the boy's father live? Does the boy renounce all of them in the end? Is there a sense in which the boy is being true to his father by betraying him?

(2) How is the principal conflict related to the "peace and joy" the boy feels at the sight of Major de Spain's house?

(3) How is the language related to the point of view? Is it always appropriate to the experience being related or undergone by the point of view character?

(4) Discuss concepts of justice that emerge from the story. What does the story say about the evolution of justice from its primitive to its more civilized forms?

(5) How do the shifts of scene and setting serve to express the meaning of the unfolding action?

(6) Is the tone essentially optimistic or pessimistic?

Film Appreciation

(1) What's the function of the general store as the first court?

(2) Why is the campfire the father built so small?

(3) What's the central image of the story/film?

(4) Which country does the rug come from? How much does it cost? How much is the compensation?

(5) What's the function of the classroom as the second court?

(6) How is the family divided into three sides, Father/brother vs. Mother/Aunt/Sarty vs. two sisters?

(7) What scenes could show the parents' love to Sarty?

(8) What's the father's motivation for the revenge?

Further Reading and Watching:

A Rose for Emily

Unit Five: Theme

Chapter 9: Almos' a Man

Chapter 10: The Sky Is Gray

Chapter 9
Almos' a Man

Richard Wright

Author Introduction:

Richard Wright (1908—1960) was born at Rucker's Plantation near Natchez, Mississippi, the grandson of slaves, the son of a mill worker and a schoolteacher. Deserted by his father at an early age, he spent most of his childhood traveling through the South as his mother looked for work as a cook or maid. The family soon dissolved after her death, and Richard was forced into a series of orphanages and foster homes. After the ninth grade, he struck out on his own, living briefly in Memphis.

In 1927 he turned up in Chicago, where he joined the Communist party and began to write. In 1937, Wright moved to New York, and he gained national attention for the collection of four short stories entitled *Uncle Tom's Children* (1938).

A growing reputation as a short story writer was solidified with the publication of his first novel, *Native Son* (1940), a pathetic and gory narrative of a young black man hurled blindly into crime. Wright moved to Paris in 1946, and became a permanent American expatriate. He died in Paris of a heart attack at the age of 52, though his daughter Julia claimed that her father was murdered.

Much of Wright's literature concerns racial themes, especially those involving the plight of African Americans during the late 19th to mid-20th centuries.

Richard Wright talks about African Civilization in *Twelve Million Black Voices* (1941), "We had our own civilization in Africa before we were captured off to this land. You may smile when we call the way of life we lived in Africa 'civilization', but in numerous respects the culture of many of our tribes was equal to that of the lands from which the slave captors came. We smelted iron, danced, made music, and recited folk poems; we sculptured, worked in glass, spun cotton and wool, wove baskets and cloth; we invented a medium of exchange; mined silver and gold, made pottery and cutlery; we fashioned tools and utensils of brass, bronze, ivory, quartz, and granite; we had our own literature, our own systems of law, religion, medicine, science, and education; we painted in color upon rocks; we raised cattle, sheep, and goats; we planted and harvested grain—in short, centuries before the Romans ruled, we lived as men."

Black boy (1945), a vivid personal narrative, was followed by the novel *The Outsider* (1953) and *Black Power* (1954), an extensive report on the African Gold Coast countries. Many of his stories are collected in *Uncle Tom's Children* (1938) and *Eight Men* (1961).

Story Summary:

Dave is a black teenage farm worker in the late 1930s. Misunderstood by his family, patronized by his elders, taken for granted by the man he works for, he is at the stage in his life when he is no longer a boy and not yet a man. With a second-hand gun that he persuades his mother to let him buy—"I'm almos' a man," he argues—he accidentally shoots a mule and opens himself anew to misunderstanding and ridicule. In a final act of resolve, he retrieves the gun he buried in panic—the very object that symbolizes his adulthood—and hops a passing freight train, to be borne off to somewhere he could "be a man," free at last from the bonds of family and place.

We should learn from the naïve Dave, who is poised between boyhood and adulthood, desiring to achieve manhood with a gun but shifting his responsibility through escape.

Key Terms:

Adolescence: Dave is a young boy of seventeen, desiring to be a man, and he stands within the period of adolescence and on the threshold of manhood.

Powerlessness: Dave works very hard every day, but still gets treated like a boy, powerless at home and on the farm. His payment goes directly to his mother, and his father often beats him.

Adulthood: Dave desires to achieve the adulthood, and he believes the attaining of a gun could guarantee his maturity and manhood, only leading to further loss of his pride and autonomy.

Responsibility: As the elder son of the family, Dave has a responsibility to support the family and help his father, but Dave simply escapes from such an obligation.

Identity: Dave is poised between boyhood and adulthood. Dave's parents, Mr. Hawkins, and people he works with threaten Dave's fragile sense of identity.

Almos' a Man[①]

Dave struck out across the fields, looking homeward through parting light. Whut's the usa talkin wid em niggers in the field? Anyhow, his mother was putting supper on

---

① The story first appeared in *Harper's Bazaar* in 1940 under the title "Almos' a Man." The final version of "The Man Who Was Almost a Man" was not published until 1960—the year of Wright's death—in a collection of short stories entitled *Eight Men*.

the table. Them niggers can't understan nothing. One of these days he was going to get a gun and practice shooting, then they couldn't talk to him as though he were a little boy. He slowed, looking at the ground. Shucks, Ah ain scareda them even ef they are biggern me! Aw, Ah know whut Ahma do. Ahm going by ol Joe's sto n git that Sears Roebuck catlog n look at them guns. Mebbe Ma will lemme buy one when she gits mah pay from ol man Hawkins. Ahma beg her t gimme some money. Ahm ol ernough to hava gun. Ahm seventeen. Almos a man. He strode, feeling his long loose-jointed limbs. Shucks, a man oughta hava little gun aftah he done worked hard all day.

He came in sight of Joe's store. A yellow lantern glowed on the front porch. He mounted steps and went through the screen door, hearing it bang behind him. There was a strong smell of coal oil and mackerel fish. He felt very confident until he saw fat Joe walk in through the rear door, then his courage began to ooze.

"Howdy, Dave! Whutcha want?"

"How yuh, Mistah Joe? Aw, Ah don wanna buy nothing. Ah jus wanted t see ef yuhd lemme look at tha catlog erwhile."

"Sure! You wanna see it here?"

"Nawsuh. Ah wans t take it home wid me. Ah'll bring it back termorrow when Ah come in from the fiels."

"You plannin on buying something?"

"Yessuh."

"Your ma lettin you have your own money now?"

"Shucks. Mistah Joe, Ahm gittin t be a man like anybody else!"

Joe laughed and wiped his greasy white face with a red bandanna[①].

"Whut you plannin on buyin?"

Dave looked at the floor, scratched his head, scratched his thigh, and smiled. Then

---

① A large handkerchief usually figured and brightly colored.

Chapter 9 Almos' a Man

he looked up shyly.

"Ah'll tell yuh, Mistah Joe, ef yuh promise yuh won't tell."

"I promise."

"Waal, Ahma buy a gun."

"A gun? Whut you want with a gun?"

"Ah wanna keep it."

"You ain't nothing but a boy. You don't need a gun."

"Aw, lemme have the catlog, Mistah Joe. Ah'll bring it back."

Joe walked through the rear door. Dave was elated. He looked around at barrels of sugar and flour. He heard Joe coming back. He craned his neck to see if he were bringing the book. Yeah, he's got it. Gawddog, he's got it!

"Here, but be sure you bring it back. It's the only one I got."

"Sho, Mistah Joe."

"Say, if you wanna buy a gun, why don't you buy one from me? I gotta gun to sell."

"Will it shoot?"

"Sure it'll shoot."

"Whut kind is it?"

"Oh, it's kinda old... a left-hand Wheeler. A pistol. A big one."

"Is it got bullets in it?"

"It's loaded."

"Kin Ah see it?"

"Where's your money?"

"Whut yuh wan fer it?"

"I'll let you have it for two dollars."

"Just two dollahs? Shucks, Ah could buy tha when Ah git mah pay."

"I'll have it here when you want it."

"Awright, suh. Ah be in fer it."

He went through the door, hearing it slam again behind him. Ahma git some money from Ma n buy me a gun! Only two dollahs! He tucked the thick catalogue under his arm and hurried.

"Where yuh been, boy?" His mother held a steaming dish of black-eyed peas.

"Aw, Ma, Ah jus stopped down the road t talk wid the boys."

"Yuh know bettah t keep suppah waitin."

He sat down, resting the catalogue on the edge of the table.

"Yuh git up from there and git to the well n wash yosef! Ah ain feedin no hogs in mah house!"

She grabbed his shoulder and pushed him. He stumbled out of the room, then came back to get the catalogue.

"Whut this?"

"Aw, Ma, it's jusa catlog."

"Who yuh git it from?"

"From Joe, down at the sto."

"Waal, thas good. We kin use it in the outhouse①."

"Naw, Ma." He grabbed for it. "Gimme ma catlog, Ma."

She held onto it and glared at him.

"Quit hollerin at me! Whut's wrong wid yuh? Yuh crazy?"

"But Ma, please. It ain mine! It's Joe's! He tol me t bring it back t im termorrow."

She gave up the book. He stumbled② down the back steps, hugging the thick book under his arm. When he had splashed water on his face and hands, he groped back to the kitchen and fumbled③ in a corner for the towel. He bumped into a chair; it clattered

---

① An outdoor toilet.
② To walk unsteadily.
③ To make one's way clumsily or blindly.

Chapter 9 Almos' a Man

to the floor. The catalogue sprawled at his feet. When he had dried his eyes he snatched up the book and held it again under his arm. His mother stood watching him.

"Now, ef yuh gonna act a fool over that ol book, Ah'll take it n burn it up."

"Naw, Ma, please."

"Waal, set down n be still!"

He sat down and drew the oil lamp close. He thumbed page after page, unaware of the food his mother set on the table. His father came in. Then his small brother.

"Whutcha got there, Dave?" his father asked.

"Jusa catlog," he answered, not looking up.

"Yeah, here they is!" His eyes glowed at blue-and-black revolvers[①]. He glanced up, feeling sudden guilt. His father was watching him. He eased the book under the table and rested it on his knees. After the blessing was asked, he ate. He scooped up peas and swallowed fat meat without chewing. Buttermilk helped to wash it down. He did not want to mention money before his father. He would do much better by cornering his mother when she was alone. He looked at his father uneasily out of the edge of his eye.

"Boy, how come yuh don quit foolin wid tha book n eat yo suppah?"

"Yessuh."

"How you n ol man Hawkins gitten erlong?"

"Suh?"

"Can't yuh hear? Why don yuh lissen? Ah ast yu how wuz yuh n ol man Hawkins gittin erlong?"

"Oh, swell, Pa. Ah plows mo lan than anybody over there."

"Waal, yuh oughta keep yo mind on whut yuh doin."

"Yessuh."

---

① A pistol having a revolving cylinder with several cartridge chambers that may be fired in succession.

He poured his plate full of molasses① and sopped it up slowly with a chunk of cornbread. When his father and brother had left the kitchen, he still sat and looked again at the guns in the catalogue, longing to muster courage enough to present his case to his mother. Lawd, ef Ah only had tha pretty one! He could almost feel the slickness of the weapon with his fingers. If he had a gun like that he would polish it and keep it shining so it would never rust. N Ah'd keep it loaded, by Gawd!

"Ma?" His voice was hesitant.

"Hunh?"

"Ol man Hawkins give yuh mah money yit?"

"Yeah, but ain no usa yuh thinking bout throwin nona it erway. Ahm keepin tha money sos yuh kin have cloes t go to school this winter."

He rose and went to her side with the open catalogue in his palms. She was washing dishes, her head bent low over a pan. Shyly he raised the book. When he spoke, his voice was husky, faint.

"Ma, Gawd knows Ah wans one of these."

"One of whut?" she asked, not raising her eyes.

"One of these," he said again, not daring even to point. She glanced up at the page, then at him with wide eyes.

"Nigger, is yuh gone plumb crazy?"

"Aw, Ma—"

"Git outta here! Don yuh talk t me bout no gun! Yuh a fool!"

"Ma, Ah kin buy one fer two dollahs."

"Not ef Ah knows it, yuh ain!"

"But yuh promised me one—"

"Ah don care whut Ah promised! Yuh ain nothing but a boy yit!"

---

① A thick, dark brown syrup which is produced when sugar is processed, usually used in cooking.

Chapter 9 Almos' a Man

"Ma, ef yuh lemme buy one Ah'll *never* ast yuh fer nothing no mo."

"Ah tol yuh t git outta here! Yuh ain gonna toucha penny of tha money fer no gun! Thas how come Ah has Mistah Hawkins t pay yo wages t me, cause Ah knows yuh ain got no sense."

"But, Ma, we needa gun. Pa ain got no gun. We needa gun in the house. Yuh kin never tell whut might happen."

"Now don yuh try to maka fool outta me, boy! Ef we did hava gun, yuh wouldn't have it!"

He laid the catalogue down and slipped his arm around her waist.

"Aw, Ma, Ah done worked hard alla summer n ain ast yuh fer nothin, is Ah, now?"

"Thas whut yuh spose t do!"

"But Ma, Ah wans a gun. Yuh kin lemme have two dollahs outta mah money. Please, Ma. I kin give it to Pa ... Please, Ma! Ah loves yuh, Ma."

When she spoke her voice came soft and low.

"Whut yu wan wida gun, Dave? Yuh don need no gun. Yuh'll git in trouble. N ef yo pa jus *thought* Ah let yuh have money t buy a gun he'd hava fit."

"Ah'll hide it, Ma. It ain but two dollahs."

"Lawd, chil, whut's wrong wid yuh?"

"Ain nothin wrong, Ma. Ahm almos a man now. Ah wans a gun."

"Who gonna sell yuh a gun?"

"Ol Joe at the sto."

"N it don cos but two dollahs?"

"Thas all, Ma. Jus two dollahs. Please, Ma."

She was stacking the plates away; her hands moved slowly, reflectively. Dave kept an anxious silence. Finally, she turned to him.

"Ah'll let yuh git tha gun ef yuh promise me one thing."

"Whut's tha, Ma?"

"Yuh bring it straight back t me, yuh hear? It be fer Pa."

"Yessum! Lernme go now, Ma."

She stooped, turned slightly to one side, raised the hem of her dress, rolled down the top of her stocking, and came up with a slender wad① of bills.

"Here," she said. "Lawd knows yuh don need no gun. But yer pa does. Yuh bring it right back t me, yuh hear? Ahma put it up. Now ef yuh don, Ahma have yuh pa lick yuh so hard yuh won fergit it."

"Yessum."

He took the money, ran down the steps, and across the yard.

"Dave! Yuuuuuh Daaaaave!"

He heard, but he was not going to stop now. "Naw, Lawd!"

The first movement he made the following morning was to reach under his pillow for the gun. In the gray light of dawn he held it loosely, feeling a sense of power. Could kill a man with a gun like this. Kill anybody, black or white. And if he were holding his gun in his hand, nobody could run over him; they would have to respect him. It was a big gun, with a long barrel② and a heavy handle. He raised and lowered it in his hand, marveling at its weight.

He had not come straight home with it as his mother had asked; instead he had stayed out in the fields, holding the weapon in his hand, aiming it now and then at some imaginary foe. But he had not fired it; he had been afraid that his father might hear. Also he was not sure he knew how to fire it.

To avoid surrendering the pistol he had not come into the house until he knew that they were all asleep. When his mother had tiptoed to his bedside late that night and

---

① A sizable roll of paper money.
② The metal, cylindrical part of a firearm through which the bullet travels.

demanded the gun, he had first played possum①; then he had told her that the gun was hidden outdoors, that he would bring it to her in the morning. Now he lay turning it slowly in his hands. He broke it, took out the cartridges②, felt them, and then put them back.

He slid out of bed, got a long strip of old flannel from a trunk, wrapped the gun in it, and tied it to his naked thigh while it was still loaded. He did not go in to breakfast. Even though it was not yet daylight, he started for Jim Hawkins' plantation. Just as the sun was rising he reached the barns where the mules and plows were kept.

"Hey! That you, Dave?"

He turned. Jim Hawkins stood eying him suspiciously.

"What're yuh doing here so early?"

"Ah didn't know Ah wuz gittin up so early, Mistah Hawkins. Ah wuz fixin t hitch up ol Jenny n take her t the fiels."

"Good. Since you're so early, how about plowing that stretch down by the woods?"

"Suits me, Mistah Hawkins."

"O.K. Go to it!"

He hitched Jenny to a plow and started across the fields. Hot dog! This was just what he wanted. If he could get down by the woods, he could shoot his gun and nobody would hear. He walked behind the plow, hearing the traces creaking, feeling the gun tied tight to his thigh.

When he reached the woods, he plowed two whole rows before he decided to take out the gun. Finally, he stopped, looked in all directions, then untied the gun and held it in his hand. He turned to the mule and smiled.

"Know whut this is, Jenny? Naw, yuh wouldn know! Yuhs jusa ol mule! Anyhow,

---

① To pretend to be sleeping or dead.
② Bullets.

this is a gun, n it kin shoot, by Gawd!"

He held the gun at arm's length. Whut t hell, Ahma shoot this thing! He looked at Jenny again.

"Lissen here, Jenny! When Ah pull this ol trigger, Ah don wan yuh t run n acka fool now!"

Jenny stood with head down, her short ears pricked straight. Dave walked off about twenty feet, held the gun far out from him at arm's length, and turned his head. Hell, he told himself, Ah ain afraid. The gun felt loose in his fingers; he waved it wildly for a moment. Then he shut his eyes and tightened his forefinger. *Bloom!* A report[①] half deafened him and he thought his right hand was torn from his arm. He heard Jenny whinnying and galloping over the field, and he found himself on his knees, squeezing his fingers hard between his legs. His hand was numb; he jammed it into his mouth, trying to warm it, trying to stop the pain. The gun lay at his feet. He did not quite know what had happened. He stood up and stared at the gun as though it were a living thing. He gritted his teeth[②] and kicked the gun. Yuh almos broke mah arm! He turned to look for Jenny; she was far over the fields, tossing her head and kicking wildly.

"Hol on there, ol mule!"

When he caught up with her she stood trembling, walling her big white eyes at him. The plow was far away; the traces had broken. Then Dave stopped short, looking, not believing. Jenny was bleeding. Her left side was red and wet with blood. He went closer. Lawd, have mercy! Wondah did Ah shoot this mule? He grabbed for Jenny's mane[③]. She flinched, snorted, whirled, tossing her head.

"Hol on now! Hol on."

---

① An explosive noise.
② To press your upper and lower teeth tightly together, usually because you are angry about something.
③ The long hair along the top and sides of the neck of horse.

Chapter 9 Almos' a Man

Then he saw the hole in Jenny's side, right between the ribs. It was round, wet, red. A crimson stream streaked down the front leg, flowing fast. Good Gawd! Ah wuzn't shootin at tha mule. He felt panic. He knew he had to stop that blood, or Jenny would bleed to death. He had never seen so much blood in all his life. He chased the mule for half a mile, trying to catch her. Finally she stopped, breathing hard, stumpy tail half arched. He caught her mane and led her back to where the plow and gun lay. Then he stooped and grabbed handfuls of damp black earth and tried to plug① the bullet hole. Jenny shuddered, whinnied, and broke from him.

"Hol on! Hol on now!"

He tried to plug it again, but blood came anyhow. His fingers were hot and sticky. He rubbed dirt into his palms, trying to dry them. Then again he attempted to plug the bullet hole, but Jenny shied away, kicking her heels high. He stood helpless. He had to do something. He ran at Jenny; she dodged him. He watched a red stream of blood flow down Jenny's leg and form a bright pool at her feet.

"Jenny ... Jenny," he called weakly.

His lips trembled. She's bleeding to death! He looked in the direction of home, wanting to go back, wanting to get help. But he saw the pistol lying in the damp black clay. He had a queer feeling that if he only did something, this would not be; Jenny would not be there bleeding to death.

When he went to her this time, she did not move. She stood with sleepy, dreamy eyes; and when he touched her she gave a low-pitched whinny and knelt to the ground, her front knees slopping in blood. "Jenny ... Jenny ..." he whispered.

For a long time she held her neck erect; then her head sank, slowly. Her ribs swelled with a mighty heave and she went over.

Dave's stomach felt empty, very empty. He picked up the gun and held it

---

① If you plug a hole, you block it with something.

gingerly① between his thumb and forefinger. He buried it at the foot of a tree. He took a stick and tried to cover the pool of blood with dirt—but what was the use? There was Jenny lying with her mouth open and her eyes walled and glassy. He could not tell Jim Hawkins he had shot his mule. But he had to tell something. Yeah, Ah'll tell em Jenny started gittin wil n fell on the joint of the plow… But that would hardly happen to a mule. He walked across the field slowly, head down.

It was sunset. Two of Jim Hawkins' men were over near the edge of the woods digging a hole in which to bury Jenny. Dave was surrounded by a knot of people, all of whom were looking down at the dead mule.

"I don't see how in the world it happened," said Jim Hawkins for the tenth time.

The crowd parted and Dave's mother, father, and small brother pushed into the center.

"Where Dave?" his mother called.

"There he is," said Jim Hawkins.

His mother grabbed him.

"Whut happened, Dave? Whut yuh done?"

"Nothin."

"C mon, boy, talk," his father said.

Dave took a deep breath and told the story he knew nobody believed.

"Waal," he drawled②. "Ah brung ol Jenny down here sos Ah could do mah plowin. Ah plowed bout two rows, just like yuh see." He stopped and pointed at the long rows of upturned earth. "Then somethin musta been wrong wid ol Jenny. She wouldn ack right a-tall. She started snortin n kickin her heels. Ah tried t hol her, but she pulled erway, rearin n goin on. Then when the point of the plow was stickin up in the air, she

---

① With extreme care or delicacy.
② To speak slowly and not very clearly.

Chapter 9 Almos' a Man

swung erroun n twisted herself back on it... She stuck herself n started t bleed. N fo Ah could do anything, she wuz dead."

"Did you ever hear of anything like that in all your life?" asked Jim Hawkins.

There were white and black standing in the crowd. They murmured. Dave's mother came close to him and looked hard into his face. "Tell the truth, Dave," she said.

"Looks like a bullet hole to me," said one man.

"Dave, whut yuh do wid the gun?" his mother asked.

The crowd surged① in, looking at him. He jammed his hands into his pockets, shook his head slowly from left to right, and backed away. His eyes were wide and painful.

"Did he hava gun?" asked Jim Hawkins.

"By Gawd, Ah tol yuh tha wuz a gun wound," said a man, slapping his thigh. His father caught his shoulders and shook him till his teeth rattled.

"Tell whut happened, yuh rascal②! Tell whut ..."

Dave looked at Jenny's stiff legs and began to cry.

"Whut yuh do wid tha gun?" his mother asked.

"Whut wuz he doin wida gun?" his father asked.

"Come on and tell the truth," said Hawkins. "Ain't nobody going to hurt you ..."

His mother crowded close to him.

"Did yuh shoot tha mule, Dave?"

Dave cried, seeing blurred white and black faces.

"Ahh ddinn gggo tt sshooot hher ... Ah ssswear ffo Gawd Ahh ddin. ... Ah wuz a-tryin t sssee ef the old gggun would sshoot—"

"Where yuh git the gun from?" his father asked.

---

① To rise and move, as in waves or billows.
② One who is playfully mischievous.

"Ah got it from Joe, at the sto."

"Where yuh git the money?"

"Ma give it t me."

"He kept worryin me, Bob. Ah had t. Ah tol im t bring the gun right back t me … It was fer yuh, the gun."

"But how yuh happen to shoot that mule?" asked Jim Hawkins.

"Ah wuzn shootin at the mule, Mistah Hawkins. The gun jumped when Ah pulled the trigger... N fo Ah knowed anythin Jenny was there a-bleedin."

Somebody in the crowd laughed. Jim Hawkins walked close to Dave and looked into his face.

"Well, looks like you have bought you a mule, Dave."

"Ah swear fo Gawd, Ah didn go t kill the mule, Mistah Hawkins!"

"But you killed her!"

All the crowd was laughing now. They stood on tiptoe and poked① heads over one another's shoulders.

"Well, boy, looks like yuh done bought a dead mule! Hahaha!"

"Ain tha ershame."

"Hohohohoho."

Dave stood, head down, twisting his feet in the dirt.

"Well, you needn't worry about it, Bob," said Jim Hawkins to Dave's father. "Just let the boy keep on working and pay me two dollars a month."

"Whut yuh wan fer yo mule, Mistah Hawkins?"

Jim Hawkins screwed up his eyes.

"Fifty dollars."

"Whut yuh do wid tha gun?" Dave's father demanded.

---

① If you poke your head through an opening or if it pokes through an opening, you push it through, often so that you can see something more easily.

Chapter 9 Almos' a Man

Dave said nothing.

"Yuh wan me t take a tree n beat yuh till yuh talk!"

"Nawsuh!"

"Whut yuh do wid it?"

"Ah throwed it erway."

"Where?"

"Ah... Ah throwed it in the creek."

"Waal, c mon home. N firs thing in the mawnin git to tha creek n fin tha gun."

"Yessuh."

"Whut yuh pay fer it?"

"Two dollahs."

"Take tha gun n git yo money back n carry it t Mistah Hawkins, yuh hear? N don fergit Ahma lam you black bottom good fer this! Now march yosef on home, suh!"

Dave turned and walked slowly. He heard people laughing. Dave glared, his eyes welling with tears. Hot anger bubbled in him. Then he swallowed and stumbled on.

That night Dave did not sleep. He was glad that he had gotten out of killing the mule so easily, but he was hurt. Something hot seemed to turn over inside him each time he remembered how they had laughed. He tossed on his bed, feeling his hard pillow. N Pa says he's gonna beat me... He remembered other beatings, and his back quivered. Naw, naw, Ah sho don wan im t beat me tha way no mo. Dam em all! Nobody ever gave him anything. All he did was work. They treat me like a mule, n then they beat me. He gritted his teeth. N Ma had t tell on[①] me.

Well, if he had to, he would take old man Hawkins that two dollars. But that meant selling the gun. And he wanted to keep that gun. Fifty dollars for a dead mule.

---

① To reveal the secret.

He turned over, thinking how he had fired the gun. He had an itch to fire it again. Ef other men kin shoota gun, by Gawd, Ah kin! He was still, listening. Mebbe they all sleepin now. The house was still. He heard the soft breathing of his brother. Yes, now! He would go down and get that gun and see if he could fire it! He eased out of bed and slipped into overalls.

The moon was bright. He ran almost all the way to the edge of the woods. He stumbled over the ground, looking for the spot where he had buried the gun. Yeah, here it is. Like a hungry dog scratching for a bone, he pawed it up. He puffed his black cheeks and blew dirt from the trigger and barrel. He broke it and found four cartridges[①] unshot. He looked around; the fields were filled with silence and moonlight. He clutched the gun stiff and hard in his fingers. But, as soon as he wanted to pull the trigger, he shut his eyes and turned his head. Naw, Ah can't shoot wid mah eyes closed n mah head turned. With effort he held his eyes open; then he squeezed. *Blooooom!* He was stiff, not breathing. The gun was still in his hands. Dammit, he'd done it! He fired again. *Blooooom!* He smiled. *Blooooom! Blooooom! Click, click.* There! It was empty. If anybody could shoot a gun, he could. He put the gun into his hip pocket and started across the fields.

When he reached the top of a ridge he stood straight and proud in the moonlight, looking at Jim Hawkins' big white house, feeling the gun sagging in his pocket. Lawd, ef Ah had jus one mo bullet Ah'd taka shot at tha house. Ah'd like t scare ol man Hawkins jusa little... Jusa enough t let im know Dave Saunders is a man.

To his left the road curved, running to the tracks of the Illinois Central. He jerked his head, listening. From far off came a faint *hoooof-hoooof; hoooof-hoooof; hoooof-hoooof...* He stood rigid. Two dollahs a mont. Les see now... Tha means it'll take bout two years. Shucks! Ah'll be dam!

---

① A metal or cardboard tube containing a bullet and an explosive substance, which is used in guns.

Chapter 9 Almos' a Man

He started down the road, toward the tracks. Yeah, here she comes! He stood beside the track and held himself stiffly. Here she comes, erroun the ben... C mon, yuh slow poke①! C mon! He had his hand on his gun; something quivered in his stomach. Then the train thundered past, the gray and brown box cars rumbling and clinking. He gripped the gun tightly; then he jerked his hand out of his pocket. Ah betcha② Bill wouldn't do it! Ah betcha. ... The cars slid past, steel grinding upon steel. Ahm ridin yuh ternight, so hep me Gawd! He was hot all over. He hesitated just a moment; then he grabbed, pulled atop of a car, and lay flat. He felt his pocket; the gun was still there. Ahead the long rails were glinting in the moonlight, stretching away, away to somewhere, somewhere where he could be a man ...

Film Comment:

Richard Wright's *Almos' a Man*: 39 minutes, color

Starring: LeVar Burton & Madge Sinclair

Screenplay by: Leslie Lee

Directed by: Stan Lathan

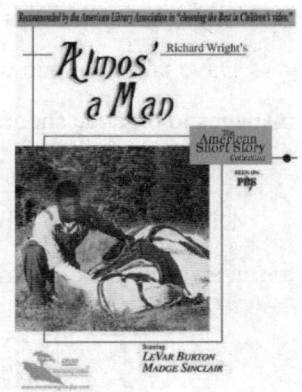

Although Dave (LeVar Burton) and his family are poor sharecroppers in the Deep South in the 1930s, this 15-year-old's problem is shared by teenagers today: he stands with one foot in adulthood and the other in childhood. "Almos' a Man," yet still treated like a child, he struggles for an identity. There's one thing, one symbol of manhood, Dave thinks, that could guarantee him instant respect—a gun.

Dave finds a way to buy a pistol and at last, is ready to pull the trigger for the first time, never again will they call him a boy...But, he trembles, the gun overpowers the

---

① Someone who moves slowly.

② Colloquial: bet you.

boy's body and he loses control—his young life forever changed.

Film Scenes:

Scene 1: to be a man

Dave wants to be a man, but the people around treat him like a boy, so he dreams to have a gun and keeps them away.

Scene 2: I want a gun

With the two dollars he begs from his mother, Dave buys a second-hand revolver from Joe, which is supposed to hand over to his father.

Scene 3: pump up!

Dave wants to practice gun shooting, but he doesn't dare to shoot the gun. Coming back at night, Dave hides the gun under his pillow.

Scene 4: the accident

Dave takes the gun with him when going to the field for the ploughing. He finally manages to practice shooting, but shoots the mule by accident.

Scene 5: running away

Killing the mule, Dave has to pay 50 dollars, 2 dollars each month. Dave chooses to run away on a freight train, leaving behind the huge debt.

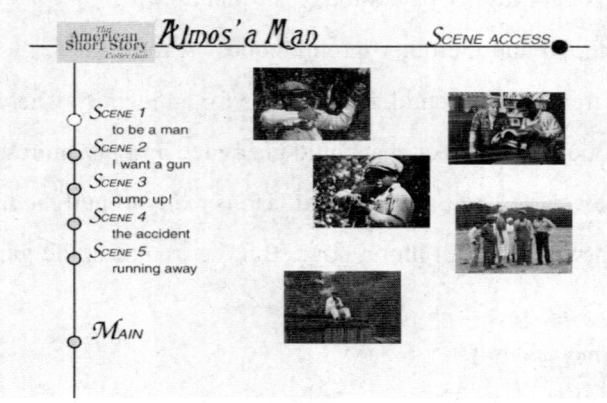

Film Clip:

The Leaving

Early in the morning, Dave leaves his home and runs almost all the way to the edge of the woods. He stumbles over the ground, looking for the spot where he has buried the gun. Digging up the gun, Dave clutches the gun stiff and hard in his fingers. But, as soon as he wants to pull the trigger, he shuts his eyes and turns his head. With much effort he holds his eyes open; then he squeezes. Blooooom! The gun is still in his hands. He shoots another three times, and then the gun is empty. If anybody could shoot a gun, Dave could. It is very important that Dave could shoot a gun, for the gun is a symbol of power, maturity and manhood for him. Dave puts the gun into his hip pocket and starts across the fields, saying goodbye to Mr. Hawkins and Jenny, getting ready for his leaving.

Dave starts down the road, toward the tracks. He stands beside the tracks and holds himself stiffly, having his hand on the gun. When the freight train thunders past, Dave grips the gun tightly; and then he jerks his hand out of his pocket. When the cars slide past, he is hot all over. Dave hesitates just a moment; and then he grabs, pulls atop of a car, and sits on top. He feels his pocket; the gun is still there. Ahead the long rails are glinting in the moonlight, stretching away and taking Dave away to somewhere where he could be a man.

Dave's leaving is naïve and highly irresponsible, leaving a huge debt to his father, his mother, and his younger brother. What kind of life will be waiting for Dave? According to the original plan of the author, Dave would possibly become a famous boxer. But whatever happens, Dave needs to get rid of being naïve and get mature quickly, finding a job, settling down, and sending money back home if possible; otherwise, he will still have to experience being beaten up by the cruel social life, without the protection of his parents this time.

Discussion Questions:

Story Discussion

(1) What is the importance of the social setting in shaping Dave's motives and course of action?

(2) How do the dialogue and limited point of view help reveal the meaning of local social pressures?

(3) To what extent is the accidental shooting of the mule crucial to Dave's departure from home? Does it merely hasten him on a course he would in any case have followed?

(4) What sort of future for Dave is implied by the last paragraphs?

(5) Discuss the role of the minor characters in shaping Dave's character and in determining his actions.

Film Appreciation

(1) Why is the father so harsh toward Dave, especially in front of the public?

(2) Why is the son so naïve at the age of seventeen?

(3) How does Dave accidentally shoot the mule?

(4) How does Dave make up the story of Jenny's death? Does anybody believe him?

(5) Why does the mother tell on Dave? What's the function of the crowd here?

(6) Why does Dave bury the gun? What's the symbolic meaning of the gun?

(7) How does Dave leave on a freight train? Is this a responsible behavior?

(8) What are the cases of film language and adapted scenes?

Further Reading and Watching:

Eight Men

Chapter 10
The Sky Is Gray

Ernest Gaines

Author Introduction:

Ernest Gaines (1933—2019) was born in Pointe Coupee Parish, Louisiana, among the fifth generation of his sharecropper family. Although born generations after the end of slavery, Gaines grew up impoverished, living in old slave quarters on a plantation. When he was 15 years old, Gaines moved to Vallejo, California, to join his mother and stepfather, who had left Louisiana during the Second World War.

After serving in the U.S. Army, he enrolled in San Francisco State College and graduated in 1957. He then won a creative writing fellowship to Stanford University. Gaines's boyhood experiences growing up in Louisiana provide the setting for many of his novels, and though none of his work is strictly autobiographical, his writing bears the distinctive stamp of the rural folk culture amid which he was raised.

Although Gaines lived much of his life in San Francisco, he maintained close contact with Louisiana, the place and the people. In the final years of his life, Gaines lived on Louisiana Highway 1 in Oscar, Louisiana, where he and his wife built a home on part of the old plantation where he grew up. Gaines died from natural causes at his home on November 5, 2019.

Gaines has created an array of characters, conflicts, and themes as rich in their variety and in their universality as any in American literature. His main works are *Of Love and Dust* (1967), *Bloodline* (1968), *The Autobiography of Miss Jane Pittman* (1971), *A Long Day in November* (1971), *In My Father's House* (1978), *A Gathering of Old Men* (1984) and *A Lesson Before Dying* (1993).

Story Summary:

Powerfully told with a convincing use of black dialect and dialogue, the story features the first-person narrator James and the lessons he learns from his personal odyssey.

James is an eight-year-old black boy in rural Louisiana in the early 1940s. He valiantly tries to ignore a raging toothache. His mother has taught him not to complain, look for sympathy or squander money. After both aspirin and prayer fail to quell the toothache, his mother takes James to town to have it pulled. In the dentist's office they hear a preacher and student quarrel about the troubles of black people. The dentist closes for lunch before getting to James. The boy and his mother must walk around hungry in the cold sleet until the office reopens, because they must save their money for bus fare home. The child hero in this odyssey begins to realize the world is complicated and neither black nor white.

We should learn from the personal odyssey of James, the eight-year-old boy who realizes that the destiny of the black is neither black nor white but gray, just like the sky.

Key Terms:

Personal Responsibility: After Daddy being taken away into the Army, it is Mama's responsibility to take care of the whole family.

Moral Behavior: Mama always makes use of every opportunity to teach James the moral behavior, like how to be a man rather than a bum.

Racial Injustice: The family are black, and Mama and James have to suffer racial injustice when going to the dentist office in the town.

Community Defined Values: There are some values defined by the white or black community, followed by most community members.

Rite of Passage: Lasting only for one day, the personal odyssey of James to the town is the rite of passage for the eight-year-old young boy.

Civil Rights Era: The destiny of black people in Civil Rights Era is neither black nor white, and it is gray, just like the sky.

The Sky Is Gray[①]

I

Go'n be coming in a few minutes. Coming round that bend down there full speed. And I'm go'n get out my handkerchief and wave it down, and we go'n get on it and go.

I keep on looking for it, but Mama don't look that way no more. She's looking down the road where we just come from. It's a long old road, and far 's you can see you don't see nothing but gravel. You got dry weeds on both sides, and you got trees on both sides, and fences on both sides, too. And you got cows in the pastures and they standing close together. And when we was coming out here to catch the bus I seen the

---

① First published in *Negro Digest* in August 1963, and then collected in *Bloodline* (1968).

Chapter 10 The Sky Is Gray

smoke coming out of the cows's noses.

I look at my mama and I know what she's thinking. I been with Mama so much, just me and her, I know what she's thinking all the time. Right now it's home—Auntie and them. She's thinking if they got enough wood—if she left enough there to keep them warm till we get back. She's thinking if it go'n rain and if any of them go'n have to go out in the rain. She's thinking 'bout the hog—if he go'n get out, and if Ty and Val be able to get him back in. She always worry like that when she leaves the house. She don't worry too much if she leave me there with the smaller ones, 'cause she know I'm go'n look after them and look after Auntie and everything else. I'm the oldest and she say I'm the man.

I look at my mama and I love my mama. She's wearing that black coat and that black hat and she's looking sad. I love my mama and I want put my arm round her and tell her. But I'm not supposed to do that. She say that's weakness and that's crybaby[①] stuff, and she don't want no crybaby round her. She don't want you to be scared, either. 'Cause Ty's scared of ghosts and she's always whipping him. I'm scared of the dark, too, but I make 'tend I ain't. I make 'tend I ain't 'cause I'm the oldest, and I got to set a good sample for the rest. I can't ever be scared and I can't ever cry. And that's why I never said nothing 'bout my teeth. It's been hurting me and hurting me close to a month now, but I never said it. I didn't say it 'cause I didn't want act like a crybaby, and 'cause I know we didn't have enough money to go have it pulled. But, Lord, it been hurting me. And look like it wouldn't start till at night when you was trying to get yourself little sleep. Then soon 's you shut your eyes—ummmummm, Lord, look like it go right down to your heartstring.

"Hurting, hanh?" Ty'd say.

I'd shake my head, but I wouldn't open my mouth for nothing. You open your

---

① A person who cries or complains frequently with little cause.

mouth and let that wind in, and it almost kill you.

I'd just lay there and listen to them snore. Ty there, right 'side me, and Auntie and Val over by the fireplace. Val younger than me and Ty, and he sleeps with Auntie. Mama sleeps round the other side with Louis and Walker.

I'd just lay there and listen to them, and listen to that wind out there, and listen to that fire in the fireplace. Sometimes it'd stop long enough to let me get little rest. Sometimes it just hurt, hurt, hurt. Lord, have mercy.

II

Auntie knowed it was hurting me. I didn't tell nobody but Ty, 'cause we buddies and he ain't go'n tell nobody. But some kind of way Auntie found out. When she asked me, I told her no, nothing was wrong. But she knowed it all the time. She told me to mash up a piece of aspirin and wrap it in some cotton and jugg it down in that hole. I did it, but it didn't do no good. It stopped for a little while, and started right back again. Auntie wanted to tell Mama, but I told her, "Uh-uh." 'Cause I knowed we didn't have any money, and it just was go'n make her mad again. So Auntie told Monsieur[①] Bayonne, and Monsieur Bayonne came over to the house and told me to kneel down 'side him on the fireplace. He put his finger in his mouth and made the Sign of the Cross on my jaw. The tip of Monsieur Bayonne's finger is some hard, 'cause he's always playing on that guitar. If we sit outside at night we can always hear Monsieur Bayonne playing on his guitar. Sometimes we leave him out there playing on the guitar.

Monsieur Bayonne made the Sign of the Cross over and over on my jaw, but that didn't do no good. Even when he prayed and told me to pray some, too, that tooth still hurt me.

"How you feeling?" he say.

---

① Used as a form of polite address for a man in a French-speaking area.

Chapter 10 The Sky Is Gray

"Same," I say.

He kept on praying and making the Sign of the Cross and I kept on praying, too.

"Still hurting?" he say.

"Yes, sir."

Monsieur Bayonne mashed harder and harder on my jaw. He mashed so hard he almost pushed me over on Ty. But then he stopped.

"What kind of prayers you praying, boy?" he say.

"Baptist," I say.

"Well, I'll be—no wonder that tooth still killing him. I'm going one way and he pulling the other. Boy, don't you know any Catholic prayers?"

"I know 'Hail Mary'[①]," I say.

"Then you better start saying it."

"Yes, sir."

He started mashing on my jaw again, and I could hear him praying at the same time. And, sure enough, after while it stopped hurting me.

Me and Ty went outside where Monsieur Bayonne's two hounds was and we started playing with them. "Let's go hunting," Ty say. "All right," I say; and we went on back in the pasture. Soon the hounds got on a trail, and me and Ty followed them all 'cross the pasture and then back in the woods, too. And then they cornered this little old rabbit and killed him, and me and Ty made them get back, and picked up the rabbit and started on back home. But my tooth had started hurting me again. It was hurting me plenty now, but I wouldn't tell Monsieur Bayonne. That night I didn't sleep a bit, and first thing in the morning Auntie told me to go back and let Monsieur Bayonne pray over me some more. Monsieur Bayonne was in his kitchen making coffee when I got there. Soon 's he seen me he knowed what was wrong.

---

① A prayer based on the greetings of Gabriel and Saint Elizabeth to Virgin Mary.

"All right, kneel down there 'side that stove," he say. "And this time make sure you pray Catholic. I don't know nothing 'bout that Baptist, and I don't want know nothing 'bout him."

III

Last night Mama say, "Tomorrow we going to town."

"It ain't hurting me no more," I say. "I can eat anything on it."

"Tomorrow we going to town," she say.

And after she finished eating, she got up and went to bed. She always go to bed early now. 'Fore Daddy went in the Army, she used to stay up late. All of us sitting out on the gallery or round the fire. But now, look like soon 's she finish eating she go to bed.

This morning when I woke up, her and Auntie was standing 'fore the fireplace. She say: "Enough to get there and get back. Dollar and a half to have it pulled. Twenty-five for me to go, twenty-five for him. Twenty-five for me to come back, twenty-five for him. Fifty cents left. Guess I get little piece of salt meat with that."

"Sure can use it," Auntie say. "White beans and no salt meat ain't white beans."

"I do the best I can," Mama say.

They was quiet after that, and I made 'tend I was still asleep.

"James, hit the floor," Auntie say.

I still made 'tend I was asleep. I didn't want them to know I was listening.

"All right," Auntie say, shaking me by the shoulder. "Come on. Today's the day."

I pushed the cover down to get out, and Ty grabbed it and pulled it back.

"You, too, Ty," Auntie say.

"I ain't getting no teef pulled," Ty say.

"Don't mean it ain't time to get up," Auntie say. "Hit it, Ty."

Ty got up grumbling.

Chapter 10 The Sky Is Gray

"James, you hurry up and get in your clothes and eat your food," Auntie say. "What time y'all coming back?" she say to Mama.

"That 'leven o'clock bus," Mama say. "Got to get back in that field this evening."

"Get a move on you, James," Auntie say.

I went in the kitchen and washed my face, then I ate my breakfast. I was having bread and syrup. The bread was warm and hard and tasted good. And I tried to make it last a long time.

Ty came back there grumbling and mad at me.

"Got to get up," he say. "I ain't having no teefes pulled. What I got to be getting up for?"

Ty poured some syrup in his pan and got a piece of bread. He didn't wash his hands, neither his face, and I could see that white stuff in his eyes.

"You the one getting your teef pulled," he say. "What I got to get up for. I bet if I was getting a teef pulled, you wouldn't be getting up. Shucks[①]; syrup again. I'm getting tired of this old syrup. Syrup, syrup, syrup. I'm go'n take with the sugar diabetes[②]. I want me some bacon sometime."

"Go out in the field and work and you can have your bacon," Auntie say. She stood in the middle door looking at Ty. "You better be glad you got syrup. Some people ain't got that—hard 's time is."

"Shucks," Ty say. "How can I be strong."

"I don't know too much 'bout your strength," Auntie say; "but I know where you go'n be hot at, you keep that grumbling up. James, get a move on you; your mama waiting."

I ate my last piece of bread and went in the front room. Mama was standing 'fore the fireplace warming her hands. I put on my coat and my cap, and we left the house.

---

① Used to express mild disappointment, disgust, or annoyance.
② An informal or dialect word for diabetes mellitus.

IV

I look down there again, but it still ain't coming. I almost say, "It ain't coming yet," but I keep my mouth shut. 'Cause that's something else she don't like. She don't like for you to say something just for nothing. She can see it ain't coming, I can see it ain't coming, so why say it ain't coming. I don't say it, I turn and look at the river that's back of us. It's so cold the smoke's just raising up from the water. I see a bunch of pool-doos not too far out—just on the other side the lilies. I'm wondering if you can eat pool-doos. I ain't too sure, 'cause I ain't never ate none. But I done ate owls and blackbirds, and I done ate redbirds, too. I didn't want kill the redbirds, but she made me kill them. They had two of them back there. One in my trap, one in Ty's trap. Me and Ty was go'n play with them and let them go, but she made me kill them 'cause we needed the food.

"I can't," I say. "I can't."

"Here," she say. "Take it."

"I can't," I say. "I can't. I can't kill him, Mama, please."

"Here," she say. "Take this fork, James."

"Please, Mama, I can't kill him," I say.

I could tell she was go'n hit me. I jerked back, but I didn't jerk back soon enough.

"Take it," she say.

I took it and reached in for him, but he kept on hopping to the back.

"I can't, Mama," I say. The water just kept on running down my face. "I can't," I say.

"Get him out of there," she say.

I reached in for him and he kept on hopping to the back. Then I reached in farther, and he pecked me on the hand.

"I can't, Mama," I say.

She slapped me again.

Chapter 10 The Sky Is Gray

I reached in again, but he kept on hopping out my way. Then he hopped to one side and I reached there. The fork got him on the leg and I heard his leg pop. I pulled my hand out 'cause I had hurt him.

"Give it here," she say, and jerked the fork out my hand.

She reached in and got the little bird right in the neck. I heard the fork go in his neck, and I heard it go in the ground. She brought him out and helt him right in front of me.

"That's one," she say. She shook him off and gived me the fork. "Get the other one."

"I can't, Mama," I say. "I'll do anything, but don't make me do that."

She went to the corner of the fence and broke the biggest switch over there she could find. I knelt 'side the trap, crying.

"Get him out of there," she say.

"I can't, Mama."

She started hitting me 'cross the back. I went down on the ground, crying.

"Get him," she say.

"Octavia?" Auntie say.

'Cause she had come out of the house and she was standing by the tree looking at us.

"Get him out of there," Mama say.

"Octavia," Auntie say, "explain to him. Explain to him. Just don't beat him. Explain to him."

But she hit me and hit me and hit me.

I'm still young—I ain't no more than eight; but I know now; I know why I had to do it. (They was so little, though. They was so little. I 'member how I picked the feathers off them and cleaned them and helt them over the fire. Then we all ate them. Ain't had but a little bitty piece each, but we all had a little bitty piece, and everybody just looked at me 'cause they was so proud.) Suppose she had to go away? That's why I had to do it. Suppose she had to go away like Daddy went away? Then who was go'n look after us? They had to be somebody left to carry on. I didn't know it then, but I know it now. Auntie and Monsieur Bayonne talked to me and made me see.

V

Time I see it I get out my handkerchief and start waving. It's still 'way down there, but I keep waving anyhow. Then it come up and stop and me and Mama get on. Mama tell me go sit in the back while she pay. I do like she say, and the people look at me. When I pass the little sign that say "White" and "Colored," I start looking for a seat. I just see one of them back there, but I don't take it, 'cause I want my mama to sit down herself. She comes in the back and sit down, and I lean on the seat. They got seats in the front, but I know I can't sit there, 'cause I have to sit back of the sign. Anyhow, I don't want sit there if my mama go'n sit back here.

They got a lady sitting 'side my mama and she looks at me and smiles little bit. I smile back, but I don't open my mouth, 'cause the wind'll get in and make that tooth ache. The lady take out a pack of gum and reach me a slice, but I shake my head. The lady just can't understand why a little boy'll turn down gum, and she reach me a slice again. This time I point to my jaw. The lady understands and smiles little bit, and I smile little bit, but I don't open my mouth, though.

They got a girl sitting 'cross from me. She got on a red overcoat and her hair's plaited in one big plait. First, I make 'tend I don't see her over there, but then I start looking at her little bit. She make 'tend she don't see me, either, but I catch her looking that way. She got a cold, and every now and then she h'ist that little handkerchief to her nose. She ought to blow it, but she don't. Must think she's too much a lady or something.

Every time she h'ist that little handkerchief, the lady 'side her say something in

Chapter 10　The Sky Is Gray

her ear. She shakes her head and lays her hands in her lap again. Then I catch her kind of looking where I'm at. I smile at her little bit. But think she'll smile back? Un-uh. She just turn up her little old nose and turn her head. Well, I show her both of us can turn us head. I turn mine too and look out at the river.

The river is gray. The sky is gray. They have pool-doos on the water. The water is wavy, and the pool-doos go up and down. The bus go round a turn, and you got plenty trees hiding the river. Then the bus go round another turn, and I can see the river again.

I look toward the front where all the white people sitting. Then I look at that little old gal[①] again. I don't look right at her, 'cause I don't want all them people to know I love her. I just look at her little bit, like I'm looking out that window over there. But she knows I'm looking that way, and she kind of look at me, too. The lady sitting 'side her catch her this time, and she leans over and says something in her ear.

"I don't love him nothing," that little old gal says out loud.

Everybody back there hear her mouth, and all of them look at us and laugh.

"I don't love you, either," I say. "So you don't have to turn up your nose, miss."

"You the one looking," she say.

"I wasn't looking at you," I say. "I was looking out that window, there."

"Out that window, my foot," she say. "I seen you. Everytime I turned round you was looking at me."

"You must of been looking yourself if you seen me all them times," I say.

"Shucks," she say, "I got me all kinds of boyfriends."

"I got girlfriends, too," I say.

"Well, I just don't want you getting your hopes up," she say.

I don't say no more to that little old gal 'cause I don't want have to bust[②] her in the mouth. I lean on the seat where Mama sitting, and I don't even look that way no

---

① Girl.
② Tame.

more. When we get to Bayonne, she jugg her little old tongue out at me. I make 'tend I'm go'n hit her, and she duck down 'side her mama. And all the people laugh at us again.

VI

Me and Mama get off and start walking in town. Bayonne is a little bitty town. Baton Rouge is a hundred times bigger than Bayonne. I went to Baton Rouge once—me, Ty, Mama, and Daddy. But that was 'way back yonder, 'fore Daddy went in the Army. I wonder when we go'n see him again. I wonder when. Look like he ain't ever coming back home… Even the pavement all cracked in Bayonne. Got grass shooting right out the sidewalk. Got weeds in the ditch, too; just like they got at home.

It's some cold in Bayonne. Look like it's colder than it is home. The wind blows in my face, and I feel that stuff running down my nose. I sniff. Mama says use that handkerchief. I blow my nose and put it back.

We pass a school and I see them white children playing in the yard. Big old red school, and them children just running and playing. Then we pass a cafe, and I see a bunch of people in there eating. I wish I was in there 'cause I'm cold. Mama tells me keep my eyes in front where they belong.

We pass stores that's got dummies, and we pass another cafe, and then we pass a shoe shop, and that baldhead man in there fixing on a shoe. I look at him and I butt into that white lady, and Mama jerks me in front and tells me stay there.

We come up to the courthouse, and I see the flag waving there. This flag ain't like the one we got at school. This one here ain't got but a handful of stars. One at school got a big pile of stars—one for every state. We pass it and we turn and there it is—the dentist office. Me and Mama go in, and they got people sitting everywhere you look. They even got a little boy in there younger than me.

Me and Mama sit on that bench, and a white lady come in there and ask me what my name is. Mama tells her and the white lady goes on back. Then I hear somebody hollering① in there. Soon 's that little boy hear him hollering, he start hollering, too. His mama pats him and pats him, trying to make him hush up, but he ain't thinking 'bout his mama.

The man that was hollering in there comes out holding his jaw. He is a big old man and he's wearing overalls and a jumper②.

"Got it, hanh?" another man ask him.

The man shakes his head—don't want to open his mouth.

"Man, I thought they was killing you in there," the other man says. "Hollering like a pig under a gate."

The man don't say nothing. He just heads for the door, and the other man follows him.

"John Lee," the white lady says, "John Lee Williams."

The little boy juggs his head down in his mama's lap and holler more now. His mama tells him go with the nurse, but he ain't thinking 'bout his mama. His mama tells him again, but he don't even hear her. His mama picks him up and takes him in there, and even when the white lady shuts the door I can still hear little old John Lee.

"I often wonder why the Lord let a child like that suffer," a lady says to my mama. The lady's sitting right in front of us on another bench. She's got on a white dress and a black sweater. She must be a nurse or something herself, I reckon.

"Not to us to question," a man says.

"Sometimes I don't know if we shouldn't," the lady says.

"I know definitely we shouldn't," the man says. The man look like a preacher. He's big and fat and he's got on a black suit. He's got a gold chain, too.

"Why?" the lady says.

"Why anything?" the preacher says.

---

① Yelling or shouting.
② A loose, protective garment worn over other clothes.

"Yes," the lady says. "Why anything?"

"Not to us to question," the preacher says.

The lady looks at the preacher a little while and looks at Mama again.

"And look like it's the poor who suffers the most," she says. "I don't understand it."

"Best not to even try," the preacher says. "He works in mysterious ways—wonders to perform."

Right then little John Lee bust out hollering, and everybody turn they head to listen.

"He's not a good dentist," the lady says. "Dr. Robillard is much better. But more expensive. That's why most of the colored people come here. The white people go to Dr. Robillard. Y'all from Bayonne?"

"Down the river," my mama says. And that's all she go'n say, 'cause she don't talk much. But the lady keeps on looking at her, and so she says, "Near Morgan."

"I see," the lady says.

VII

"That's the trouble with the black people in this country today," somebody else says. This one here's sitting on the same side me and Mama's sitting, and he is kind of sitting in front of that preacher. He looks like a teacher or somebody that goes to college. He's got on a suit, and he's got a book that he's been reading. "We don't question is exactly our problem," he says. "We should question and question and question—question everything."

The preacher just looks at him a long time. He done put a toothpick or something in his mouth, and he just keeps on turning it and turning it. You can see he don't like that boy with that book.

"Maybe you can explain what you mean," he says.

Chapter 10 The Sky Is Gray

"I said what I meant," the boys says. "Question everything. Every stripe, every star, every word spoken. Everything."

"It 'pears to me that this young lady and I was talking 'bout God, young man," the preacher says.

"Question Him too," the boys says.

"Wait," the preacher says. "Wait now."

"You heard me right," the boy says. "His existence as well as everything else. Everything."

The preacher just looks across the room at the boy. You can see he's getting madder and madder. But mad or no mad, the boy ain't thinking 'bout him. He looks at that preacher just 's hard 's the preacher looks at him.

"Is this what they coming to?" the preacher says. "Is this what we educating them for?"

"You are not educating me," the boys says. "I wash dishes at night so that I can go to school in the day. So even the words you spoke need questioning."

The preacher just looks at him and shakes his head.

"When I come in this room and seen you were with your book, I said to myself, 'There's an intelligent man.' How wrong a person can be."

"Show me one reason to believe in the existence of a God," the boy says.

"My heart tells me," the preacher says.

"'My heart tells me,'" the boy says. "'My heart tells me.' Sure, 'My heart tells me.' And as long as you listen to what your heart tells you, you will have only what the white man gives you and nothing more. Me, I don't listen to my heart. The purpose of the heart is to pump blood throughout the body, and nothing else."

"Who's your paw, boy?" the preacher says.

"Why?"

"Who is he?"

"He's dead."

"And your mon?"

"She's in Charity Hospital with pneumonia. Half killed herself, working for nothing."

"And 'cause he's dead and she's sick, you mad at the world?"

"I'm not mad at the world. I'm questioning the world. I'm questioning it with cold logic, sir. What do words like Freedom, Liberty, God, White, Colored mean? I want to know. That's why *you* are sending us to school, to read and to ask questions. And because we ask these questions, you call us mad. No sir, it is not us who are mad."

"You keep saying 'us'?"

"'Us.' Yes—us. I'm not alone."

The preacher just shakes his head. Then he looks at everybody in the room—everybody. Some of the people look down at the floor, keep from looking at him. I kind of look 'way myself, but soon 's I know he done turn his head, I look that way again.

"I'm sorry for you," he says to the boy.

"Why?" the boy says. "Why not be sorry for yourself? Why are you so much better off than I am? Why aren't you sorry for these other people in here? Why not be sorry for the lady who had to drag her child into the dentist office? Why not be sorry for the lady sitting on that bench over there? Be sorry for them. Not for me. Some way or the other I'm going to make it."

"No, I'm sorry for you," the preacher says.

"Of course, of course," the boy says, nodding his head. "You are sorry for me because I rock that pillar you're leaning on."

"You can't ever rock the pillar I'm leaning on, young man. It's stronger than anything man can never do."

"You believe in God because a man told you to believe in God," the boy says. "A white man told you to believe in God. And why? To keep you ignorant so he can keep

Chapter 10 The Sky Is Gray

his feet on your neck."

"So now we the ignorant?" the preacher says.

"Yes," the boy says. "Yes." And he opens his book again.

The preacher just looks at him sitting there. The boy done forgot all about him. Everybody else make 'tend they done forgot the squabble, too.

Then I see that preacher getting up real slow. Preacher's a great big old man and he got to brace himself to get up. He comes over where the boy is sitting. He just stands there a little while looking down at him, but the boy don't raise his head.

"Get up, boy," preacher says.

The boy looks up at him, then he shuts his book real slow and stands up. Preacher just hauls back and hit him in the face. The boy falls back 'gainst the wall, but he straightens himself up and looks right back at that preacher.

"You forgot the other cheek," he says.

The preacher hauls back and hit him again on the other side. But this time the boy braces himself and don't fall.

"That hasn't changed a thing," he says.

The preacher just looks at the boy. The preacher's breathing real hard like he just run up a big hill. The boy sits down and opens his book again.

"I feel sorry for you," the preacher says. "I never felt so sorry for a man before."

The boy makes 'tend he don't even hear that preacher. He keeps on reading his book. The preacher goes back and gets his hat off the chair.

"Excuse me," he says to us. "I'll come back some other time. Y'all, please excuse me."

And he looks at the boy and goes out the room. The boy h'ist his hand up to his mouth one time to wipe 'way some blood. All the rest of the time he keeps on reading. And nobody else in there say a word.

VIII

Little John Lee and his mama come out the dentist office, and the nurse calls somebody else in. Then little bit later they come out, the nurse calls another name. But fast 's she calls somebody in there, somebody else comes in the place where we sitting, and the room stays full.

The people coming in now, all of them wearing big coats. One of them says something 'bout sleeting①, another one says he hope not. Another one says he think it ain't nothing but rain. 'Cause, he says, rain can get awful cold this time of year.

All around the room they talking. Some of them talking to people right by them, some of them talking to people clear 'cross the room, some of them talking to anybody'll listen. It's a little bitty room, no bigger than us kitchen, and I can see everybody in there. The little old room's full of smoke, 'cause you got two old men smoking pipes over by that side door. I think I feel my tooth thumping me some, and I hold my breath and wait. I wait and wait, but it don't thump me no more. Thank God for that.

I feel like going to sleep, and I lean back 'gainst the wall. But I'm scared to go to sleep. Scared 'cause the nurse might call my name and I won't hear her. And Mama might go to sleep, too, and she'll be mad if neither one of us heard the nurse.

I look up at Mama. I love my mama. I love my mama. And when cotton come I'm go'n get her a new coat. And I ain't go'n get a black one, either. I think I'm go'n get her a red one.

"They got some books over there," I say. "Want read one of them?"

Mama looks at the books, but she don't answer me.

"You got yourself a little man there," the lady says.

Mama don't say nothing to the lady, but she must've smiled, 'cause I seen the lady

---

① A mixture of rain and snow or hail.

Chapter 10 The Sky Is Gray

smiling back. The lady looks at me a little while, like she's feeling sorry for me.

"You sure got that preacher out here in a hurry," she says to that boy.

The boy looks up at her and looks in his book again. When I grow up I want be just like him. I want clothes like that and I want keep a book with me, too.

"You really don't believe in God?" the lady says.

"No," he says.

"But why?" the lady says.

"Because the wind is pink," he says.

"What?" the lady says.

The boy don't answer her no more. He just reads in his book.

"Talking 'bout the wind is pink," that old lady says. She's sitting on the same bench with the boy and she's trying to look in his face. The boy makes 'tend the old lady ain't even there. He just keeps on reading. "Wind is pink," she says again. "Eh, Lord, what children go'n be saying next?"

The lady 'cross from us bust out laughing.

"That's a good one," she says. "The wind is pink. Yes, sir, that's a good one."

"Don't you believe the wind is pink?" the boy says. He keeps his head down in the book.

"Course I believe it, honey," the lady says. "Course I do." She looks at us and winks her eye. "And what color is grass, honey?"

"Grass? Grass is black."

She bust out laughing again. The boy looks at her.

"Don't you believe grass is black?" he says.

The lady quits her laughing and looks at him. Everybody else looking at him, too. The place quiet, quiet.

"Grass is green, honey," the lady says. "It was green yesterday, it's green today, and it's go'n be green tomorrow."

"How do you know it's green?"

"I know because I know."

"You don't know it's green," the boy says. "You believe it's green because someone told you it was green. If someone had told you it was black you'd believe it was black."

"It's green," the lady says. "I know green when I see green."

"Prove it's green," the boy says.

"Sure, now," the lady says. "Don't tell me it's coming to that."

"It's coming to just that," the boy says. "Words mean nothing. One means no more than the other."

"That's what it all coming to?" that old lady says. That old lady got on a turban[①] and she got on two sweaters. She got a green sweater under a black sweater. I can see the green sweater 'cause some of the buttons on the other sweater's missing.

"Yes ma'am," the boy says. "Words mean nothing. Action is the only thing. Doing. That's the only thing."

"Other words, you want the Lord to come down here and show Hisself to you?" she says.

"Exactly, ma'am," he says.

"You don't mean that, I'm sure?" she says.

"I do, ma'am," he says.

"Done, Jesus," the old lady says, shaking her head.

"I didn't go 'long with that preacher at first," the other lady says; "but now—I don't know. When a person say the grass is black, he's either a lunatic or something's wrong."

"Prove to me that it's green," the boy says.

---

① A woman's close-fitting hat that consists of material wound around a small inner cap.

Chapter 10 The Sky Is Gray

"It's green because the people say it's green."

"Those same people say we're citizens of these United States," the boy says.

"I think I'm a citizen," the lady says.

"Citizens have certain rights," the boy says. "Name me one right that you have. One right, granted by the Constitution, that you can exercise in Bayonne."

The lady don't answer him. She just looks at him like she don't know what he's talking 'bout. I know I don't.

"Things changing," she says.

"Things are changing because some black men have begun to think with their brains and not their hearts," the boy says.

"You trying to say these people don't believe in God?"

"I'm sure some of them do. Maybe most of them do. But they don't believe God is going to touch these white people's hearts and change things tomorrow. Things change through action. By no other way."

Everybody sit quiet and look at the boy. Nobody says a thing. Then the lady 'cross the room from me and Mama just shakes her head.

"Let's hope that not all your generation feel the same way you do," she says.

"Think what you please, it doesn't matter," the boy says. "But it will be men who listen to their heads and not their hearts who will see that your children have a better chance than you had."

"Let's hope they ain't all like you, though," the old lady says. "Done forgot the heart absolutely."

"Yes ma'am, I hope they aren't all like me," the boy says. "Unfortunately, I was born too late to believe in your God. Let's hope that the ones who come after will have your faith—if not in your God, then in something else, something definitely that they can lean on. I haven't anything. For me, the wind is pink, the grass is black."

IX

The nurse comes in the room where we all sitting and waiting and says the doctor won't take no more patients till one o'clock this evening. My mama jumps up off the bench and goes up to the white lady.

"Nurse, I have to go back in the field this evening," she says.

"The doctor is treating his last patient now," the nurse says. "One o'clock this evening."

"Can I at least speak to the doctor?" my mama says.

"I'm his nurse," the lady says.

"My little boy's sick," my mama says. "Right now his tooth almost killing him."

The nurse looks at me. She's trying to make up her mind if to let me come in. I look at her real pitiful. The tooth ain't hurting me at all, but Mama say it is, so I make 'tend for her sake.

"This evening," the nurse says, and goes on back in the office.

"Don't feel 'jected, honey," the lady says to Mama, "I been round them a long time—they take you when they want to. If you was white, that's something else; but we the wrong color."

Mama don't say nothing to the lady, and me and her go outside and stand 'gainst the wall. It's cold out there. I can feel that wind going through my coat. Some of the other people come out of the room and go up the street. Me and Mama stand there a little while and we start walking. I don't know where we going. When we come to the other street we just stand there.

"You don't have to make water[①], do you?" Mama says.

"No, ma'am," I say.

We go on up the street. Walking real slow. I can tell Mama don't know where

---

① To pass water; pee.

Chapter 10 The Sky Is Gray

she's going. When we come to a store we stand there and look at the dummies. I look at a little boy wearing a brown overcoat. He's got on brown shoes, too. I look at my old shoes and look at his'n again. You wait till summer, I say.

Me and Mama walk away. We come up to another store and we stop and look at them dummies, too. Then we go on again. We pass a cafe where the white people in there eating. Mama tells me keep my eyes in front where they belong, but I can't help from seeing them people eat. My stomach starts to growing 'cause I'm hungry. When I see people eating, I get hungry; when I see a coat, I get cold.

A man whistles at my mama when we go by a filling station①. She makes 'tend she don't even see him. I look back and I feel like hitting him in the mouth. If I was bigger, I say; if I was bigger, you'd see.

We keep on going. I'm getting colder and colder, but I don't say nothing. I feel that stuff running down my nose and I sniff.

"That rag," Mama says.

I get it out and wipe my nose. I'm getting cold all over now—my face, my hands, my feet, everything. We pass another little cafe, but this'n for white people, too, and we can't go in there, either. So we just walk. I'm so cold now I'm 'bout ready to say it. If I knowed where we was going I wouldn't be so cold, but I don't know where we going. We go, we go, we go. We walk clean out of Bayonne. Then we cross the street and we come back. Same thing I seen when I got off the bus this morning. Same old trees, same old walk, same old weeds, same old cracked pave—same old everything.

I sniff again.

"That rag," Mama says.

I wipe my nose real fast and jugg that handkerchief back in my pocket 'fore my hand gets too cold. I raise my head and I can see David's hardware store. When we

---

① Gas station.

come up to it, we go in. I don't know why, but I'm glad.

It's warm in there. It's so warm in there you don't ever want to leave. I look for the heater, and I see it over by them barrels. Three white men standing round the heater talking in Creole[①]. One of them comes over to see what my mama want.

"Got any axe handles?" she says.

Me, Mama and the white man start to the back, but Mama stops me when we come up to the heater. She and the white man go on. I hold my hands over the heater and look at them. They go all the way to the back, and I see the white man pointing to the axe handles 'gainst the wall. Mama takes one of them and shakes it like she's trying to figure how much it weighs. Then she rubs her hand over it from one end to the other end. She turns it over and looks at the other side, then she shakes it again, and shakes her head and puts it back. She gets another one and she does it just like she did the first one, then she shakes her head. Then she gets a brown one and do it that, too. But she don't like this one, either. Then she gets another one, but 'fore she shakes it or anything, she looks at me. Look like she's trying to say something to me, but I don't know what it is. All I know is I done got warm now and I'm feeling right smart better. Mama shakes this axe handle just like she did the others, and shakes her head and says something to the white man. The white man just looks at his pile of axe handles, and when Mama pass him to come to the front, the white man just scratch his head and follows her. She tells me come on and we go on out and start walking again.

We walk and walk, and no time at all I'm cold again. Look like I'm colder now 'cause I can still remember how good it was back there. My stomach growls and I suck it in to keep Mama from hearing it. She's walking right 'side me, and it growls so loud you can hear it a mile. But Mama don't say a word.

---

① Language of European descent born in the West Indies or Spanish America.

Chapter 10 The Sky Is Gray

X

When we come up to the courthouse, I look at the clock. It's got quarter to twelve. Mean we got another hour and a quarter to be out here in the cold. We go and stand 'side a building. Something hits my cap and I look up at the sky. Sleet's falling.

I look at Mama standing there. I want stand close 'side her, but she don't like that. She say that's crybaby stuff. She say you got to stand for yourself, by yourself.

"Let's go back to that office," she says.

We cross the street. When we get to the dentist office I try to open the door, but I can't. I twist and twist, but I can't. Mama pushes me to the side and she twist the knob, but she can't open the door, either. She turns 'way from the door. I look at her, but I don't move and I don't say nothing. I done seen her like this before and I'm scared of her.

"You hungry?" she says. She says it like she's mad at me, like I'm the cause of everything.

"No, ma'am," I say.

"You want eat and walk back, or you rather don't eat and ride?"

"I ain't hungry," I say.

I ain't just hungry, but I'm cold, too. I'm so hungry and cold I want to cry. And look like I'm getting colder and colder. My feet done got dumb. I try to work my toes, but I don't even feel them. Look like I'm go'n die. Look like I'm go'n stand right here and freeze to death. I think 'bout home. I think 'bout Val and Auntie and Ty and Louis and Walker. It's 'bout twelve o'clock and I know they eating dinner now. I can hear Ty making jokes. He done forgot 'bout getting up early this morning and right now he's probably making jokes. Always trying to make somebody laugh. I wish I was right there listening to him. Give anything in the world if I was home around the fire.

"Come on," Mama says.

We start walking again. My feet so numb I can't hardly feel them. We turn the corner and go on back up the street. The clock on the courthouse starts hitting for twelve.

The sleet's coming down plenty now. They hit the pave and bounce like rice. Oh, Lord; oh, Lord, I pray. Don't let me die, don't let me die, don't let me die, Lord.

XI

Now I know where we going. We going back of town where the colored people eat. I don't care if I don't eat. I been hungry before. I can stand it. But I can't stand the cold.

I can see we go'n have a long walk. It's 'bout a mile down there. But I don't mind. I know when I get there I'm go'n warm myself. I think I can hold out. My hands numb in my pockets and my feet numb, too, but if I keep moving I can hold out. Just don't stop no more, that's all.

The sky's gray. The sleet keeps on falling. Falling like rain now—plenty, plenty. You can hear it hitting the pave. You can see it bouncing. Sometimes it bounces two times 'fore it settles.

We keep on going. We don't say nothing. We just keep on going, keep on going.

I wonder what Mama's thinking. I hope she ain't mad at me. When summer come I'm go'n pick plenty cotton and get her a coat. I'm go'n get her a red one.

I hope they'd make it summer all the time. I'd be glad if it was summer all the time—but it ain't. We got to have winter, too. Lord, I hate the winter. I guess everybody hate the winter.

I don't sniff this time. I get out my handkerchief and wipe my nose. My hands's so cold I can hardly hold the handkerchief.

I think we getting close, but we ain't there yet. I wonder where everybody is. Can't see a soul but us. Look like we the only two people moving round today. Must be too cold for the rest of the people moving round today. Must be too cold for the rest of

Chapter 10   The Sky Is Gray

people to move round in.

I can hear my teeth. I hope they don't knock together too hard and make that bad one hurt. Lord, that's all I need, for that bad one to start off.

I hear a church bell somewhere. But today ain't Sunday. They must be ringing for a funeral or something.

I wonder what they doing at home. They must be eating. Monsieur Bayonne might be there with his guitar. One day Ty played with Monsieur Bayonne's guitar and broke one of the strings. Monsieur Bayonne was some mad with Ty. He say Ty wasn't go'n ever 'mount to nothing. Ty can go just like Monsieur Bayonne when he ain't there. Ty can make everybody laugh when he starts to mocking Monsieur Bayonne.

I used to like to be with Mama and Daddy. We used to be happy. But they took him in the Army. Now, nobody happy no more… I be glad when Daddy comes home.

Monsieur Bayonne say it wasn't fair for them to take Daddy and give Mama nothing and give us nothing. Auntie say, "Shhh, Etienne. Don't let them hear you talk like that." Monsieur Bayonne say, "It's God truth. What they giving his children? They have to walk three and a half miles to school hot or cold. That's anything to give for a paw? She's got to work in the field rain or shine just to make ends meet. That's anything to give for a husband?" Auntie say, "Shhh, Etienne, shhh." "You are right," Monsieur Bayonne say. "Best don't say it in front of them now. But one day they go'n find out. One day." "Yes, I suppose so," Auntie say. "Then what, Rose Mary?" Monsieur Bayonne say. "I don't know, Etienne," Auntie say. "All we can do is us job, and leave everything else in His hand…"

We getting closer, now. We getting closer. I can even see the railroad tracks.

We cross the tracks, and now I see the cafe. Just to get in there, I say. Just to get in there. Already I'm starting to feel little better.

XII

We go in. Ahh, it's good. I look for the heater; there 'gainst the wall. One of them little brown ones. I just stand there and hold my hands over it. I can't open my hands too wide 'cause they almost froze.

Mama's standing right 'side me. She done unbuttoned her coat. Smoke rises out of the coat, ant the coat smelled like a wet dog.

I move to the side so Mama can have more room. She opens out her hands and rubs them together. I rub mine together too, 'cause this keep them from hurting. If you let them warm too fast, they hurt you sure. But if you let them warm just little bit at a time, and you keep rubbing them, they be all right every time.

They got just two more people in the cafe. A lady back of the counter, and a man on this side the counter. They been watching us ever since we come in.

Mama gets out the handkerchief and count up the money. Both of us know how much money she's got there. Three dollars. No, she ain't got three dollars, 'cause she had to pay us way up here. She ain't got but two dollars and a half left. Dollar and a half to get my tooth pulled, and fifty cents for us to go back on, and fifty cents worth of salt meat.

She stirs the money round with her finger. Most of the money is change 'cause I can hear it rubbing together. She stirs it and stirs it. Then she looks at the door. It's still sleeting. I can hear it hitting 'gainst the wall like rice.

"I ain't hungry, Mama," I say.

"Got to pay them something for they heat," she says.

She takes a quarter out the handkerchief and ties the handkerchief up again. She looks over her shoulder at the people, but she still don't move. I hope she don't spend the money. I don't want her spending it on me. I'm hungry, I'm almost starving I'm so hungry, but I don't want her spending the money on me.

She flips the quarter over like she's thinking. She's must be thinking 'bout us

Chapter 10 The Sky Is Gray

walking back home. Lord, I sure don't want walk home. If I thought it'd do any good to say something, I'd say it. But Mama makes up her own mind 'bout things.

She turns 'way from the heater right fast, like she better hurry up and spend the quarter 'fore she change her mind. I watch her go toward the counter. The man and the lady look at her, too. She tells the lady something and the lady walks away. Then man keeps on looking at her. Her back's turned to the man, and she don't even know he's standing there.

The lady puts some cakes and a glass of milk on the counter. Then she pours up a cup of coffee and sets it 'side the other stuff. Mama pays her for the things and comes on back where I'm standing. She tells me sit down at the table 'gainst the wall.

The milk and the cakes's for me; the coffee's for Mama. I eat slow and I look at her. She's looking outside at the sleet. She's looking real sad. I say to myself, I'm go'n make all this up one day. You see, one day, I'm go'n make all this up. I want say it now; I want tell her how I feel right now; but Mama don't like for us to talk like that.

"I can't eat all this," I say.

They ain't got but just three little old cakes there. I'm so hungry right now, the Lord knows I can eat a hundred times three, but I want my mama to have one.

Mama don't even look my way. She knows I'm hungry, she knows I want it. I let it stay there a little while, then I get it and eat it. I eat just on my front teeth, though, 'cause if cake touch that back tooth I know what'll happen. Thank God it ain't hurt me at all today.

After I finish eating I see the man go to the juke box[①]. He drops a nickel in it, then he just stand there a little while looking at the record. Mama tells me keep my eyes in front where they belong. I turn my head like she say, but then I hear the man coming toward us.

---

① A machine that plays CDs in a place such as a bar. You put money in and choose the song you want to hear.

"Dance, pretty?" he says.

Mama gets up to dance with him. But 'fore you know it, she done grabbed the little man in the collar and done heaved him 'side the wall. He hit the wall so hard he stop the juke box from playing.

"Some pimp," the lady back of the counter says. "Some pimp."

The little man jumps up off the floor and starts toward my mama. 'Fore you know it, Mama sprung open her knife and she's waiting for him.

"Come on," she says. "Come on. I'll gut you from your neighbo to your throat. Come on."

I go up to the little man to hit him, but Mama makes me come and stand 'side her. The little man looks at me and Mama and goes back to the counter.

"Some pimp," the lady back of the counter says. "Some pimp." She starts laughing and pointing at the little man. "Yes sir, you a pimp, all right. Yes sir-ree."

XIII

"Fasten your coat, let's go," Mama says.

"You don't have to leave," the lady says.

Mama don't answer the lady, and we right out in the cold again. I'm warm right now—my hands, my ears, my feet—but I know this ain't go'n last too long. It done sleet so much now you got ice everywhere you look.

We cross the railroad tracks, and soon's we do, I get cold. That wind goes through this little old coat like it ain't even there. I got on a shirt and a sweater under the coat, but that wind don't pay them no mind. I look up and I can see we got a long way to go. I wonder if we go'n make it 'fore I get too cold.

We cross over to walk on the sidewalk. They got just one sidewalk back here, and it's over there.

After we go just a little piece, I smell bread cooking. I look, then I see a baker

Chapter 10   The Sky Is Gray

shop. When we get closer, I can smell it more better. I shut my eyes and make 'tend I'm eating. But I keep them shut too long and I butt up 'gainst a telephone post. Mama grabs me and see if I'm hurt. I ain't bleeding or nothing and she turns me loose.

I can feel I'm getting colder and colder, and I look up to see how far we still got to go. Uptown is 'way up yonder. A half mile more, I reckon. I try to think of something. They say think and you won't get cold. I think of that poem, "Annabel Lee"[①]. I ain't been to school in so long—this bad weather—I reckon they done passed "Annabel Lee" by now. But passed it or not, I'm sure Miss Walker go'n make me recite it when I get there. That woman don't never forget nothing. I ain't never seen nobody like that in my life.

I'm still getting cold. "Annabel Lee" or no "Annabel Lee," I am still getting cold. But I can see we getting closer. We getting there gradually.

Soon 's we turn the corner, I see a little old white lady up in front of us. She's the only lady on the street. She's all in black and she's got a long black rag over her head.

"Stop," she says.

Me and Mama stop and look at her. She must be crazy to be out in all this bad weather. Ain't got but a few other people out there, and all of them's men.

"Y'all done ate?" she says.

"Just finish," Mama says.

"Y'all must be cold then?" she says.

"We headed for the dentist," Mama says. "We'll warm up when we get there."

"What dentist?" the old lady says. "Mr. Bassett?"

"Yes, ma'am," Mama says.

"Come on in," the old lady says. "I'll telephone him and tell him y'all coming."

Me and Mama follow the old lady in the store. It's a little bitty store, and it don't

---

① A poem by Edgar Allan Poe, published in 1849.

have much in there. The old lady takes off her head rag and folds it up.

"Helena?" somebody calls from the back.

"Yes, Alnest?" the old lady says.

"Did you see them?"

"They're here. Standing beside me."

"Good. Now you can stay inside."

The old lady looks at Mama. Mama's waiting to hear what she brought us in here for. I'm waiting for that, too.

"I saw y'all each time you went by," she says. "I came out to catch you, but you were gone."

"We went back of town," Mama says.

"Did you eat?"

"Yes, ma'am."

The old lady looks at Mama a long time, like she's thinking Mama might be just saying that. Mama looks right back at her. The old lady looks at me to see what I have to say. I don't say nothing. I sure ain't going 'gainst my mama.

"There's food in the kitchen," she says to Mama. "I've been keeping it warm."

Mama turns right around and starts for the door.

"Just a minute," the old lady says. Mama stops. "The boy'll have to work for it. It isn't free.'

"We don't take no handout," Mama says.

"I'm not handing out anything," the old lady says. "I need my garbage moved to the front. Ernest has a bad cold and can't go out there."

"James'll move it for you," Mama says.

"Not unless you eat," the old lady says. "I'm old, but I have my pride, too, you know."

Mama can see she ain't go'n beat this old lady down, so she just shakes her head.

Chapter 10 The Sky Is Gray

"All right," the old lady says. "Comes into the kitchen."

She leads the way with that rag in her hand. The kitchen is a little bitty little old thing, too. The table and the stove just 'bout fill it up. They got a little room to the side. Somebody in there laying 'cross the bed—'cause I can see one of his feet. Must be the person she was talking to; Ernest or Alnest—something like that.

"Sit down," the old lady says to Mama. "Not you," she says to me. "You have to move the cans."

"Helena?" the man says in the other room.

"Yes, Alnest?" the old lady says.

"Are you going out there again?"

"I must show the boy where the garbage is, Alnest," the old lady says.

"Keep that shawl over your head," the old man says.

"You don't have to remind me, Alnest. Come, boy," the old lady says.

We got out in the yard. Little old back yard ain't no bigger than the store or the kitchen. But it can sleet here just like it can sleet in any big back yard. And 'fore you know it, I'm trembling.

"There," the old lady says, pointing to the cans. I pick up one of the cans and set it right back down. The can's so light, I'm go'n see what's inside of it.

"Here," the old lady says. "Leave that can alone."

I look back at her standing there in the door. She's got that black rag wrapped round her shoulders, and she's pointing one of her little old fingers at me.

"Pick it up and carry it to the front," she says. I go by her with the can, and she's looking at me all the time. I'm sure the can's empty. I'm sure she could've carried it herself—maybe both of them at the same time. "Set it on the sidewalk by the door and come back for the other one," she says.

I go and come back, and Mama looks at me when I pass her. I get the other can and take it to the front. It don't feel a bit heavier than that first one. I tell myself I ain't go'n be nobody's fool, and I'm go'n look inside this can to see just what I been hauling. First, I look up the street, then down the street. Nobody coming. Then I look over my shoulder toward the door. That little old lady done slipped up there quiet 's mouse, watching me again. Look like she knowed what I was go'n do.

"Ehh, Lord," she says. "Children, children. Come in here, boy, and go wash your hands."

I follow her in the kitchen. She points toward the bathroom, and I go in there and wash up. Little bitty old bathroom, but it's clean, clean. I don't use any of her towels; I wipe my hands on my pants legs.

When I come back in the kitchen, the old lady done dished up the food. Rice, gravy[①], meat—and she even got some lettuce and tomato in a saucer. She even got a glass of milk and a piece of cake there, too. It looks so good, I almost start eating 'fore I say my blessing.

"Helena?" the old man says.

"Yes, Alnest?"

"Are they eating?"

"Yes," she says.

"Good," he says. "Now you'll stay inside."

The old lady goes in there where he is and I can hear them talking. I look at Mama. She's eating slow like she's thinking. I wonder what's the matter now. I reckon she's thinking 'bout home.

The old lady comes back in the kitchen.

"I talked to Dr. Bassett's nurse," she says. "Dr. Bassett will take you as soon as you get there."

"Thank you, ma'am," Mama says.

---

① The juices that drip from cooking meat.

"Perfectly all right," the old lady says. "Which one is it?"

Mama nods toward me. The old lady looks at me real sad. I look sad, too.

"You're not afraid, are you?" she says.

"No, ma'am," I say.

"That's a good boy," the old lady says. "Nothing to be afraid of. Dr. Bassett will not hurt you."

When me and Mama get through eating, we thank the old lady again.

"Helena, are they leaving?" the old man says.

"Yes, Alnest."

"Tell them I say good-bye."

"They can hear you, Alnest."

"Good-bye both mother and son," the old man says. "And may God be with you."

Me and Mama tell the old man good-bye, and we follow the old lady in the front room. Mama opens the door to go out, but she stops and comes back in the store.

"You sell salt meat?" she says.

"Yes."

"Give me two bits worth."

"That isn't very much salt meat," the old lady says.

"That's all I have," Mama says.

The old lady goes back to the counter and cuts a big piece off the chunk. Then she wraps it up and puts it in a paper bag.

"Two bits," she says.

"That looks like awful lot of meat for a quarter," Mama says.

"Two bits," the old lady says. "I've been selling salt meat behind this counter twenty-five years. I think I know what I'm doing."

"You got a scale there," Mama says.

"What?" the old lady says.

"Weigh it," Mama says.

"What?" the old lady says. "Are you telling me how to run business?"

"Thanks very much for the food," Mama says.

"Just a minute," the old lady says.

"James," Mama says to me. I move toward the door.

"Just one minute, I said," the old lady says.

Me and Mama stop again and look at her. The old lady takes the meat out of the bag and unwraps it and cuts 'bout half of it off. Then she wraps it up again and juggs it back in the bag and gives the bag to Mama. Mama lays the quarter on the counter.

"Your kindness will never be forgotten," she says. "James," she says to me.

We go out, and the old lady comes to the door to look at us. After we go a little piece I look back, and she's still there watching us.

The sleet's coming down heavy, heavy now, and I turn up my coat collar to keep my neck warm. My mama tells me turn it right back down.

"You not a bum[①]," she says. "You a man."

Film Comment:

Ernest Gaines's *The Sky Is Gray*: 47 minutes, color

Starring: Olivia Cole & James Bond III

Screenplay by: Charles Fuller

Directed by: Stan Lathan

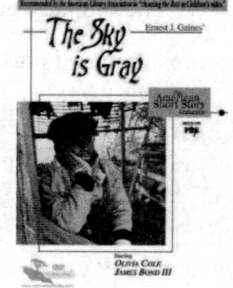

From Ernest J. Gaines, author of *The Autobiography of Miss Jane Pittman*, comes a deceptively simple, yet emotionally complex tale of a young boy's discovery of what it's like to be black in Louisiana during the 1940s.

---

① A tramp; a vagrant.

Chapter 10 The Sky Is Gray

James, the boy in question, has a raging toothache that necessitates a trip to the dentist. His mother (Olivia Cole, Emmy Award Winner), accompanies James to town on an eye opening odyssey where the boy gains valuable insights into poverty, racism—and his own sense of pride.

With an exciting musical score by Webster Lewis, this multi-award winning film explores a child's discovery that the world is a complicated place … where things are never truly black or white… only shades of gray.

Film Scenes:

Scene 1: the tooth ache

James is suffering from the tooth ache, and it is necessary to go to the dentist in the town to have it pulled, which is a heavy burden for his family.

Scene 2: killing a bird

Though unwilling, James has to kill the birds like a man to bring some food for the family, and Mama also worries that she has to go someday, just like Daddy.

Scene 3: going to town

James takes the bus to the town together with Mama, meeting a lovely girl on the bus, and starts his eye-opening odyssey trip.

Scene 4: the dentist visit

When waiting in the dentist office, James experiences the squabble between the preacher and the student as well as the argument between the lady and the student.

Scene 5: the dance

When the stranger asks Mama to dance, she has to protect herself with a knife, for the husband is absent and the son is still young.

Scene 6: the benefactor

The old couple invite James and Mama into their store, providing them with food and heat in return for James' carrying the empty cans for them. They give their help without hurting the pride of Mama, and their kindness will never be forgotten.

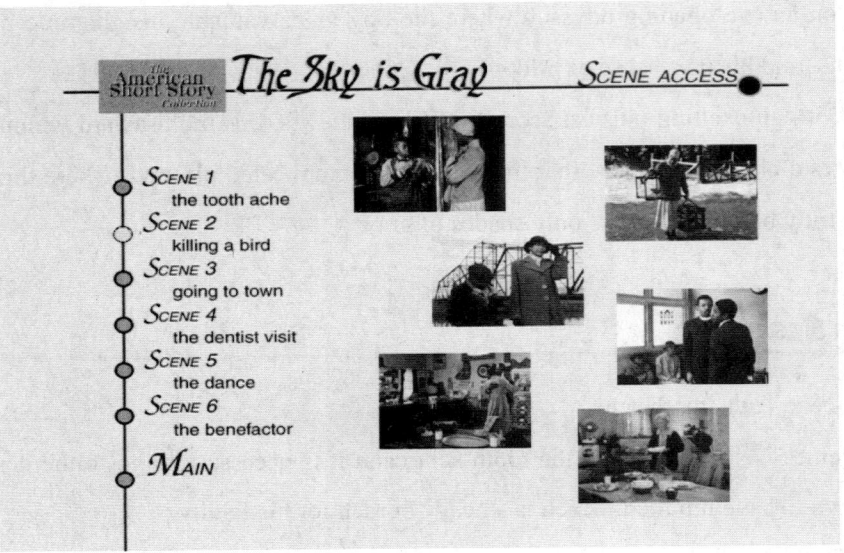

Film Clip:

The Squabble

The student sits on the same side with James and Mama, in front of the preacher. He is dressed on a suit, having a book that he has been reading. According to the student, the trouble with the black people in this country is that they don't question. They should question everything. The preacher and the lady are talking about God, but the student insists to question Him, too. The preacher thinks he is mad at the world. The student doesn't think he is mad at the world. He is questioning the world. He wants to know what the words like Freedom, Liberty, God, White and Colored mean. That's why they are sent to school, to read and to ask questions. Yet, the preacher insists that he is sorry for the student. According to the student, the preacher believes in God because a man tells him to believe in God. A white man tells him to believe in God to keep him

Chapter 10 The Sky Is Gray

ignorant so the white man can keep his feet on his neck.

The preacher gets up slowly and comes over where the student is sitting. The preacher asks him to get up. The student looks up at him, and then he shuts his book slowly and stands up. The preacher just hauls back and hits him in the face. The student straightens himself up and looks right back at that preacher, saying that he has forgot the other cheek. The preacher hauls back and hits him again on the other side. The student says the slap from the preacher hasn't changed anything. The preacher just looks at the student, breathing real hard, while the student sits down and opens his book again. The preacher again says he feels sorry for the student. The student pretends he doesn't hear the preacher, and he keeps on reading his book. The preacher goes back and gets his hat off the chair. He apologizes to all of them, looking at the student and going out of the room.

The other lady doesn't go along with the preacher at first, but now she doesn't know, for when a person says the wind is pink and the grass is black, he is either a lunatic or something is wrong. How to prove that the grass is green? It's green because people say it's green. It is the same people who say that the black are citizens of the United States. Citizens have certain rights. The black can hardly name one right that they have, granted by the Constitution, that they can exercise in Bayonne. The student believes that the men who listen to their heads rather than their hearts will see that their children have a better chance. The student doesn't believe in God. He has nothing to lean on. For him, the wind is pink, and the grass is black. He hopes that the future generation will have faith they can lean on.

The whole process of the squabble is narrated through the perspective of the young James, who possibly doesn't understand the argument between the preacher and the student, but just gives an objective description with his eyes. The squabble between the preacher and the student as well as the argument between the other lady and the student seems to make no sense at first, but it somewhat reflects the actual situation of the black in American South during the Civil Rights Era. The young generation are waking up to the reality and struggling to get their own rights with action rather than only with words.

Discussion Questions:

Story Discussion

(1) What takes James to town?

(2) What can we learn from the quarrel between the preacher and the student? What about the argument between the old lady and the student in the dentist's office?

(3) How do you read the walking of the mother and son back and forth of the street?

(4) What does James learn from this eye-opening trip?

(5) What do you think of the color image in the story, such as black, green, pink, white, red, and grey? What is the color of sky?

Film Appreciation

(1) What troubles have the family met with the father's absence from the house?

(2) Why does the preaching of Monsieur Bayonne fail to cure James' toothache?

(3) Why does Mama have to make James kill the birds?

(4) What's happening on the bus? Does it still have a sign labelling the white and the colored today?

(5) How does the student quarrel with the preacher and argue with the old lady?

(6) What's the symbolic meaning of different colors in the story, such as black, green, pink, white, red, and grey?

(7) How does Mama protect herself when the husband is absent and the son is still young?

(8) How does Mama keep her pride when facing the kindness from the old couple?

(9) What are the adapted scenes in the film?

Further Reading and Watching:

A Long Day in November

Appendix

I. A Brief Chronology of the American Short Story

1819—Washington Irving's "Rip Van Winkle" and "The Legend of Sleepy Hollow"

1821—*The Saturday Evening Post* established

Romantic Period: 1828—1865

1837—Nathaniel Hawthorne's *Twice-Told Tales*

1840—Edgar Allan Poe's *Tales of the Grotesque and Arabesque*

1843—*The Prose Romances of Edgar Allan Poe*

1846—Nathaniel Hawthorne's *Mosses from an Old Manse*

1850—Herman Melville's "Hawthorne and His Mosses"

1857—*Atlantic Monthly* established

Realistic Period: 1865—1900

1865—Mark Twain's "The Celebrated Jumping Frog of Calaveras County"

1868—Bret Harte's "The Luck of Roaring Camp"

1892—*The Yale Review* established

1893—Henry James' *The Real Thing and Other Tales*

1898—Stephen Crane's *The Open Boat and Other Tales of Adventure*

Naturalistic Period: 1900—1914

1900—Mark Twain's *The Man That Corrupted Hadleyburg and Other Stories*

Appendix

1901—Edith Wharton's *Crucial Instances*

1905—Willa Cather's *The Troll Garden*

1906—O. Henry's *The Four Million*

1907—Jack London's *Love of Life*

Period of Modernism: 1914—1945

1922—F. Scott Fitzgerald's *Tales of the Jazz Age*

1925—*The New Yorker* established

1927—Ernest Hemingway's *Men without Women*

1933—Sherwood Anderson's *Death in the Woods and Other Stories*

1935—Katherine Anne Porter's *Flowering Judas and Other Stories*

1938—Richard Wright's *Uncle Tom's Children*

1942—William Faulkner's *Go Down, Moses*

      James Thurber's *My World—and Welcome to It*

Postwar Period: 1945—1963

1949—Shirley Jackson's *The Lottery*

1950—William Faulkner's *Collected Stories of William Faulkner*

1953—J. D. Salinger's *Nine Stories*

1955—Flannery O'Connor's *A Good Man is Hard to Find*

1962—John Updike's *Pigeon Feathers and Other Stories*

"Confessional" Period: 1963—1980

1963—Frank O'Connor's *The Lonely Voice*

1969—*Collected Stories of Jean Stafford*, winning Pulitzer Prize

1971—*The Complete Short Stories of Flannery O'Connor*

1972—Ernest Hemingway's *The Nick Adams Stories*

1978—Isaac B. Singer winning the Nobel Prize for his life's work in the short story genre

Postmodern Period: 1980—

1980—*The Collected Short Stories of Eudora Welty*

1983—John Gardner's *The Art of Fiction*

1985—Bob Shacochis' *Easy in the Islands,* winning the American Book Award

1990—Stuart Dybek's *The Coast of Chicago*

1997—Annie Proulx's "Brokeback Mountain"

II. A Brief Glossary of Literary Terms

Antagonist—a character in a story that deceives, frustrates, or works against the main character, or protagonist, in some way. The antagonist doesn't necessarily have to be a person. It could be death, the devil, an illness, or any challenge that prevents the main character from living "happily ever after."

Character—a person who is responsible for the thoughts and actions within a story. Characters are extremely important because they are the medium through which a reader interacts with a piece of literature. Every character has his or her own personality, which a creative author uses to assist in forming the plot of a story or creating a mood.

Genre—a type of literature. We say a poem, novel, story, or other literary work belongs to a particular genre if it shares at least a few conventions, or standard characteristics, with other works in that genre.

Irony—a literary term referring to how a person, situation, statement, or circumstance is not as it would actually seem. Many times it is the exact opposite of what it appears to be. There are many types of irony, the three most common being verbal irony, dramatic irony, and cosmic irony.

Narrative—a collection of events that tells a story, which may be true or not, placed in a particular order and recounted through either telling or writing.

Narrator—one who tells a story, the speaker or the "voice" of an oral or written work. Although it can be, the narrator is not usually the author. The narrator is one of three types of characters: 1) participant (protagonist or participant in any action that may take place in the story); 2) observer (someone who is indirectly involved in the action of a story); or 3) non participant (one who is not at all involved in any action of the story).

Plot—the plot in a dramatic or narrative work is constituted by its events and actions, as these are rendered and ordered toward achieving particular emotional and artistic effects.

Point of View—a way the events of a story are conveyed to the reader, it is the "vantage point" from which the narrative is passed from author to the reader. The point of view can vary from work to work.

Protagonist—a protagonist is considered to be the main character or lead figure in a novel, play, story, or poem. It may also be referred to as the "hero" of a work.

Setting—the time, place, physical details, and circumstances in which a situation occurs. Settings include the background, atmosphere or environment in which characters live and move, and usually include physical characteristics of the surroundings.

Symbol—a word or object that stands for another word or object. The object or word can be seen with the eye or not visible.

Theme—a common thread or repeated idea that is incorporated throughout a literary work. A theme is a thought or idea the author presents to the reader that may be deep, difficult to understand, or even moralistic.

(The literary terms here are excerpted from M. H. Abrams' *A Glossary of Literary Terms*.)

III. A Brief Glossary of Film Terms
Types of Shots

Long Shot—(a relative term) a shot taken from a sufficient distance to show a landscape, a building or a large crowd.

Medium Shot—(also relative) a shot between a long shot and a close-up that might show two people in full figure or several people from the waist up.

Close-up—a shot of one face or object that fills the screen completely.

Extreme Close-up—a shot of a small object or part of a face that fills the screen.

Camera Angles

High Angle—the camera looks down at what is being photographed.

"Eye Level"—a shot that approximates human vision—a camera presents an object so that the line between camera and object is parallel to the ground.

Low Angle—the camera looks up at what is being photographed.

Camera Movement

Pan—the camera moves horizontally on a fixed base.

Tilt—the camera points up or down from a fixed base.

Tracking (Dolly) Shot—the camera moves through space on a wheeled truck (or dolly), but stays in the same plane.

Boom—the camera moves up or down through space.

Zoom—not a camera movement, but a shift in the focal length of the camera lens to give the impression that the camera is getting closer to or farther from an object.

Duration of Shots

Shots also vary in time from subliminal (a few frames) to quick (less than a second) to "average" (more than a second but less than a minute) to lengthy (more than a minute).

Editing

Cut—the most common type of transition in which one scene ends and a new one immediately begins.

Fade-out/Fade-in—one scene gradually goes dark and the new one gradually emerges from the darkness.

Dissolve—a gradual transition in which the end of one scene is superimposed over the beginning of a new one.

Wipe—an optical effect in which one shot appears to "wipe" the preceding one from the screen. Special wipes include flip wipes, iris wipes, star wipes, etc.

Sources of Sound in Film

Voice—over narration, dialogue, sound effects, and soundtrack music (underscoring).

(The film terms here are excerpted from Teasley & Wilder's *Reel Conversations: Reading Films with Young Adults*.)

IV. The American Short Story Collection

1. "Almos' a Man"—Richard Wright
2. Barn Burning—William Faulkner
3. Bernice Bobs Her Hair—F. Scott Fitzgerald
4. Blue Hotel, The—Stephen Crane
5. Displaced Person, The—Flannery O'Connor
6. Golden Honeymoon, The—Ring Lardner
7. Greatest Man in the World, The—James Thurber
8. Hollow Boy, The—Hortense Calisher
9. I'm a Fool—Sherwood Anderson
10. Jilting of Granny Weatherall, The—Katherine Anne Porter
11. Jolly Corner, The—Henry James
12. Love and Other Sorrows—Harold Brodkey
13. Man That Corrupted Hadleyburg, The—Mark Twain
14. Music School, The—John Updike
15. Parker Adderson, Philosopher—Ambrose Bierce
16. Paul's Case—Willa Cather
17. Pigeon Feathers—John Updike
18. Rappaccini's Daughter—Nathaniel Hawthorne
19. Revolt of Mother, The—Mary E. Wilkins Freeman
20. Sky Is Gray, The—Ernest J. Gaines
21. Soldier's Home—Ernest Hemingway

References

Primary Sources

Anderson, Sherwood. "I'm a Fool" in *Horses and Men*. B.W. Huebsch, 1923.

Cather, Willa. "Paul's Case" in *The Troll Garden*. McClure, Phillips & Co., 1905.

Crane, Stephen. "The Blue Hotel" in *The Monster and Other Stories*. Harper & Brothers Publishers, 1899.

Faulkner, William. "Barn Burning" in *Collected Stories of William Faulkner*. Random House, Inc., 1950.

Fitzgerald, F. Scott. "Bernice Bobs Her Hair" in *Flappers and Philosophers*. Curtis Publishing Co, 1921.

Gaines, Ernest J. "The Sky Is Gray" in *Bloodline*. The Dial Press, 1963.

Hawthorne, Nathaniel. "Rappaccini's Daughter" in *Mosses from an Old Manse*. Ohio State University Press, 1974.

Hemingway, Ernest. "Soldier's Home" in *In Our Time*. Charles Scribner's Sons, 1925.

Thurber, James. "The Greatest Man in the World" in *The Middle-Aged Man on the Flying Trapeze*. Harper & Row, Publishers, Inc., 1935.

Wright, Richard. "Almos' a Man" in *Eight Men*. World Publishing Company, 1960.

Secondary Sources

Abrams, M. H. *A Glossary of Literary Terms* (10th edition). Wadsworth, Cengage Learning, 2012.

Beaty, Jerome, ed. *The Norton Introduction to Fiction* (6th edition). Norton, 1995.

Bendixen, Alfred & James Nagel, eds. *A Companion to the American Short Story*. Wiley-Blackwell, 2010.

Bordwell, David & Kristin Thompson. *Film Art: An Introduction* (7th edition). McGraw-Hill, 2004.

Cartmell, Deborah & Imelda Whelehan, eds. *The Cambridge Companion to Literature on Screen*. Cambridge University Press, 2007.

Cassill, R. V., ed. *The Norton Anthology of Short Fiction* (7th edition). Norton, 2006.

Charters, Ann. *The Story and Its Writer: An Introduction to Short Fiction* (7th edition). Bedford/St. Martin's, 2007.

Chatman, Seymour. *Story and Discourse: Narrative Structure in Fiction and Film*. Cornell University Press, 1980.

Corrigan, Timothy, ed. *Film and Literature: An Introduction and Reader* (2nd edition). Routledge, 2012.

Desmond, John M. & Peter Hawkes. *Adaptation: Studying Film and Literature*. McGraw-Hill, 2006.

Emmens, Carol A. *Short Stories on Film and Video* (2nd edition). Libraries Unlimited, 1985.

Gelfant, Blanche H., ed. *The Columbia Companion to the Twentieth-Century American Short Story*. Columbia University Press, 2000.

Gordon, Jane Bachman & Karen Kuehher. *Fiction: An Introduction to the Short Story*. NTC/Contemporary Publishing Group, 1999.

Harrison, Stephanie, ed. *Adaptations: From Short Story to Big Screen*. Three Rivers Press, 2005.

Hayward, Susan. *Cinema Studies: The Key Concepts* (3rd edition). Routledge, 2006.

Hitchcock, Bert & Virginia M. Kouidis. *American Short Stories* (8th edition). Pearson Longman, 2007.

Kennedy, X. J. & Dana Gioia. *An Introduction to Fiction* (9th edition). Pearson

Longman, 2005.

Lothe, Jakob. *Narrative in Fiction and Film: An Introduction*. Oxford University Press, 2000.

McFarlane, Brian. *Novel to Film: An Introduction to the Theory of Adaptation*. Claredon Press, 1996.

Palmer, R. Barton, ed. *Nineteenth-Century American Fiction on Screen*. Cambridge University Press, 2007.

Palmer, R. Barton, ed. *Twentieth-Century American Fiction on Screen*. Cambridge University Press, 2007.

Pickering, James H., ed. *Fiction 100: An Anthology of Short Stories* (10th edition). Prentice-Hall, 2003.

Sage, Howard. *Incorporating Literature in ESL Instruction*. Prentice-Hall, 1987.

Scofield, Martin. *The Cambridge Introduction to the American Short Story*. Cambridge University Press, 2006.

Semali, Ladislaus M. *Literacy in Multimedia America: Integrating Media Education across the Curriculum*. Falmer Press, 2000.

Skaggs, Calvin, ed. *The American Short Story*. Dell Publishing, 1977.

Stam, Robert & Alessandra Raengo, eds. *A Companion to Literature and Film*. Blackwell Publishing, 2004.

Stam, Robert & Alessandra Raengo, eds. *Literature and Film: A Guide to the Theory and Practice of Film Adaptation*. Blackwell Publishing, 2005.

Stevick, Philip. *The American Short Story 1900—1945: A Critical History*. Twayne Publishers, 1984.

Teasley, Alan B. & Ann Wilder. *Reel Conversations: Reading Films with Young Adults*. Boynton/Cook Publishers, 1997.

Weaver, Gordon. *The American Short Story 1945—1980: A Critical History*. Twayne Publishers, 1984.